Punishing Disease

The publisher and the University of California Press Foundation gratefully acknowledge the generous support of the Anne G. Lipow Endowment Fund in Social Justice and Human Rights.

Punishing Disease

HIV and the Criminalization of Sickness

Trevor Hoppe

UNIVERSITY OF CALIFORNIA PRESS

University of California Press, one of the most
distinguished university presses in the United States,
enriches lives around the world by advancing scholarship
in the humanities, social sciences, and natural sciences. Its
activities are supported by the UC Press Foundation and
by philanthropic contributions from individuals and
institutions. For more information, visit www.ucpress.edu.

University of California Press
Oakland, California

Design/Art Direction: Jonathan Lefrançois and Pulp &
Pixel. Illustrations: Justin Karas for Pulp & Pixel.

Library of Congress Cataloging-in-Publication Data

Names: Hoppe, Trevor, 1983– author.
Title: Punishing disease : HIV and the criminalization of
    sickness / Trevor Hoppe.
Description: Oakland, California : University of
    California Press, [2018] | Includes bibliographical
    references and index. | Identifiers: LCCN
    2017020960 (print) | LCCN 2017023297 (ebook) |
    ISBN 9780520965300 (ebook) | ISBN 9780520291584
    (cloth : alk. paper) | ISBN 9780520291607 (pbk. : alk.
    paper)
Subjects: LCSH: AIDS (Disease)—Social aspects—United
    States. | AIDS (Disease)—Law and legislation—United
    States.
Classification: LCC RA643.83 (ebook) | LCC RA643.83 .H67
    2018 (print) | DDC 362.19697/92—dc23
LC record available at https://lccn.loc.gov/2017020960

Manufactured in the United States of America

26 25 24 23 22 21 20 19 18 17
10 9 8 7 6 5 4 3 2 1

Contents

Illustrations

TABLES

BOX

Acknowledgments

This book would not have been possible without the tremendous support of many generous institutions, supportive friends, critical reading groups, emotional happy hours, thoughtful advisers, and patient parents and family members. First of all, I feel so incredibly lucky and grateful to have benefited so tremendously from the mentorship of David Halperin. This book would not exist without his tireless assistance, thoughtful feedback, and unwavering support and stewardship—from our first meeting when I was an undergraduate student to our continued friendship today. Thank you, David, for teaching me "How to Be Gay" and for never letting me get away with second-rate scholarship (or, at the very least, for desperately doing your best to save me from myself).

This book (as well as my career) truly is the product of a kind of gay mentorship that should not go unspoken in these pages. When I moved to San Francisco in 2005, Eric Rofes brought me into the gay men's health movement and challenged me to rethink my naïve and stale assumptions about the HIV epidemic. When I began to casually express frustration with an HIV prevention campaign billboard later that year, he plainly instructed me to "write about it." That instruction led to my first commentary on the epidemic, an editorial in San Francisco's *Bay Area Reporter*, which planted the seeds of chapter 2 in this very book nearly a dozen years later. His untimely death in 2006 was devastating, and his loss continues to leave a void in my life and in the broader gay men's health community and movement. I would not be the scholar I am today were it not for Eric and for the many other gay men whose critical leadership shaped my understanding of the world. They include (but are not limited to) Barry Adam, Chris Bartlett, Edwin Bernard, David Caron, Héctor Carrillo, Alex Garner, David John Frank, Michael Hurley, Eric Mykhalovskiy, Mark Padilla, Kane Race, Sean Strub, Tony Valenzuela, and Fred Wherry. Perhaps at a greater distance, I also feel indebted for the leadership of gay and queer male scholars such as Juan Battle, John D'Emilio, Steve Epstein, Amin Ghaziani, Adam Green, and Salvador Vidal-Ortiz.

That's not to say that women and heterosexuals did not also help, of course! I am lucky to have had a co-advisor through graduate school, Renee Anspach, who has been my enthusiastic cheerleader ever since I set foot on campus at University of Michigan. Renee's brilliant mind and tireless work have been instrumental in forming the basis of my scholarship and the basis of this book. Renee logged countless hours helping me to develop the historical and theoretical arguments found in these pages, and for that I am especially grateful.

In addition, I'm grateful for the consistent support and enthusiasm from my editor at UC Press, Maura Roessner, as well as their entire editorial team (including my eagle-eyed copyeditor, Barbara Armentrout). Special thanks also go out to the anonymous reviewers who helped me to improve this manuscript, as well as to several readers who provided sage feedback at various stages of its development, including Judith Auerbach, Edwin Bernard, Sarah Burgard, Scott Burris, Adam Green, Sandra Levistsky, David Pedulla, and Kane Race. I am also grateful for the assistance of Twin Oaks indexing, who created the index for this book.

Perhaps no editor was more helpful than Brad Gorman, my soon-to-be husband, who transformed many a clunky sentence into far more accessible prose. I love you and I am so grateful to have you in my life.

There are many more to name, particularly my friends whose support during graduate school and beyond made writing this book a lot more tolerable, including Matt Aslesen, Aaron Boalick, Jay Borchert, Jackson Bowman, Matt Burgess, Redd Carter, Win Chesson, Scott De Orio (homo potluck!), Spencer Derrico, Matthieu Dupas, Karen Paxton Erbe, Maxime Foerster, Aston Gonzalez, Jessica Lowen, Rostom Mesli, Matt Leslie Santana, Jack Tocco, Bryan Victor, and Cookie Woolner.

Financially, this book was made possible by the support of many institutions that have been generous enough to support my research over the years. The funding I received from the University of Michigan was especially instrumental in supporting this project—particularly funds provided by the Rackham Graduate School, the Department of Sociology, the Department of Women's Studies, the Ford School of Public Policy, the Institute for Research on Women and Gender, and the Center for the Education of Women. The University of California at Irvine Department of Criminology, Law, and Society; the Social Science Research Council; and the University at Albany, SUNY also provided critical support.

Invaluable research assistance was provided by Dean Bock, Jake Carias, and Christine Walsh at the University at Albany; Jazzmine Lorenzana, Nolan Phillips, and Tien Truong at UC-Irvine; and Matthew Lavigueur, Ruben Macias, Dana Nelson, and Brittany Rouchou at the HIV Law Project.

Last and certainly not least, I must thank my family. My parents, Robert and Susan, have been unwavering in their support of my academic development. They might not have always understood what I was up to or why, but they were always there to support me as I worked toward my dream. I am eternally grateful for their love and support. And last but not least, my siblings—Derek and Lindsay—who have managed to treat this middle child with a lot of love, tolerance, and patience.

Punishment

AIDS in the Shadow of an American Institution

The states should pass laws and/or step up enforcement of
their laws against homosexual activity. As much of a moral
issue as it is, homosexual activity is also now a health threat
of epidemic proportions, and it simply cannot be allowed.

—Rev. Jimmy Swaggart, July 20, 1986[1]

It is time for the homosexual community to publicly chastise
itself for its promiscuous sexual practices that is causing the
spread of AIDS more to its own people and now the heterosexual community.

—Louis Sheldon, October 5, 1985[2]

AIDS carriers are a threat to society, and the state has a
compelling interest in protecting the uninfected. I am weary
of politicians who pander to perverts with an eye to the next
election.

—Former Indiana Representative Don Boys, June 24, 1988[3]

We sue for everything that our forefathers would never have
done, and we blame everybody for everything. Now that we
have done all of this, we have AIDS, child abuse, wife abuse,
satanic cults, gang killings, rampant dope dealers and users,
children killing children, people wanting everything free,
having children to get more, AFDC, murder rising, rape
more than ever in history, and the police cannot get the paper
work done before some judge lets those arrested back out on
the street.

—Joan Parrish, February 28, 1989[4]

From the very beginning of the epidemic, AIDS was linked to punishment. For evangelical Americans, AIDS represented divine punishment for the moral depravity sweeping America—namely, what conservatives derisively termed the "homosexual lifestyle." According to a 1987 Gallup poll, 61 percent of American evangelicals and 50 percent of non-evangelicals agreed with the statement "I sometimes think AIDS is a punishment for the decline in moral standards."[5] Televangelists like Jimmy Swaggart and Pat Robertson took to the airways to publicly condemn homosexuality as the cause of AIDS. Their like-minded political counterparts, activists such as William F. Buckley and Lyndon LaRouche, spearheaded campaigns aimed at getting states to pass punitive laws: to criminalize homosexuality, to tattoo newly diagnosed patients, to raid gay establishments.[6]

AIDS activists fiercely resisted these policies as draconian efforts to trample on civil liberties—policies that they argued were stigmatizing and thus likely to be counterproductive in the fight against AIDS.[7] Activists argued that freedom and privacy, not coercion and intrusive surveillance, were the keys to a successful disease control strategy. Despite their efforts, in the late 1980s state lawmakers around the country began to introduce criminal legislation targeting people living with HIV, whom they viewed as recklessly exposing their sexual partners to the disease. Echoing the sentiments of many Americans, a California newspaper editorial argued in 1987 that these laws were needed "to prevent unstable AIDS victims from passing on a death sentence to others."[8] Although they are sometimes mislabeled as "HIV transmission laws," most criminal laws enacted in the United States governing HIV exposure and/or disclosure make no mention of transmission or even the risk of that outcome. Instead, these new offenses resemble what prosecutors call a "crime of omission": by failing to reveal their HIV status to their partners, HIV-positive people in dozens of states can now face stiff prison penalties if charged under these felony statutes.

Although AIDS crystallized a specific set of social anxieties about sex, drugs, and death, the brand of punitive rhetoric and policies it spirited was not unique to AIDS in the 1980s. While President Reagan's administration is notorious for its callous indifference to the epidemic, First Lady Nancy Reagan is equally notorious for her Just Say No campaign against drugs. President Nixon first announced a war on drugs in 1971, but it was ratcheted up to new heights in the 1980s as federal and state authorities instituted a swath of new policies aimed at keeping drug users behind bars for as long as possible.[9] In the midst of these heated policy debates, some authorities even made extremely sensational calls for drug dealers to be put to death. In 1986, for example, Vice President George Bush told reporters that he would probably support the death penalty for large-scale drug dealers.[10] Four years later, Los Angeles Police Chief Daryl Gates (founder of the D.A.R.E. school program) testified before Congress that he believed casual drug users were treasonous and "ought to be taken out and shot."[11]

There are striking similarities between the conservative backlash to AIDS and the crackdown on drugs. While conservatives promoted policies that targeted homosexuality in the face of AIDS, so too did they promote policies that targeted stigmatized minorities in their war on drugs. The racism underlying the Reagan-era drug war was belied by its special focus on a drug that was disproportionately used by poor Black Americans: crack cocaine.[12] Indeed, Congress enacted the Anti-Drug Abuse Act of 1986 that mandated extremely different sentences for crack cocaine (five years for five grams) and its powdered cousin more commonly used by Whites (five years for *five hundred* grams); while this one hundred-to-one disparity was on its face "color-blind," critics nonetheless viewed it as racist because of its devastatingly disparate impact on Black men.[13] By the end of the decade, America's jail and prison population had doubled to over one million inmates; while African Americans constituted just 12.1 percent of the American population in 1990, they made up a lopsided 48.4 percent of its booming prison population.[14] Like the homophobia that haunted the conservative backlash to AIDS in America, racism drove America's obsession with punishing crack cocaine.

The war on drugs and the punitive response to HIV are but two examples of a more seismic shift in American corrections policy; lawmakers increasingly turned away from the rehabilitative spirit of the 1960s and 1970s in favor of far more punitive approaches that were rooted in retribution—or punishment for punishment's sake. This trend away from rehabilitation was driven by three key social factors. First, crime rates had risen sharply from the 1960s, reaching historically high levels just as AIDS began to emerge in the early 1980s.[15] Second, inconsistent social science findings had eroded the confidence of American criminal justice authorities in the effectiveness of such programs, although they had seen rehabilitation as a key part of their mission during the 1960s and 1970s.[16] Third, conservatives organized a racist backlash to civil rights activism that linked criminality with race and frequently portrayed young Black men as lawless "superpredators" that needed to be controlled and punished.[17] These three factors struck fear into the hearts and minds of middle-class and White Americans, leading to escalating calls for "tough-on-crime" policies that disproportionately impacted the poor and racial minorities.[18]

This network of punitive policies led to dramatically higher rates of incarceration in the United States. Since 2002, America has had the highest incarceration rate in the world—surpassing even repressive regimes such as Russia.[19] Although the total correctional population peaked in 2007, 716 of 100,000 Americans were behind bars in 2013 (the latest year this figure was available at the time of publication).[20] Far from being a reflection of increasing crime rates, incarceration rates have skyrocketed while crime rates have plummeted. This spike in incarceration cannot be entirely explained by increasing crime or even a rise in the number of arrests; sociologists instead explain that much of the increase in incarceration can be explained by determinations made after arrest: rather than issuing warnings or minor citations, criminal justice authorities are incarcerating a greater share of arrested defendants than ever before.[21] This panoply of punishment has reinforced and deepened racial inequality in American society, leading to some to charge that it represents a new era of Jim Crow.[22] For example, researchers estimate that in 2004, 33.4 percent of African American adult males had a felony conviction as compared to 7.5 percent of adults overall.[23] Higher rates of incarceration are associated with numerous negative outcomes, from unemployment to worsened health and family dissolution.[24] This "mass incarceration" has led sociologists to argue that punishment has become a new American institution that is fundamentally disrupting the way our society is organized.[25]

The story of mass incarceration is now well known among social scientists and even among many Americans as popular books such as Michelle Alexander's *The New Jim Crow* have helped to disseminate its central thesis: that a highly racialized war on drugs in the 1980s and 1990s helped to propel a massive spike in incarceration rates, with particularly devastating consequences for African Americans. However, scholars have recently pointed out that the war on drugs is but one of many theaters in the American war on crime. For example, experts argue that an undeclared war on sex simmered and eventually erupted just as Americans had begun to lose confidence in the war on drugs.[26] Even as the number of Americans under correctional supervision (including those in jail, in prison, on probation, and on parole) flattened and declined slightly between 2006 and 2013, the rolls of state sex offender registries ballooned 35 percent to include nearly 750,000 Americans.[27] A recent study found that Black Americans are registered at rates twice that of White Americans—reflecting the broader racialized dynamic of American criminal justice.[28]

Because HIV is sexually transmitted and was immediately linked to homosexuality, it may be tempting to view efforts to criminalize HIV as merely another example of efforts to criminalize nonnormative sexuality. However, *Punishing Disease* reveals that punitive policies toward people living with HIV are not driven solely by an interest in policing sexual morality. The first three chapters of *Punishing Disease* reveal that, instead, the criminalization of HIV is but one of the more recent examples in public health history of an effort to control disease by coercion and punishment—what this book terms *punitive disease control*. Although calls for punitive HIV control measures quickly became intertwined with (and at times nearly indistinguishable from) calls to police sexual norms, these two social projects are not the same. As this book reveals, the impetus to control, segregate, and punish the sick has a long history that stretches back to plagues such as smallpox and the Spanish flu, epidemics whose spread had little to do with sex.

The popularity of punitive approaches to public health practice has waxed and waned over time in concert with a changing medical landscape. Public health began to make headway against infectious disease mortality in the early twentieth century through an emphasis on promoting nutrition and sanitation. There has been considerable debate over whether these improvements in quality of life were responsible for reducing mortality as compared to the advent of vaccines, antibiotics, and other new medical technologies in the mid-twentieth-century.[29] Whatever the true causes may have been, however, many medical authorities attributed much of the twentieth-century declines in mortality to medical technologies and, as such, came to view pills and needles as the public health tools of tomorrow. In light of this changing medical landscape, many medical authorities were hopeful that coercive measures would be unnecessary in a new era of low mortality associated with infectious disease. As *Punishing Disease* reveals, however, AIDS gravely undermined this new optimism as a chorus of critics trumpeted a return to the coercive strategies of the past.

Although the history of punitive disease control stretches back centuries, no disease in modern American history has been met with a similarly systematic campaign to criminalize people living with an infectious disease. The second half of this book examines a second story: how a social problem typically perceived as medical—in this case, infectious disease—

became a target for criminalization. This story flips on its head the classic approach in medical sociology to studying the process of "medicalization," or how social problems previously understood as nonmedical come under the jurisdiction of medical authorities and institutions. Although this concept may seem foreign to readers new to medical sociology, many may recognize the sociological critique of its most famous example: attention deficit hyperactivity disorder (ADHD). Before that diagnosis was popularized in the 1960s, the same set of behaviors among children that would be diagnosed as disease today was historically viewed instead as kids behaving badly.[30] Crucially, pharmaceutical companies quickly began profiting off the sale of new stimulant therapies as doctors diagnosed ever-greater numbers of American children with the disorder.[31] Medicalization is therefore often described as the transformation "from badness to sickness."[32]

The second half of *Punishing Disease* looks, instead, at how HIV was transformed from sickness to badness under the criminal law, or what this book terms the *criminalization of sickness*. Under what circumstances do police and prosecutors claim jurisdiction over social problems typically thought of as medical problems? How is HIV litigated in a criminal court? And what are the effects of criminalizing sickness? The final three chapters of this book grapple with these questions.

It is no mistake that authorities responded to the HIV epidemic with a new punitiveness. Three historical factors helped to shape the punitive response to AIDS. First, the coincidence of HIV's emergence with the birth of mass incarceration as a social institution meant that lawmakers were already in the habit of proposing handcuffs and prisons as solutions to social problems. *Punishing Disease* reveals the consequences of the emergence of AIDS in the shadow of this American institution's ascent.

Second, HIV was immediately linked to stigmatized social groups that were, at that historical moment, particularly hated and, in many cases, already viewed as suspected criminals. In 1981, when the first cases of AIDS were reported, consensual sex between same-sex partners was a criminal offense in twenty-two states and the District of Columbia. Initial news reports described the disease as a "gay cancer" that was linked to marginalized social groups collectively known as the 4-H club: homosexuals, Haitians, heroin users, and hemophiliacs.[33] That the epidemic was symbolically synonymous with so many highly stigmatized and potentially criminal classes of people—rather than housewives, babies, or some other sympathy-engendering group—made criminalization a more obvious response.

Third, during the early 1980s, there was widespread uncertainty and fear over the cause and effects of AIDS. This uncertainty created an opportunity for alternative theories to emerge, particularly the theory that AIDS was caused not by a virus but by a deviant lifestyle (namely, drug use and promiscuous homosexual sex).[34] Early missteps by medical authorities allowed these alternative theories to thrive. For example, by originally naming the disease gay-related immune deficiency (G.R.I.D.), authorities communicated an implicitly causal relationship between homosexuality and infection to the general public.[35] Such lifestyle theories of AIDS were bolstered by the disease's bizarre and terrifying progression; instead of presenting with a unique set of symptoms, AIDS patients were instead disfigured and/or killed by a litany of normally rare and horrifying diseases described as "opportunistic infections." Sometimes analogized by conservatives to the Biblical plagues of Egypt, these diseases included Kaposi's sarcoma (a cancer that causes purplish splotches on the skin), cytomegalovirus (a virus that causes blindness), and toxoplasmosis (a fungal infection that can cause seizures and swelling of the brain).

Taken together, these three historical factors created a perfect storm for punitive rhetoric and criminalization on a level not seen before in the modern history of American disease control.

Although many readers are likely to associate punishment most readily with the criminal justice system, the analysis contained in these pages is not limited to that institution. The first section of the book examines how institutions of public health shaped punitive policies toward infectious disease historically and, more recently, toward AIDS. Although some readers may view public health as a comparatively benevolent institution, this book does not view either public health or criminal justice as inherently good or bad. Instead, this book adopts the classic sociological approach to examining how public health and the law label and control *deviance*—defined by sociologists as behavior perceived as violating social expectations.[36] *Punishing Disease* tracks the historical origins of these norms as well as the punitive responses to their violation. From this labeling perspective, understanding how punishment became a legitimate disease control strategy requires an examination of both institutions of criminalization and institutions of disease control. In this way, this book not only contributes to an understanding of how public health labels, surveils, controls, and *punishes* people living with infectious diseases ("punitive disease control"); it also illuminates how the criminal justice system has come to control a conventionally medical category and with what effects ("the criminalization of sickness").

Punitive disease control and the criminalization of sickness represent two sides of the same coin; they share an interest in enforcing social norms and sanctioning behavior labeled deviant but differ in their institutional contexts (for example, public health versus criminal justice). In some cases, the norms in question are literally spelled out, as is the case in the twenty-eight states with criminal statutes that require people living with HIV to disclose their HIV-status to sexual partners before having sex. In other cases, these norms may be less formalized and subject to greater degrees of interpretation, such as public health laws that grant health officials authority to sanction people living with infectious diseases whose behavior they determine constitutes a "health threat to others."

While criminal justice and public health policies may determine how authorities *ought* to respond to such norm violations, their enforcement is not automated; legal and health authorities (prosecutors, judges, health officials, nurses, and others) must investigate rule breakers and decide how to proceed in each case. Taken together, their actions bring the criminal, civil, and administrative law to life. In this way, *Punishing Disease* continues the long tradition in sociolegal studies of examining the gap between the law on the books and the law in action.[37]

As this book shows, however, punishment is more than just the sum of state laws and policies and the actions of state authorities who enforce them. Stigma and ignorance often serve as invisible hands guiding the wheel as lawmakers draft statutes and authorities determine how they are applied.[38] Stigma—against HIV, against gay men, against prostitution—can lubricate the transition from "sickness to badness," while ignorance about how HIV is transmitted can facilitate punitive responses to scenarios that involve little or no risk of transmitting the disease.

This book also examines how individual events and actors can provoke the spread of criminalization under the right conditions. For example, sensationally reported crimes can quickly prompt a legislator to introduce a bill aiming to punish related future offenses. This is especially true when moral entrepreneurs (or individuals who champion a particular cause) lobby for lawmakers to draft legislation or for prosecutors to press charges.

Each chapter of *Punishing Disease* examines a different facet of a social problem that is collectively referred to as "the criminalization of HIV." While that moniker implies a unidirectional and monolithic social process, the reality is far less tidy; it involves a wide array of players operating in different institutional contexts and is dependent on numerous cultural and political variables. Moreover, the pathways to criminalization and end products vary tremendously by state and sometimes even by county. Laws might be passed but never enforced. Or lawmakers may have shunned HIV-specific criminal laws, but creative prosecutors nonetheless find ways to punish under general statutes (typically felony assault). Nor is criminalization a dichotomous state, with HIV being "criminalized" in some states and "not criminalized" in others; punitive approaches to HIV instead fall along a spectrum of possibilities. No single book could reasonably claim to have told all the stories about the relationship between punishment and HIV. Instead, each chapter of *Punishing Disease* tells a different slice of a complicated story.

As such, this book should not be read as an exhaustive review of every attempt by health and legal authorities to control infectious disease or even just HIV throughout recent history. For example, public health practitioners reading this book from progressive coastal cities such as San Francisco or New York City may find the punitive strain of public health practice described by some of their Midwestern counterparts in chapter 3 to be entirely foreign or even objectionable. In highlighting these punitive strategies, the goal is not to erase or negate less punitive approaches to controlling disease that certainly do exist. Instead, the goals of *Punishing Disease* are (1) to examine under what conditions an impulse to punish becomes fused to the social project of controlling disease, and (2) to analyze the effects of this marriage.

OVERVIEW OF THE BOOK

The chapters in the first section, "Punitive Disease Control," collectively analyze policies and enforcement practices. This analysis focuses on a strain of public health and policy that promotes coercive and punitive strategies for controlling disease. This is sometimes evidenced through the direct action of health officials who surveil and coerce people living with diseases. Or punitive disease control may be achieved indirectly, by promoting the idea that people living with infectious diseases are (at least in part) individually responsible and thus culpable for their infection and the infection of others.

Chapter 1, "Controlling Typhoid Mary," mines the history of infectious disease control to analyze how AIDS prompted calls for a return to the coercive techniques of the past. For centuries, quarantine was a staple of public health efforts to combat such scourges as the plague and Spanish flu. However, that begin to change as improved nutrition and sanitation and then the advent of vaccines, antibiotics, and new treatments effectively put an end to diseases that had once killed or maimed millions, such as polio and smallpox. In this optimistic context, public health practitioners in the mid-twentieth century began to view quarantine and coercive public health tactics as retrograde approaches of yesteryear. As chronic illness replaced infectious disease as the leading cause of death in the twentieth century, public health began to view individual health behaviors—such as smoking and diet—as the primary causes of disease. But the rise of an unknown and terrifying infectious disease eventually called AIDS threatened to turn back the clock on public health practice, as conservative advocates demanded that public health tattoo everyone diagnosed with HIV and quarantine or imprison those individuals deemed a threat to public health.

Chapter 2, "'HIV Stops with Me,'" examines how shifts in HIV prevention policy and practice have deepened the notion that HIV-positive people are individually responsible for the epidemic. While many Americans still imagine HIV prevention campaigns as billboards telling HIV-negative people to use a condom, that approach is increasingly a relic of the past. In practice, health authorities reorganized the entire prevention enterprise beginning in the 2000s: people already infected with HIV were urged not to infect their partners and, more recently, to take their medication. The most visible break in the nation's prevention strategy came in 2003, when the Centers for Disease Control and Prevention (CDC) announced its new priorities for HIV prevention. Critics expressed alarm that condoms were virtually absent from the document. This announcement came on the heels of a growing sentiment among public health experts that declining rates of condom use required new strategies for keeping the epidemic in check. This chapter tells the story of how a series of CDC policy shifts over the next decade worked to "repolarize" the very notion of doing HIV prevention away from targeting HIV-negative people and toward targeting people living with HIV. As it turns out, there is a very fine line between assigning individual responsibility and assigning blame. By advocating for HIV-positive people to take individual responsibility for preventing new infections, public health has inadvertently contributed to the notion that people with communicable disease are responsible for their illness and, as such, blameworthy for its continued spread.

Chapter 3, "The Public Health Police," examines how local health officials police the behavior of people living with HIV in their efforts to end new infections. As the HIV epidemic wore on in the 2000s, public health authorities became enamored with the idea of ending AIDS. Health departments began to track HIV-positive clients more closely, aiming to control their behavior and ensure their adherence to treatment regimens. This chapter explores how local health authorities in Michigan ensure that HIV-positive clients behave in a manner officials deem responsible—and how they catch and punish those who do not. While the state maintains that the work of local health officials is done solely in the interest of promoting public health, their efforts to control HIV-positive clients reveal that they are also engaged in policing and law enforcement.

The second section of the book, "The Criminalization of Sickness," examines the history and application of HIV exposure and disclosure laws in the United States. Taken together, these chapters reveal how stigma, fear, and ignorance have driven efforts to criminalize people living with HIV—sometimes with unexpected effects.

Chapter 4, "Making HIV a Crime," analyzes the state legislative debates that led lawmakers to pass new, HIV-specific criminal laws across the United States. Initially, prosecutors pressed charges against HIV-positive people under general assault and attempted murder statutes. However, prosecutors repeatedly fumbled efforts to legally secure defendants' medical records or, in other cases, failed to prove that they had acted with criminal intent—a key element in common law known as *mens rea*. In the wake of a series of high-profile dismissals and acquittals under general statutes, calls for HIV-specific criminal legislation grew louder. Police organized early campaigns to criminalize HIV by publicly shaming HIV-positive women arrested for prostitution. Misdemeanor prostitution statutes, they argued, failed to protect society from their recklessness; new felony laws were needed. In other cases, the impulse to criminalize HIV grew out of simultaneous debates over the decriminalization of sodomy. Lawmakers invoked the specter of legal gay sex in their calls for new, HIV-specific criminal legislation. Finally, one state lawmaker helped to institutionalize HIV criminalization when a bill she introduced in Illinois formed the basis of a widely disseminated American Legislative Exchange Council (ALEC) model statute. Together, these social anxieties and interest-group campaigns sparked an epidemic of legislation that ultimately spread to forty-five states.

Chapter 5, "HIV on Trial," goes inside American courtrooms to analyze how HIV exposure and disclosure laws were enforced between 1992 and 2010. After a widely reported and sensationalized conviction in Michigan in 1992, the number of criminal cases against HIV-positive people quickly grew throughout the 1990s. While medical advances dramatically changed HIV outside the courtroom, those changes were scarcely evident in Michigan and Tennessee courtrooms over the next two decades: prosecutors and judges continually justified their harsh sentences by calling HIV-positive defendants murderers and by casting HIV as a deadly weapon—even in cases where HIV could not have plausibly been transmitted. By tracing the impact that stigmatizing language has on courtroom decisions, this chapter demonstrates that courtroom talk is more than "just words."[39]

Finally, Chapter 6, "Victim Impact," analyzes which communities are most affected under HIV exposure and disclosure laws. In the wake of a sensational 2014 case involving a Black gay male defendant, some critics charged that HIV-specific criminal laws could be used to target Black gay men. This chapter draws on an original dataset of convictions under HIV-specific criminal laws in six states to evaluate whether the enforcement of HIV exposure and disclosure laws has discriminatory effects. Findings show that victim characteristics—rather than defendant demographics—shape uneven patterns in the application of the law. This "victim impact" flips expected patterns of discrimination, resulting in disproportionately high rates of convictions among heterosexual male defendants; yet, at sentencing, Black defendants are punished more severely, women are treated more leniently, and men accused of not disclosing to women are punished more harshly than those accused by men. This chapter digests these trends using the tools of sociology, epidemiology, and criminology to offer a specific diagnosis for reform.

The conclusion threads the needle of these six chapters, building a cohesive model of the engines driving the criminalization of sickness. In addition, the conclusion makes explicit the pitfalls of using the criminal justice system to tackle disease. Put simply, punishment is not the appropriate response to infectious disease; the criminal justice system is poorly suited for managing epidemics. The conclusion explains why this is so and what an alternative approach might look like.

At the heart of *Punishing Disease* is a central question: Why punishment? Although public health and medical institutions are designed to manage epidemics and viruses, punishment as an institution is built to manage crime. The tools designed for one job—pills versus handcuffs, hospitals versus prisons—are not effective for the other. The tool for punishing deviance is a hammer ill-suited for managing disease. In criminalizing sickness, HIV exposure and disclosure laws threaten to erode the boundary between sickness and crime, paving the way for a new era of criminalization that targets disease.

Punishing Disease reveals that criminalization has predictable effects. It reproduces stigma. It does not prevent disease. And it codifies outdated and deeply flawed ideas about HIV into law. Now that the door to criminalizing sickness is open, what other ailments will follow? When our colleague shows up to work with the flu in the future, will we wonder whether we should call the police? While we cannot predict what will happen tomorrow, moves in several state legislatures to extend their HIV-specific criminal laws to include new diseases such as hepatitis and meningitis demonstrate that this possibility is more than academic.

PART ONE

Punitive Disease Control

CHAPTER 1

Controlling Typhoid Mary

When reports began to emerge in October 2014 that a New York City doctor had fallen ill with Ebola, media outlets whipped themselves into a frenzy. Mayor Bill de Blasio attempted to reassure the public that there was no risk of an Ebola outbreak in the Big Apple at a press conference announcing that Dr. Craig Spencer had tested positive for Ebola. "We want to state at the outset—there is no reason for New Yorkers to be alarmed," de Blasio said. The mayor's efforts to assuage the public, however, did not dissuade a flurry of Twitter commenters, bloggers, and even mainstream media reporters from feeding public hysteria. Predictably, the New York City tabloids ran sensational front-page headlines that capitalized on New Yorkers' fears: "EBOLA HERE!" (*New York Post*) and "NY DOC HAS EBOLA" (*New York Daily News*).

Over the next twenty-four hours, reporters began to piece together the timeline of Dr. Spencer's movements through a combination of news releases from the governor, the New York City Health Department, and even the ride-sharing service Uber. New Yorkers were collectively outraged by the story that crystallized: not only did Spencer not remain in his apartment under self-quarantine, but he took an Uber to go bowling in Williamsburg! The *New York Times*—the city's standard-bearer— ran a short, dry online piece headlined "Can You Get Ebola from a Bowling Ball?"[1] The *New York Daily News* ran a more sensational piece, "New Yorkers, Twitter Users Wonder Why Dr. Craig Spencer Went Bowling," that featured a collection of more than a dozen angry posts from Twitter users condemning the doctor's actions.[2] That article cited a post from Twitter user ericbolling that encapsulated much of the public anger expressed towards Spencer online: "ABSOLUTELY NO SYM-PATHY for a doctor who knows he's been in contact w/Ebola, goes bowling, takes 2 subways, has contact with girl, Uber. None."[3] Online comment threads predictably devolved into angry disputes over issues as diverse as gentrification (keywords: uber, Williamsburg) and Ebola transmission pathways (keywords: saliva, bowling ball).

Dr. Spencer's infection came on the heels of the death of Thomas Eric Duncan, a Liberian man who became ill after traveling to the United States.[4] Furious debate centered on Duncan's first visit to the hospital after he initially developed symptoms. Although he told a nurse he had traveled to Africa, that information was not communicated to other medical staff.[5] When his providers asked him if he had been in contact with Ebola patients, he reportedly said no—a statement that was not true. Medical staff discharged him with a prescription for antibiotics, sending him back out into the world, where he might have inadvertently exposed others to the disease.[6] Authorities in Liberia were outraged—not with medical providers or their failure to catch his infection earlier, but with Duncan himself. Liberian president Ellen Johnson Sirleaf char-acterized his failure to report contact with Ebola patients as "unpar-donable."[7] Airport officials went further, threatening to file criminal charges against Duncan should he ever return home.

Across the Hudson River, Nurse Kaci Hickox returned to New Jersey from Sierra Leone, where she had been treating Ebola patients. After being quarantined in New Jersey by health officials for two days, she was allowed to return home to Maine, where health officials pressured her to quarantine herself.[8] She openly defied those calls and was photographed biking around her hometown (a fact jokingly cited in a *Saturday Night Live* skit about her case: "that's Kaci with an 'I'—as in I don't care if I got Ebola, I'm riding my damn bike!"[9]). Maine governor Paul LePage threatened to take action but hesitated to follow New Jersey's lead in instituting mandatory twenty-one-day quarantine policies for anyone who had been in contact with Ebola patients after Centers for Disease Control and Prevention (CDC) director Anthony Fauci called such poli-cies "a little bit draconian."[10] Backed by the American Civil Liberties Union, Hickox sued New Jersey for depriving her of her liberty in a case that remains pending.[11]

The range of responses to these three cases—moral outrage, criminali-zation, and quarantine—illustrates the spectrum of coercive and punitive attitudes toward the sick, which have deep roots in public health history. The tension between individual liberty and public health stretches as far back as Typhoid Mary, an Irish immigrant and asymptomatic typhoid carrier who was quarantined in 1907 by New York authorities. For centuries, public health officials have waged a battle—sometimes against overwhelming odds—to promote and protect the health of populations and to prevent the spread of disease. Controlling the actions of individuals and communities believed to spread disease has been a core public health strategy, including persuading people to take up practices believed to be "healthy" while discouraging or regulating those actions believed to be "unhealthy."[12] In its battle to preserve population health, a key weapon of public health has been what sociologists refer to as social control.

This chapter traces the history of coercion, persuasion, and regulation in American disease control—first, by examining the rise of coercive practices such as quarantine in the face of deadly and rapidly spreading infectious diseases like the plague; second, by turning to the rise of persuasion and regulation in the twentieth century as improved sanitation, better nutrition, and the advent of antibiotics and vaccines erased the most horrific diseases from the American epidemiological landscape; and third, by revealing how the emergence of new infectious diseases in the late twentieth century such as AIDS and Ebola, as well as new antibiotic-resistant strains of old scourges like tuberculosis, sparked renewed demands for coercive and punitive approaches to disease control.

COERCION AND PUNISHMENT IN THEORY AND PRACTICE

Coercion and punishment are not necessarily the same.[13] Health authorities have an interest in controlling disease and that has at times required restricting the freedom and movement of individuals and even entire communities. In the context of public health law, *coercion* is defined as restricting the liberty of a person or a group of people in the interest of protecting or promoting the public's health; it does not necessarily imply that the person or group of people has committed an offense.[14] Punishment, on the other hand, is a social response to a person's wrongdoing; while it necessarily involves coercion (through fines, jail time, or other means), it is also specifically intended to punish.

Although on paper this distinction between coercion and punishment appears straightforward, in practice it can become muddied. For example, the Supreme Court has upheld "civil confinement" programs under which convicted sex offenders are detained well beyond their court-ordered prison sentences, potentially indefinitely, as deemed necessary by corrections officials. The court has ruled that this continued detention does not violate constitutional guarantees against double jeopardy because the procedures are civil rather than criminal in nature; the prisoner's extended detention, the court further reasoned, is therefore not punishment at all because "the commitment determination is made based on a 'mental abnormality' or 'personality disorder' rather than on one's criminal intent."[15] The fact that the conditions of civil commitment are virtually indistinguishable from prison is treated almost as a coincidence; the programs' intended function differentiates their constitutional standing. Public health experts have made similar observations of the state's power to quarantine: under certain conditions, the deprivation of liberty imposed through isolation exceeds what is constitutionally permitted under the criminal justice system.[16]

These legal and philosophical distinctions may prove cold comfort to the detained sex offender or the quarantined person; whatever the state's intent, the effect of detention may well be experienced as *punitive*. Although the coercive practices critically examined in this chapter may not constitute punishment in the strict, constitutional-law sense of the term, this chapter nonetheless considers historical cases in which public health practice has taken on characteristics of state-sanctioned punishment.[17]

When and how does coercion turn punitive in public health practice? The hallmark of a punitive campaign is the attribution of blame: punishment is meted out by the state against individuals who have been found culpable. Calls to blame someone for their actions are nearly invariably followed by calls for their punishment. This is most obvious in cases of criminalization in which individuals are tried before a court of law, found guilty, and punished accordingly. But criminal justice authorities do not have a monopoly on blame. Although medical problems are supposed to be handled neutrally, many people—including some doctors and public health officials—nonetheless ascribe blame to individuals who become sick.[18] This chapter examines moments in public health history in which the line between coercion and punishment has been blurred.

QUARANTINE AND COERCION IN PUBLIC HEALTH HISTORY

On an otherwise ordinary winter afternoon in 1907, authorities arrived at a Park Avenue home in New York City to take the cook, Mary

Mallon, into custody. Mallon was accused not of theft or murder but instead of unwittingly spreading typhoid to several members of the households in which she worked as a cook. Authorities had tracked Mallon down by following a trail of "breadcrumbs" left in her wake: a string of typhoid infections and deaths. Antibiotics did not yet exist, and nearly 10 percent of those infected with the disease died.[19]

Authorities told Mallon that she could have her freedom if she allowed them to remove her gallbladder (where the disease was believed to be festering) or agreed to change her profession. Mallon refused, in large part because she did not believe that she was a carrier of the disease, and, as such, she argued that her detention was unjust. In 1910, Mallon finally relented and agreed to stop cooking and work instead as a laundress. However, after her release, she became frustrated with the lower wages of laundry workers. Adopting an alias to conceal her widely reported identity, she returned to cooking. In 1915, authorities detained her again after food she had prepared was found to be the source of another outbreak. She spent the next twenty-three years in isolation on North Brother Island at Riverside Hospital, which was largely used to quarantine tuberculosis patients. The facility was notoriously isolating and poorly managed. One historian describes the site in this way:

> Five miles up the East River, approximately 1,500 feet east of 140th Street in the South Bronx and, on a bad day, downwind from the city's garbage dump on Riker's Island, was the city lazaretto, Riverside Hospital on North Brother Island. Even a century later, when one stands on the rocky shoals of the island, peering into the distance, the city seems remote and inaccessible. The sense of loneliness on North Brother Island is almost palpable. The site had been used as a small hospital for the poor afflicted with contagious diseases since the 1850s. . . . The facilities lacked space, financial resources, adequate medical equipment, and nursing personnel.[20]

Mallon spent the remainder of her life on North Brother Island's "rocky shoals," where she died in 1938. Soon after her first quarantine, a 1908 issue of the *Journal of the American Medical Association* labeled her "typhoid Mary"—a moniker that would live on in notoriety long after her death.[21]

Although Mallon's case is perhaps the most widely reported quarantine in public health history, she was hardly the first person in history to be quarantined. The fact that the hospital she called home was located on an island is the relic of a much longer history that begins in medieval Europe during the fourteenth century. The bubonic plague—colloquially known as the Black Death—claimed the lives of millions. (It has been estimated that 75–200 million Europeans died of the plague between 1346 and 1353.) Scholars believe the epidemic began in central Asia and traveled along trading routes to Western Europe by way of Italian merchants. Sicily was wracked by one of the first known outbreaks in October 1347, followed quickly by Genoa and Venice in January 1348. Confronted with this rapidly spreading and poorly understood affliction, officials in the Italian city states forced ships from plague-infested countries to remain anchored for a period of time at island isolation stations known as *lazarettos*. Infected sailors were confined to hospitals on the island. Sailors and ships were originally confined for thirty days under a *trentino* policy; when it was extended to forty days, the policy became known as *quarantino*.[22]

On land, infected people were isolated to their homes in cities across Europe. Authorities erected cordons sanitaires, blockades that sectioned off whole neighborhoods to prevent anyone from entering or leaving. Unfortunately, cordons sanitaires were rarely successful because the plague was not primarily spread by human-to-human contact. Instead, most scholars today agree that the disease was spread primarily through rodents infested with a species of flea that carried the bacteria *Yersinia pestis* in its gut; while blockades could restrict the movement of humans, they did little to prevent rodents from freely moving across cities.[23] But this fact was not yet known so authorities continued to cordon off homes and entire neighborhoods.

When colonists left Europe for the New World, they brought these practices with them. Quarantine and isolation were widely used from the seventeenth through the nineteenth century as America faced epidemics of smallpox, yellow fever, cholera and typhus.[24] Although the late-eighteenth-century sanitarian movement—which focused on providing clean water, sewage disposal, and hygienic housing—had a profound impact on infectious disease long before effective medical treatments or vaccines were developed, equally important were the more coercive practices of quarantine and isolation.

In the United States, two systems of quarantine gradually emerged. In ports, a system of maritime quarantine stations—eventually managed by the federal government—detained and inspected cargo, crew, and immigrants from countries with outbreaks of contagious diseases. In cities and towns, local outbreaks were managed by state and local health officials. In the wake of the Industrial Revolution, overcrowding, unsanitary living conditions, and urban poverty led to frequent outbreaks of infectious diseases. Local officials ordered the isolation and confinement of infected individuals and suspected carriers to "pest-houses," hospital wards, or their homes.[25] Nineteenth-century public health officials adopted other methods that were only slightly less coercive: compulsory vaccination, imposing fines or confinement of those who refused, mandatory reporting of infected patients by physicians to disease registries, contact tracing, and other surveillance techniques.

Better nutrition, improved sanitation, and the advent of vaccines and modern medicine began to turn the tide against many widespread infectious diseases in the twentieth century. In the wake of these shifts in mortality and morbidity, many public health experts came to view coercive strategies for containing epidemics as old-fashioned or even regressive. Medical historian Eugenia Tognotti describes the perspective at the turn of the century:

> In 1911, the eleventh edition of *Encyclopedia Britannica* emphasized that "the old sanitary preventive system of detention of ships and men" was "a thing of the past." At the time, the battle against infectious diseases seemed about to be won, and the old health practices would only be remembered as an archaic scientific fallacy. No one expected that within a few years, nations would again be forced to implement emergency measures in response to a tremendous health challenge.[26]

That challenge came in the form of the devastating influenza epidemics that traveled around the world in 1918, claiming the lives of between 20 and 40 million people. In the face of such a rapidly spreading and deadly disease, local municipalities closed churches, schools, and movie theaters and prohibited attendance at funerals and other public gatherings.[27]

New York City health authorities tried to control the rapidly spreading influenza outbreak while allowing for a certain amount of freedom of movement.[28] Instead of shutting down businesses altogether, the city's health commissioner, Dr. Royal S. Copeland, implemented staggered business hours in an attempt to limit congestion in public places. "Offices opened at 8:40 A.M. and closed at 4:30 P.M., while wholesalers started their days earlier, and nontextile manufacturers moved their start time to 9:30."[29] The effectiveness of these policies is not known, but historical analyses suggest the death rate may have been slightly mitigated in the Big Apple as compared to its neighbors, Boston and Philadelphia, which did not implement similar policies.[30]

Confinement and isolation continued through the first half of the twentieth century, used occasionally during outbreaks of scarlet fever and polio and more frequently for tuberculosis. Until antibiotic treatments for tuberculosis were developed in the 1940s, confinement in a sanatorium for three to six months was the standard treatment for tuberculosis.[31] Even with the development of antibiotics, however, coercive practices for containing tuberculosis did not end. Tuberculosis patients who refused treatment were handled especially aggressively. In 1949, for example, Seattle's Firland Sanatorium established a locked ward intended for the treatment of only the most noncompliant and "recalcitrant" of tuberculosis patients, who were deemed a threat to public health. In practice, however, the facility was used much more widely and ultimately housed over a thousand patients. The vast majority of patients quarantined at Firland were poor alcoholics living in one destitute neighborhood, Seattle's Skid Road, who were detained even if they were noncontagious or adhering to treatment protocols. Medical historian Barron Lerner describes the facility in stark terms:

> Known as Ward 6 and located in the old naval brig, the unit was equipped with both locked doors and heavily screened windows. All patients admitted to Ward 6 (most of whom were intoxicated) spent the first 24 hours in one of seven locked cells, which contained only concrete slabs covered by thin mattresses.[32]

Historical examples like Firland reveal how well-intentioned disease control strategies can turn punitive when disproportionately applied to specific marginalized groups. The facility—described as a "model" for others around the country—persisted and even expanded for over a decade despite accusations that the facility had effectively institutionalized quarantine as a form of punishment without due process for poor alcoholics.[33]

Sexually transmitted infections (STIs) were also the target for a wide array of coercive policies aimed at controlling infectious diseases in United States history. During World War I, states implemented policies in response to public anxiety over "venereal diseases," such as mandatory screening to obtain a marriage license and screening of newborns. However, just as Seattle's tuberculosis program targeted poor alcoholics, America's venereal disease response during World War I reserved the most invasive and punitive policies for commercial sex workers. Authorities believed prostitutes were carriers and repositories for STIs. By March 1918, over thirty-two states had passed laws requiring that individuals arrested for prostitution be screened for STIs.[34] Just as in Seattle, this frequently involved medical detention that was not subject to the normal legal safeguards of the criminal justice system. Medical historian Allan Brandt offers a telling example:

In San Francisco, the Department of Health provided arrested women with circulars explaining, "You are in quarantine and cannot be released on bail. . . . If you are found ill with venereal disease you will go to the hospital and stay there until found negative. . . . No lawyer or other person can obtain your release."[35]

That their detention was done in the name of public health rather than in the name of punishment perversely allowed the state to more severely restrict the liberty of commercial sex workers. Despite the public health label attached to their detention, however, the fact that women engaged in a criminal offense, prostitution, were singled out for detention by the state suggests a punitive motive.

On the other side of the country, the Virginia State Board of Health provided its officers with the authority to detain anyone "reasonably suspected" of carrying an STI, which included "vagrants, prostitutes, keepers, inmates, and frequenters of houses of ill fame, prostitution and assignation, persons not of good fame, persons guilty of fornication, adultery, and lewd and lascivious conduct."[36] Despite such broadly construed categories, however, no efforts were made during the time to quarantine men for STIs; these policies were systematically enforced against women.

STIs again became the subject of coercive and punitive policies during World War II. For example, a 1945 Baltimore ordinance gave public health officials the power to isolate patients with syphilis or gonorrhea who refused penicillin treatment.[37] But just as before, the most aggressive tactics were reserved for female sex workers. The Army appointed former Prohibition champion Eliot Ness (whose efforts to take down Al Capone were fictionalized most recently in the HBO series *Boardwalk Empire*) to lead a campaign against prostitution. Sex workers were once again detained in large numbers, subjected to mandatory STI screening, and placed under quarantine until treated. During this time, estimates suggest that over seven hundred cities and towns closed down their red-light districts. With so many women arrested for sex work, many jails became overcrowded. Ness attempted to ease the strain on local corrections facilities by setting up nearly thirty "civilian conservation camps" to house detained prostitutes. These facilities offered more than just medical testing and treatment. Public health scholar Troy Thompson describes one Florida woman who ended up in such a camp in 1944:

In light of the 1943 Florida laws on prostitution, the police apprehended Jean and gave her an invasive vaginal examination. The court then convicted her and sent her to one of Florida's newly converted civilian conservation camps. Jean spent the next five weeks there receiving treatment, job training, and lessons in socially sanctioned morality.[38]

Despite detaining thousands of prostitutes, the Army's efforts failed to eliminate new STI infections among troops. Officials lamentingly changed their tune, blaming not prostitutes but "amateur girls—teenagers and older women—popularly known as 'khaki-wackies,' 'victory girls,' and 'good-time Charlottes.'"[39]

Estimates suggest that more than thirty thousand prostitutes were detained between World War I and World War II. These strident efforts reflect a pattern noted by historians: from their inception in the Middle Ages, campaigns to control the spread of infectious disease through coercion have frequently targeted particular groups: disfavored immigrant groups, the poor, the "deviant," and the "disenfranchised." Typhoid Mary is a telling example not just for her brazen resistance to public health quarantine but also because she was a poor immigrant woman working in service for wealthier families—a woman in a precarious social position, a woman without the resources to contest her detention. Mary Mallon became historical legend not just for her actions, but also because of her denigrated social standing. Other typhoid carriers living at the same time are all but forgotten—carriers such as Frederick Moersch, a German-born immigrant working as a confectioner, who infected more people with typhoid fever than Mallon. Moersch, like Mallon, was confined on North Brother Island in 1915 but, as a father and "skilled workman," was viewed far more favorably by the staff; after a brief detention, he was allowed to live at home, where the state even arranged for his rent to be paid.[40] Despite the similarities in their cases, Moersch was treated far more leniently, and his case is all but unknown to history.

This disparity is not unique to American public health history: public health measures have been enforced in deeply discriminatory ways for centuries, with the harshest, most coercive measures reserved for the most marginalized communities and people. It is in these historical moments that coercion becomes punitive. It would be impossible to review every example of this trend. Instead, figure 1 illustrates key examples of coercion and discrimination in public health history. In each case listed in figure 1, coercive measures intended to combat disease were aimed at marginalized groups. In fact, labeling a person or a community a threat to public health casts the sick as hostile aggressors rather than sympathetic victims. During epidemics, fear and stigma of contagion have heightened the social exclusion of already-stigmatized groups. Viewed in this light, quarantine comes dangerously close to being a metaphor for the need of elites to protect themselves from the "dangerous" classes.

The policies that this chapter describes did not go uncontested. Coercive measures, such as compulsory vaccination programs, mandatory treatment, quarantine, and isolation, often provoked popular resistance and were the subject of many legal challenges. However, these challenges rarely proved successful. Presented with a choice between promoting the freedom of the sick and protecting the health of the masses, U.S. courts have typically deferred to public health authorities and affirmed their prerogative to use coercive measures to control epidemics.

Perhaps the most important such decision came over a century ago with the Supreme Court's ruling in *Jacobson v. Massachusetts*. The case was brought by a Swedish immigrant to the United States, Henning Jacobson, who objected to an order from the Cambridge, Massachusetts, city council requiring that all adults be vaccinated for smallpox. The penalty for not complying was set by the state at $5 (about $100 today), and there was no set procedure for actually forcing anyone to be vaccinated. Jacobson was already familiar with state vaccination programs, which were in place in his home country of Sweden, but he objected to Cambridge's program on the grounds that he and his son had experienced adverse reactions to previous inoculations. The court ruled 7–2 against Jacobson, ruling that the state had the power to impose punishment (either a fine or imprisonment) for failing to comply, but that it could not force anyone to be vaccinated.[41]

The sweeping power of public health authorities to quarantine and isolate sick people against their will falls within the civil law, but it rivals the power of the criminal justice system to infringe on individual liberties. Moreover, "until relatively recently," notes medical ethics expert Ronald Bayer, "the protections accorded to defendants in criminal prosecutions have not been extended to those viewed as a threat to the public health."[42] This changed during the 1970s when courts began to reconsider due process claims from mental patients who were facing civil commitment against their wishes. After a federal district court struck down Wisconsin's commitment law in *Lessard v. Smith* (1972), other courts began to rule that patients were entitled to the due process protections of the Fourteenth Amendment: the rights to notice, to a fair hearing, to be represented by counsel, to cross-examine witnesses, and to hold the state to a clear and convincing standard of proof. One of the most important doctrines to come out of these decisions was the least

Coercion and Punishment in Modern Public Health History

1892   Following outbreaks of typhus and cholera, nativist sentiments led to quarantines of Jewish immigrants who arrived in New York City, while Italians arriving on the same boat were detained only briefly; that same year, first-class passengers were confined to hotels, while those in steerage consigned to an overcrowded quarantine facility with squalid conditions.[1]

1894   Milwaukee officials forced immigrants and poor residents into a quarantine hospital for smallpox.

1900   A San Francisco ordinance required that all Chinese residents of the city receive a dangerous experimental vaccine for plague. Following reports of nine deaths from plague, city officials roped off the Chinese quarter, quarantining 25,000 residents and closing Chinese businesses, while explicitly exempting non-Asians. The court overturned both ordinances, ruling that officials had acted with "an evil eye and an uneven hand."[2]

1902   After smallpox cases were identified in Boston, public health officials, with police in tow, forcibly inoculated African Americans and immigrants.[3]

1907   New York health authorities quarantined Mary Mallon, a poor immigrant woman working as a cook in a private home and carrier of Typhoid. Nicknamed "Typhoid Mary," Mallon would become synonymous with the spread of infectious disease.

1. Markel, *Quarantine!*
2. Parmet, "Legal Power and Legal Rights"; Tyson, "Short History of Quarantine."
3. George J. Annas, Wendy K. Mariner, and Wendy E. Parmet, *Pandemic Preparedness: The Need for a Public Health—Not a Law Enforcement/National Security—Approach* (New York: American Civil Liberties Union, 2008).

FIGURE I. Coercion and punishment timeline. Design: Jonathan Lefrançois. Illustration: Justin Karas for Pulp & Pixel.

1916   During the 1916 polio epidemic in New York City, health workers conducted door-to-door searches, forcibly removing sick children from their homes, but allowing the children of wealthy families to remain in a separate room in their homes.[4]

1944   Military officials set up civilian conservation camps in the United States to house imprisoned prostitutes, who were rounded up in raids in an unsuccessful effort to squash sexually transmitted infections among American servicemen.

1949   Seattle's Firland Sanatorium opened its tuberculosis ward, which was used to quarantine over 1,000 mostly alcoholic tuberculosis patients—whether or not they were contagious or compliant with their treatment regimen.

1987   Author Randy Shilts published *And the Band Played On*, which blamed the spread of HIV in the United States on a promiscuous gay male flight attendant referred to as"Patient Zero."

1993   New York City began a program of directly observed treatment and quarantine in response to an outbreak of tuberculosis, disproportionately detaining poor and homeless patients who were deemed likely to be noncompliant.[5]

2014   Liberian president Ellen Johnson Sirleaf characterized Thomas Eric Duncan's failure to report contact with Ebola patients to Texas health care providers as "frankly, unpardonable." Airport officials threatened to file criminal charges against Duncan should he ever return home.

4. Guenter B. Risse, "Epidemics and History: Ecological Perspectives and Social Responses," in *AIDS: The Burdens of History*, ed. Elizabeth Fee and Daniel M. Fox (Berkeley: University of California Press, 1988), 33–66.
5. Gostin, Burris, and Lazzarini, "Law and the Public's Health"; and M. Rose Gasner, Khin Lay Maw, Gabriel E. Feldman, Paula I. Fujiwara, and Thomas R. Frieden, "The Use of Legal Action in New York City to Ensure Treatment of Tuberculosis," *New England Journal of Medicine* 340, no. 5 (1999): 359–66.

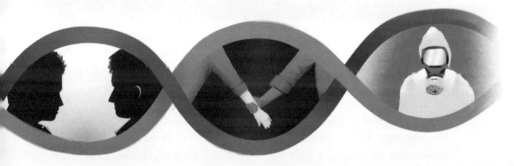

restrictive alternative doctrine, which holds that patients have the right to be treated in the least restrictive setting that meets their needs.[43]

CONTROLLING CHRONIC DISEASE THROUGH EDUCATION, PERSUASION, AND REGULATION

At the dawn of the twentieth century, infectious disease claimed more lives than any other cause of death. According to the CDC, the five leading causes of death in the United States in 1900 were[44]

- influenza and pneumonia (202.2 deaths per 100,000 people);
- tuberculosis (194.4 deaths per 100,000 people);
- gastrointestinal infections (142.7 deaths per 100,000 people);
- heart disease (137.4 deaths per 100,000 people);
- stroke and other cerebrovascular diseases (106.9 deaths per 100,000 people).

By 1950, however, dying in America had changed drastically. With dramatic improvements in nutrition, sanitation, and, finally, the advent of antibiotics and vaccines, infectious disease was dethroned as the leading cause of death in America and was replaced by heart disease (355.5 deaths per 100,000 people) and cancer (139.8 deaths per 100,000 people).[45]

This radical shift in mortality in the United States had a profound impact on public health practice. Better nutrition, improved sanitation, vaccines, and antibiotics had effectively stomped out diseases like smallpox, polio, and the measles—diseases that once maimed or killed millions. In their place were more complex diseases, such as heart disease and cancer, that were not communicable and that could not be traced to a single bacterial or viral agent. Instead, public health argued that these diseases were linked to specific "lifestyle" behaviors such as smoking, drinking alcohol, not getting enough physical exercise, and eating high-calorie foods.

Communicating this new model of disease to the public proved challenging for public health practitioners. For the past century, Americans had gradually come to understand the germ theory of disease, which linked disease and infection to the spread of bacteria and viruses. Public health now had to explain that behaviors, too, could cause disease—but the scientific link between them was harder to demonstrate. Exactly how many hamburgers does one need to eat to get fat? To get diabetes?

How many cigarettes does one need to smoke to get lung cancer? The answers were not black and white.

Smoking proved to be the low-hanging fruit. Although scientists are still debating whether x amount of salt or y amount of saturated fat causes heart disease, there has long been consensus that smoking tobacco causes lung cancer. Beginning in the 1950s, epidemiological studies came out in rapid succession demonstrating a causal relationship between smoking and lung cancer. Based on this research, the Surgeon General's Advisory Committee on Smoking and Health released its first report on smoking in 1964; the report analyzed over seven thousand studies to conclude that smoking directly causes lung cancer, emphysema, and other diseases.[46]

Once the public health establishment agreed that smoking caused cancer, they needed to find ways to convince the sizable proportion of the American public to give up the habit. That proportion was, indeed, sizable: the CDC estimates that in 1965 42.4 percent of adults in the United States smoked tobacco.[47] The mandatory vaccination, quarantine, and coercive strategies of yesteryear were obviously not the right tools for the job.

In their place, public health experts developed new strategies for disease control aimed at getting individuals to take care of their own well-being by avoiding "risky" behaviors—in this case, smoking. Authorities turned to two primary strategies to get Americans to stop smoking: regulation and persuasion. First, they regulated tobacco companies' business practices, the sale of tobacco products, and the locations in which people were allowed to smoke. In 1965, Congress passed the Cigarette Labeling and Advertising Act requiring that all cigarettes sold in the United States carry a warning label advising consumers that "Caution: Cigarette Smoking May Be Hazardous to Your Health."[48] Authorities followed quickly to ban cigarette advertisements on television and radio in 1969; to limit the ability of smokers to use tobacco in public places beginning in the 1970s; and to increase federal excise taxes on cigarettes beginning in the 1980s.[49] Over the next fifty years, local, state, and federal lawmakers would continue to ratchet up regulations on advertising and smoking in public while continuing to increase the cost to consumers through taxation.

Alongside these regulations, public health authorities at all levels began designing education programs and mass media campaigns to persuade the public to stop smoking. Young people, whose habits were perceived to be still malleable, were typically the target of media campaigns that cast smoking as unhealthy, unsexy, and uncool. Health departments were aided by Federal Communications Commission (FCC) regulations implemented in 1967 that required broadcasters to air one antismoking message for every three cigarette commercials.[50] In 1988, California voters approved Proposition 99, which raised taxes on cigarettes by twenty-five cents and required that 20 percent of the tax revenue collected be used to establish a statewide antitobacco education program featuring a mass media campaign.[51] Other states followed suit, implementing similar programs that significantly increased the scope and production quality of antitobacco messaging.

The implicit goal of these efforts was to erode the number of tobacco users in the United States while appearing to support freedom of individual choice. No one was coerced to stop smoking or quarantined for doing so. Instead, authorities regulated smoking to make it more costly and more difficult to do in public places while also persuading Americans that smoking was dangerous and uncool. This combination of strategies at local, state, and national levels had a sizable impact: between 1965 and 2014, the proportion of American adults who smoked tobacco fell from 42.4 percent to 16.8 percent.[52]

The model of regulation and persuasion proved to be a useful framework for public health efforts in many areas. Health educators persuaded through advertising campaigns and other interventions designed to change health behaviors by promoting driving with seat belts and helmets, making healthy choices based on the food pyramid, and, more generally, prodding Americans to determine their risk profile.[53] Occasionally, public health turned to regulation, enacting policies requiring that people wear seat belts and helmets and that restaurants post the caloric content of their food, and in New York, lobbying for legislation that would prohibit the sale of large sugary drinks.[54]

Despite success in domains like smoking, public health's focus on individual health behaviors has troubled some. Opponents criticized these regulations as paternalistic products of a "nanny state," while proponents pointed to the harmful effects of careless, risky health behavior on both the risk-taker's body and society at large. Instead of debating their legitimacy, social theorists have drawn attention to the ways in which focusing on health behaviors have both echoed and reinforced a general trend in American society toward emphasizing individual responsibility.[55] By promoting the notion that individuals need to take responsibility for their own health as well as the health of the collectivity, public health has ushered in an era in which the smoker, the drinker, the obese person, and the careless driver have become the new "health threat." Their behavior is not just viewed as unhealthy but is blamed for a wide array of negative consequences, from soaring health care costs to moral decay.

This shifting approach to social control—from coercion to regulation and persuasion—was not unique to public health. French social theorist Michel Foucault has shown how approaches to punishment followed a similar path; he tracks the rise of Western penal systems from the eighteenth to the twentieth century to show how governments phased out the public torture and executions of medieval times in favor of building prisons to discipline prisoners.[56] The idealized form of this new penal system was the Panopticon, a circular prison in which inmates are always visible to a single guard; under such surveillance, prisoners are trained to believe that they are always being watched and, thus, ought to police their own behavior. In many ways, the Panopticon and the food pyramid, emblematic of this "new public health," have similar aims: to prod individuals to police their own behavior rather than coercing them to change their ways.[57]

Experts have noted that morality messages are deeply embedded in modern public health campaigns that blame individuals for engaging in "risky" behaviors, blurring the line between risk and sin.[58] While ostensibly a neutral term, the way in which health authorities attach risk to some practices but not others reveals its moral underpinnings. Many people die in car accidents every year, yet we do not label driving as a risky behavior. Gay men having sex without condoms is described by public health practitioners as risky and labeled as "bareback"; sex between heterosexuals is almost never similarly described by health authorities—except, perhaps, when it is done by the poor (especially African Americans, women, and people receiving public benefits). Every step we take in life carries some form of risk, but only certain steps taken by certain people in certain contexts are labeled and controlled as risk.

CONTAGION REDUX: THE PUNITIVE TURN IN MODERN AMERICAN DISEASE CONTROL

In the early 1970s, scientists reported a cluster of unusual rheumatoid arthritis cases affecting children in Lyme, Connecticut. After exploring a number of possible causes, researchers noted that all of the children who were ill lived near wooded areas and that their symptoms typically began during the summer. Although researchers began referring to the set of symptoms as "Lyme disease," it would take nearly a decade to conclusively identify the cause: a bacteria, *Borrelia burgdorferi,* spread by deer-tick bites.[59]

Not far from Lyme, 221 attendees of a July 1976 American Legion convention in Philadelphia fell ill with strange symptoms: pneumonia and fevers reaching over 107 degrees. Within a month, news outlets were reporting that between six and fourteen men had died of what was colloquially known as Legionnaires' disease. The cause was a mystery. Fearing a major outbreak, the Pennsylvania health secretary reportedly "contemplated seizing control of all hospitals in the state and imposing quarantines."[60] Apart from the Legionnaires, however, no new cases emerged; in total, 221 cases were documented, including thirty-four deaths. After a six-month investigation, medical authorities determined the cause: a bacteria spread through the conference hotel's air conditioning system.

As the twentieth century wore on, outbreaks of new diseases like Lyme and Legionnaires' cast doubt on the optimistic claims of the 1950s that modern medicine would forever vanquish infectious disease. Alongside these new, unknown diseases came outbreaks of old scourges such as tuberculosis and the mutation of old microbes into antibiotic-resistant strains such as MRSA (methicillin-resistant *Staphylococcus aureus*). Across the globe, even more deadly epidemics of diseases such as Ebola, SARS, and avian flu shook the public confidence in medicine. Both at home and abroad, inequality appeared to be driving many of these new outbreaks; experts cite local factors such as overcrowding in prisons and homeless shelters and broader patterns such as poverty, malnutrition, homelessness, and HIV infection, which increase susceptibility to disease.[61] With global travel and migration reaching historic levels, experts feared that the epidemics of the future would quickly become global.

In the United States, this resurgence in infectious disease coincided with the rise of neoliberalism (commonly defined as the twentieth-century emphasis on laissez-faire economic policies, namely through deregulation, free trade, and privatization) in the Reagan-Thatcher years and the growing influence of religious conservatism, or the New Right.[62] Evangelical conservatives played to Americans' fear and ignorance of diseases like HIV, blaming those they deemed responsible for the spread of disease. Public health was not immune to these politics, especially as it had spent the last several decades promoting the idea that individuals and their risky health behaviors were to blame for modern epidemics. Given this context, public health officials not only returned to the restrictive measures that had been used to control the spread of infectious disease historically, but they also developed new, sometimes more coercive laws and practices. This was most apparent in the response to two of the most common diseases of the late twentieth century: tuberculosis and HIV.

Tuberculosis (TB) is a disease primarily affecting the lungs and is caused by a range of bacteria, most commonly *Mycobacterium tuberculosis*. Humans have suffered from the disease throughout much of documented history, with evidence of the disease stretching back to the spines of Egyptian mummies.[63] Most people who are infected with TB are asymptomatic—so-called latent carriers—and cannot transmit the disease. However, about 10 percent of infections progress to what is known as active TB, which is extremely contagious via coughing or sneezing; characteristic symptoms of active TB include blood-tinged sputum, fever, night sweats, and weight loss (giving the disease its historic nickname, consumption). Left untreated, more than half of people with active TB die.

As noted earlier in the chapter, TB was once a leading cause of death in the United States, second only to influenza and pneumonia. The prognosis for infected patients remained poor until streptomycin was discovered in 1946. This new treatment, along with other public health efforts to control the disease, helped to dramatically reduce the number of new TB cases by the 1950s. However, driven in part by rising rates of drug use, poverty, and homelessness, several U.S. cities saw new TB outbreaks in 1985 that disproportionately impacted racial minorities, including Latinos, African Americans, and Asians.[64] Public health authorities were especially troubled because many new TB cases were resistant to standard antibiotic treatments and thus harder to treat and more deadly.

Rather than citing a lack of access to affordable housing or poverty as the forces behind these new outbreaks, some in public health blamed these new resistant cases instead on *patients* who failed to complete the six- to eight-month treatment protocol required for curing TB. Most patients who are otherwise healthy can be successfully treated and cured of the disease.[65] Most patients do take their medication during the acute phase of their illness when they feel sick, but many drop out during the post-acute phase when they feel relatively healthy. In New York City, for example, only 53 percent of all patients completed treatment during these outbreaks (although completion rates have risen to over 90 percent more recently).[66] While these patients may feel healthy and are no longer contagious, their TB infection could come back. Worse yet, it could return as a newly mutated strain resistant to antibiotic treatments.[67]

To ensure that patients followed through with a lengthy treatment protocol, scientists pioneered direct observed therapy (commonly known as DOT) in Madras, India, and Hong Kong in the 1960s.[68] These programs typically require a patient to routinely visit a health care provider who can directly observe the patient swallowing the antibiotic treatment. Initially, DOT was mandated only for patients deemed likely to be noncompliant. But in practice, this often meant that doctors disproportionately targeted the poor and homeless as they were most likely to be viewed as potential health threats. For these reasons, some experts suggested that all patients treated for tuberculosis should be required to undergo mandatory DOT. However, this proposal was ultimately rejected as too broad and too intrusive on patients' civil liberties. Moreover, blanket DOT programs turned out to be unnecessary; most patients accept DOT and complete treatment, especially when their alternative is quarantine.[69]

Faced with the new outbreaks of TB, the New York City Public Health Department revised its health code to allow coercive actions to protect against these threats to public health. Under the new regulations, the health commissioner could order compulsory examinations for patients suspected of having tuberculosis, require that patients continue treatment until cured, order mandatory treatment under direct observation, and issue orders for involuntary detention of those deemed unwilling or unable to comply with treatment.[70] The city's new regulations proved controversial. Critics charged that the requirement that patients undergo treatment until cured expanded the notion of a health threat beyond just those individuals with active TB who were contagious. Under the new rules, individuals with latent infections who were not presently contagious but might at some point become contagious could be labeled a health threat and detained accordingly. Such a broad policy could set the stage for a repeat of Seattle's previously discussed approach to tuberculosis in 1949 that ended up systematically quarantining poor alcoholics. Further, the city was not required to provide social supports, such as transportation and housing for homeless patients, that would enable them to complete treatment. Finally, the ordinance violated the least-restrictive doctrine by not requiring the city to explore less restrictive measures before issuing confinement orders.

In actual practice, the city did attempt to remove barriers to nonadherence by providing housing, bus tokens, and incentive payments for patients undergoing DOT. Moreover, department policy was to use less restrictive measures before restrictions were imposed—for example, to offer voluntary DOT before imposing mandatory treatment, and DOT before confinement.[71] This led the authors of a study of the program in its first two years to conclude, "For most patients with tuberculosis, even those with severe social problems, completion of treatment can usually be achieved without regulatory intervention."[72] Although involuntary confinement was imposed on only 2 percent of the eight thousand tuberculosis patients, the actual number of patients subjected to involuntary confinement was notable: between 1993 and 1995, New York City confined more than one hundred patients who refused voluntary treatment, most of them confined to the secure ward of a hospital for six months.[73]

At nearly the same time that tuberculosis outbreaks were being reported, health authorities also began to report cases of a new deadly disease that seemed to be primarily affecting homosexuals. In June 1981, the CDC first reported a cluster of unusual cases of *Pneumocystis* pneumonia that appeared to be killing otherwise healthy young gay men.[74] The outbreak coincided with the election of Ronald Reagan and the ascendance of the New Right, a coalition of conservative politicians and the Christian conservatives who would become a formidable force in American politics. Health authorities were flummoxed by the new disease, and Americans were increasingly terrified. Conservatives capitalized on American's fear and ignorance of the disease, which they heralded as a symbol of America's moral decline. Medical authorities originally called the disease G.R.I.D. (gay-related immunodeficiency), a grave misstep that facilitated the New Right's characterization of the disease as a gay plague—divine retribution for sexual sin, or in the words of Jerry Falwell, "the wrath of a just God against homosexuals."[75]

Combining racism, homophobia, and xenophobia, commentators began to speak of the 4-H risk groups: homosexuals, heroin addicts, hemophiliacs, and Haitians. However, the New Right focused most of its ire on the perceived transgressions of gay men. Political pundits fed the homophobia of a terrified public with doomsday proclamations about the plague imposed on general public by the hedonistic lifestyles of drug addicts and homosexuals. A 1987 Gallup Poll showed that, like conservative religious leaders, 43 percent of Americans said that AIDS was a punishment for moral decline.[76] In communities across the country, tensions were high. When a Florida couple successfully sued the DeSoto County School District to allow their three hemophiliac, HIV-positive sons to attend school, they found their house had burned down, forcing them to leave town.[77]

By the mid-1980s conservative politicians and religious leaders, such as Jesse Helms and Pat Robertson, argued for draconian and excessively coercive measures: mandatory testing of all those "at risk" of spreading the disease, branding people with AIDS with a visible tattoo, and quarantine and criminal incarceration of "recalcitrant" AIDS carriers.[78] In their call for coercion, conservatives were joined by members of a public increasingly frightened by the spread of an incurable disease. Public opinion polls conducted in 1985 and 1986 showed that between 28 and 51 percent of respondents agreed that "people with AIDS should be put into quarantine to keep them away from the general public."[79]

At the center of many public debates was a murky figure blamed for the disease's rapid spread in gay communities. "Patient Zero," as he was called, was a French-Canadian, gay male air steward who reportedly had infected numerous of his partners in his travels. Although the CDC did interview the man and strongly urged him to stop having sex, scientists and health authorities did not, in fact, suspect him of being the source of HIV in the United States. But he made for a great story for San Francisco journalist Randy Shilts, who was putting the finishing touches on his 1987 book chronicling the government's lackluster response to AIDS, *And the Band Played On*. His publisher worried that the book would fall flat and pressured Shilts to find a way to make it more sensational:

> [Shilts's publisher] described the initial dismal prospects for *And the Band Played On* that motivated them to find a more creative way to promote the book. The solution was to use Patient Zero and present him as the handsome, promiscuous French-Canadian airline steward who may have brought AIDS to America. This was the pathway to the bestseller list, and it worked.

Just as nearly a century before Mary Mallon had been blamed for the spread of typhoid fever, so too was Canadian air steward Gaëtan Dugas blamed for the spread of HIV. While Shilts had hoped his book would be a boon to AIDS activists in calling out the federal government's inaction, debates over Patient Zero and his culpability overshadowed the rest of the book—playing right into the hands of religious conservatives:

> Shilts's salacious story of Patient Zero was ideal propaganda for conservatives because it played into the tenets of their latest campaign to isolate [people living with HIV] and gays. As an immigrant with AIDS, Gaëtan stood in for others like him who should be kept out of the country. Meanwhile, as both a gay man with an unchecked libido and an AIDS carrier who recklessly infected others, he embodied those who deserved to be locked up for their sociopathic behavior.[80]

In the minds of many Americans, the AIDS epidemic was a dangerous and deadly disease fueled by the reckless sexual behaviors of unrepentant gay men. The Patient Zero mythology represented that recklessness, providing the perfect villain for angry and fearful Americans.

Despite the fiery rhetoric on the Right, however, AIDS activists resisted these calls for invasive and coercive measures against people living with HIV—but only in part. Conservatives such as Jerry Falwell and Pat Buchanan demanded that lawmakers institute blanket quarantine measures such as Cuba's policy of indefinitely confining all HIV-positive people to a sanitorium upon diagnosis.[81] Legislators rejected such blanket measures, but in several states they did debate and ultimately enact quarantine and isolation procedures for HIV-positive individuals classified as a "health threat to others." Discussed in greater detail in chapter 3, these policies target people living with HIV who have been warned by health authorities to change their behavior but continue to engage in conduct expressly prohibited by public health authorities—typically sexual intercourse without first disclosing one's HIV-positive status.

In many states, however, legislators went a step further and enacted even more coercive measures aimed squarely at punishing HIV-positive people labeled a health threat. Between 1986 and 2011, thirty-three states enacted HIV-specific criminal statutes that made it a crime (usually a felony) for people who know that they are HIV-positive to engage in a wide range of behaviors without first disclosing their HIV-status.[82] According to a recent report coauthored by CDC and Department of Justice staff, twenty-five states criminalize one or more behaviors that pose a low or negligible risk for HIV transmission, such as oral sex, biting, spitting, or throwing blood.[83] Several statutes do not specify which behaviors are criminalized; it is a crime simply to expose another person to HIV—wording that one observer calls "unconstitutionally vague."[84] Even HIV-positive people living in a state without an HIV-specific law have been incarcerated under similar circumstances. In states like Texas and New York without such a recalcitrant criminal law, prosecutors charge HIV-positive defendants under general criminal laws against assault and battery, reckless endangerment, or attempted murder.

Many of these statutes reflect the climate of the period in which they were enacted: a time when there was an exaggerated perception of the risk of transmission of HIV and punitive attitudes toward persons living with HIV. In 2010, however, the Obama White House released its national HIV/AIDS strategy, stating that "in some cases, it may be appropriate for legislators to reconsider whether existing laws continue to further the public interest and public health."[85] For the many critics of these laws, these recommendations may come as welcome news. However, given that many of these points had been made as early as the late 1980s and that antiretroviral drugs have been in use since 1996, some may also wonder why these recommendations came so late.[86]

PUNISHING PATIENT ZERO

The impulse to punish the sick has a long history in public health—a history shot through with calls to coerce and quarantine the sick. Those efforts have repeatedly disproportionately impacted the poor, racial minorities, sex workers, and other stigmatized communities—sometimes by design, but more often as a matter of practice. Yet, despite the long, sordid affair between sickness and stigma, disease control remained a matter of civil law for most of American public health history. What begat this punitive turn?

As the HIV epidemic crystallized, it did so alongside the New Right's calls for Americans to take personal responsibility for their lives by putting an end to New Deal welfare programs. Conservatives in federal and state legislatures worked in concert to gut welfare programs while declaring a war on crime that prompted a rise in incarceration rates unprecedented in human history.[87] Funding to higher education was drastically cut while the number of prisons exploded, leading modern activists to demand "schools, not prisons."[88] For Black men especially, sociologists have demonstrated that incarceration has become a normal and even *probable* life event.[89]

It is in this context that the first cases of HIV began to be reported in major urban areas in the United States—cities such as San Francisco and New York City, which conservatives already associated with hedonism and immorality. Perhaps if the disease had struck middle-class heterosexuals in the suburbs, the New Right's reaction to HIV might have been different. Instead, the disease was immediately associated with gay men, sex workers, Haitians, and injection drug users—some of the most stigmatized communities in the United States at the time. As many of these groups were already suspected criminals, criminalization was already top of mind for authorities tasked with managing these populations.

Evangelical conservatives capitalized on this association, issuing damning proclamations that the "gay plague" would cross over and infect middle-class American families. The cover of the July 1983 issue of Jerry Falwell's *Moral Majority Report* perfectly encapsulates the stigmatizing narrative invented by conservatives. Featuring a photo of a White, middle-class family with two children whose faces are covered with medical surgical masks, the headline read: "Homosexual Diseases Threaten American Families."

Although far more extreme, this punitive view of the epidemic resonates with public health's message that risky individual health behaviors cause disease and need to be prevented. The logical leap from arguing that we need to prevent individual health behaviors that cause disease to blaming individuals for engaging health behaviors labeled "risky" was not so great. Medical historian Allan Brandt observed in 1997 that

> AIDS has been placed strongly within the paradigm of responsibility. If one "merely" avoids the risk behaviors associated with transmission of the virus—unprotected sexual intercourse and sharing needles for intravenous drug use—one can avoid AIDS. Therefore, infection is a clear—and usually terminal—marker of individual risk taking, of engaging in behaviors typically held to be deviant or criminal. According to this view, those who are infected are *responsible* for their plight. AIDS is *caused* by a moral failure of the individual.[90]

In ushering in a new era of risk avoidance in which the responsibility for one's health was placed on each individual's shoulders, public health inadvertently contributed to a context in which blame and punishment seem apt disease control strategies.

Patient Zero proved a compelling narrative not simply as an exercise in tracing the epidemiological origins of the epidemic; rather, his story helped *And the Band Played On* become a best seller because many Americans desperately wanted someone to blame. A gay male flight attendant made the perfect scapegoat for a terrified public. The conservative magazine *The National Review* branded Dugas the "Columbus of AIDS" and blamed him for bringing the disease to America. In such a context, criminalizing HIV was a logical response in this march of shame and blame.

Although Patient Zero was a fictional character invented by a journalist, his story fueled calls for public health to institute coercive and punitive measures in response to AIDS. These demands for control resembled many of the historical cases reviewed in this chapter in that they typically singled out especially marginalized people for control: in the case of Patient Zero, an immigrant gay man; in other cases reviewed in this chapter, the poor, racial minorities, sex workers, and even alcoholics. When public health institutions discriminatorily targets specific groups of people for coercive measures that are not applied to other groups, their efforts reinforce the view that certain social groups are to blame for the spread of disease. Their implicit offense is not their risky behaviors but their social difference. In this way, the history of punitive disease control is at times indistinguishable from America's troubled history of social marginalization.

We cannot know what would have happened if more cases of Ebola had been brought to American shores, or what will happen when the next infectious disease becomes epidemic in the United States. As this book reveals, however, disease and punishment are more closely linked than even before in modern history.

CHAPTER 2

"HIV Stops with Me"

The Repolarization of Post-AIDS HIV Prevention

Last year the Centers for Disease Control and Prevention (CDC) announced an initiative that would essentially eliminate the culturally and psychologically sensitive HIV prevention gay men have achieved over these past two decades. Little in the CDC's [initiative] is actually new. Rather, it invokes the "enforcement" model that spawned the discipline of public health in the TB epidemic of early twentieth-century America. . . . Perhaps most disturbingly, the initiative imposes, in the guise of "prevention," the humanly repressive values of the political right that now controls CDC funding.
—Walt Odets, *POZ Magazine*[1]

When the CDC announced its new priorities for HIV prevention in 2003, many public health advocates were alarmed: *where were the condoms?* Although there was a growing sense in the field that condoms were failing as an HIV prevention strategy, no one was prepared to admit defeat publicly. The announcement came in the pages of the CDC's *Morbidity and Mortality Weekly Report*. The report outlined "four key strategies" that would guide the organization's future HIV prevention efforts:

1. increase the number of people tested for HIV;
2. increase access to twenty-minute rapid HIV tests;
3. focus prevention efforts on individuals already diagnosed as HIV positive;
4. decrease mother-to-child transmission of HIV.[2]

For decades, the very *notion* of doing HIV prevention had become practically synonymous with promoting "safer sex" to the masses. When it came to HIV, condoms were public health's bread and butter. The CDC's announcement seemed to be signaling the end of an era. As it would turn out, that's exactly what it would be.

For most Americans, the term *HIV prevention* conjures images of unsexy posters asking HIV-negative people to "wrap it up" or "use protection." But that approach has largely been abandoned in public health practice. In the decade that followed its 2003 announcement, the CDC moved further away from promoting safer sex to HIV-negative people and toward developing new strategies specifically targeting HIV-positive people. How and why did this happen?

This chapter explores that "repolarization"—from negative to positive—in HIV prevention. The chapter explains how the notion of targeting people living with HIV for HIV prevention—or what became known as "positive prevention"—came about. While positive prevention has long roots, it began to gain traction in the late 1990s as new treatments transformed HIV from a terminal illness into a chronic, manageable disease—simultaneously transforming HIV-positive people from passive victims into active managers of their disease. However, even as public health practitioners came to agree that targeting HIV-positive people was important and necessary in this new context, there remained considerable debate over the content and character of the interventions. Social scientists cautioned against framing people living with HIV as individually responsible for HIV prevention, arguing instead for situating their lives and challenges within a broader social context. Failure to do so, they warned, could facilitate shaming and blaming individuals viewed as acting irresponsibly. As this chapter shows, their warnings were not always heeded in practice. The repolarization of HIV prevention analyzed in this chapter ushered in a new era in public health practice in which the HIV-positive person is portrayed as being individually responsible for ending the epidemic—and, implicitly, the one to blame when things go wrong.[3]

It is important to note that these efforts to endow people living with HIV with a sense of personal, individual responsibility for ending HIV were not punitive in intent or in their most immediate effects. Indeed, many of the campaigns analyzed in this chapter were explicitly and directly informed by people living with HIV who genuinely want to do their part to end HIV and contribute to fighting the epidemic. This chapter should not be read as an attack on that altruistic spirit. Instead, this chapter argues that the execution of these campaigns has at times characterized the responsibility in individualistic terms—an approach that can resonate with efforts to assign blame, punish, and, ultimately, criminalize individuals viewed as failing to live up those individual responsibilities. In this way, this chapter reveals how even well-intentioned disease control strategies that portray people living with infectious disease as individually responsible can have punitive ripple effects.

AIDS VICTIMS NO MORE

The notion that public health campaigns should target individuals already infected with HIV seems almost obvious today. We live in a world where public health campaigns routinely promote individual responsibility for people who are suffering from all kinds of ailments, from obesity to heart disease: Make better choices. Take care of your own health. Eat your vegetables. However, in 1985, any notion that people living with HIV might be considered responsible for managing their disease stood in conflict with harrowing images of helpless AIDS patients suffering a horrible, untimely death: how could we possibly describe these poor souls as "responsible" for anything?

When nighttime news programs first began reporting a new, strange disease affecting homosexuals, people suffering from AIDS were depicted in bleak terms. Newsreels cut to heart-wrenching images of shrunken figures dying in hospital beds. There was no treatment for the disease itself or for the many bizarre and extremely rare opportunistic infections that colonized defenseless HIV-positive immune systems. With gay men dying left and right, AIDS activists likened the havoc wreaked on communities and on HIV-positive bodies to the Holocaust.[4] The images of AIDS victims broadcast into American homes were hardly that of people ready to take responsibility for their own health; instead, they were *victims* of a tragic, mysterious illness that left doctors scratching their heads (or worse yet, running in the opposite direction).

This powerful AIDS-victim narrative controlled media representations of HIV for many years, ultimately crafting a public understanding of people living with HIV as isolated, disfigured, and dying. But two important factors helped shift public perception. First, AIDS activist organizations like the AIDS Coalition to Unleash Power (ACT UP) explicitly advocated against the label "AIDS victim." Even before ACT UP began organizing in the late 1980s, people living with HIV rejected the "victim" label." In a 1983 manifesto colloquially known as the

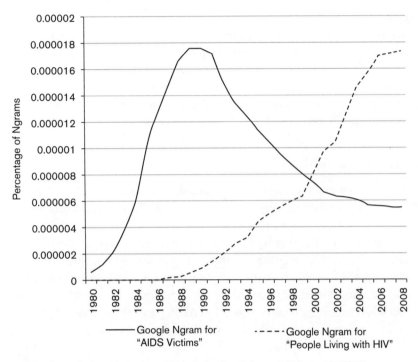

FIGURE 2. Google Ngrams for "AIDS victims" and "people living with HIV,"
1980–2008. Source: Trevor Hoppe.

Denver Principles, a small group of people living with HIV condemned
"attempts to label us as 'victims,' a term which implies defeat."[5] Activists promoted language that focused on *living with* the illness rather
than *dying from* it.[6] Instead of focusing endlessly on people dying, ACT
UP demanded coverage examining the institutions that were failing
communities affected by AIDS. ACT UP pointed the finger at government agencies' callous indifference and at pharmaceutical companies'
greed. Their chants—"ACT UP, fight back, fight AIDS!"—came to the
doorsteps of powerful organizations across the country.

    Their organizing had profound effects, changing government policies
and, ultimately, the way medical research was done.[7] It also reshaped
how we talked about AIDS. Data analyzing how often particular words
and phrases are used in Google's massive collection of digitized books
and other publications help demonstrate these effects. According to
these data (see figure 2), the term *AIDS victims* begins to fall out of
favor in the early 1990s. After 1992, the term loses traction year over

year as *people living with HIV* gains in popularity—until *people living with HIV* outpaces *AIDS victims* in 2000.

But even though ACT UP's activism was important in driving this shift in language, it was not the only variable at work. Science played an equally important part in reshaping how we understood people living with HIV. While an HIV-positive test result was a largely terminal diagnosis in the 1980s, the introduction of effective treatment in 1996 dramatically changed the outlook for people living with the disease. These drugs—called antiretrovirals, or ARVs for short—removed the threat of impending doom that prevented many people from seeing HIV-positive people as anything other than victims. Immediately after ARVs' introduction, mortality rates plummeted. CDC surveillance data indicate that AIDS-related deaths declined, from a peak of 50,489 in 1995, by over 25 percent in 1996, over 50 percent by 1997, and by nearly 65 percent by 1998.[8] Once expected to die a quick and untimely death, those diagnosed as HIV positive were suddenly expected to live for decades. Seemingly overnight, HIV-positive individuals were transformed from victims of a terminal illness to active managers of a chronic disease.

And with management comes responsibility.

POSITIVE PREVENTION AND SHIFTING RESPONSIBILITY IN HIV PREVENTION

In 2000, one of the nation's leading HIV research centers, the Centers for AIDS Prevention Studies (CAPS) at University of California at San Francisco, issued an early report outlining the need for prevention targeting HIV-positive people. The report, *Designing Primary Prevention for People Living with HIV,* cites the changing landscape for HIV-positive people as a primary rationale: "The success of new treatments for HIV infection means that there are now more people living with HIV disease than ever before, and many of these individuals are feeling healthier and are better able to participate in the normal activities of life, including sex."[9] The implication was that if HIV-positive people are going to live long lives with the virus, public health agencies needed to devise strategies to make sure they keep the virus to themselves.

In order to justify the need for positive prevention, the report points to one HIV-positive man's story in particular. In the late 1990s, American media outlets exploded with the news that an African American man in New York had been arrested after allegedly infecting nearly a dozen White women. Some of the girls were underage, making the case ripe for a sensational news cycle. The report's authors point to this "chilling" case as evidence for the need to target HIV-positive people for prevention:

> In October 1997, a chilling story out of Chautauqua County, New York, manifested the fears of AIDS advocates and the general public alike. A man named Nushawn Williams, in jail for the sale of crack, admitted to public health authorities that he had had unprotected sex with 50 to 75 young women, most of them teenagers. The story was exceptional, since only isolated incidents of willful exposure to HIV had ever been reported in the press. But the political reaction was swift, with a state assemblywoman calling for mandatory names reporting of HIV infection and proposing a new category of crime from knowingly exposing someone to HIV.[10]

Sensational media reports depicted Williams as an "HIV monster."[11] Because New York did not have an HIV-specific criminal law at the time, Williams was ultimately convicted for sexual assault and, at the time of publication, remains incarcerated despite the completion of his court-ordered prison sentence in 2010.[12]

That scholars chose William's controversial case to evidence the need for positive prevention highlights the delicate politics of responsibility involved. In early scientific papers on positive prevention, public health experts urged caution when framing responsibility for HIV-positive people. In one of the earliest academic publications on the subject, the authors urged public health practitioners to take care in framing the responsibility for preventing HIV in "collective" terms:

> The concept of collective responsibility emphasizes that all of us, infected or not, low risk or high, bear a responsibility to change our attitudes and behaviors that may promote HIV infection. Without this balance, calls for personal responsibility become almost indistinguishable from that of blaming the victim and are likely to be counterproductive to prevention efforts.[13]

A commitment to promoting collective responsibility for preventing HIV would require depicting it as something shared by everyone in a community, by both HIV-positive people and their HIV-negative counterparts, not just certain individuals.

Other scholars echoed these concerns. In a set of principles designed to guide public health practitioners developing positive prevention campaigns, sociologist and HIV policy expert Judith Auerbach goes even further by suggesting that efforts to promote individual or collective responsibility must be "embedded in larger and more comprehensive efforts to promote positive physical and emotional development, life skills and chances, poverty alleviation, and gender equity."[14] In short, it takes a village; individual responsibility can reasonably go only so far. Without also highlighting the broad range of needs facing both HIV-negative and HIV-positive people and communities, Auerbach argues that calls for HIV-positive people to take responsibility for ending the epidemic will likely be unproductive.

The CDC first signaled its interest in positive prevention in 2001 when it announced the Serostatus Approach to Fighting the Epidemic (SAFE) in the pages of the prestigious *American Journal of Public Health*.[15] The SAFE model included five strategies:

1. increase the number of HIV-infected persons who know their serostatus;

2. increase the use of health care and preventive services;

3. increase high-quality care and treatment;

4. increase adherence to therapy by individuals with HIV;

5. increase the number of individuals with HIV who adopt and sustain HIV-STI risk reduction behavior.[16]

In developing SAFE, the CDC had largely reoriented prevention around the surveillance and medical treatment of HIV-positive people. The responsibilities assigned to HIV-positive people were far more numerous than those assigned to HIV-negative individuals.

Two years later, the CDC gave SAFE teeth by announcing new funding priorities built largely around this approach, which sparked an explosion in research on positive prevention. Between 1992 and 2002, the phrase *positive prevention* appears no more than a handful of times in academic publications indexed by Google Scholar. However, beginning in 2003, the number of citations of this phrase increases rapidly, to nearly three hundred citations per year by 2013.[17] Further, while roughly one-third of the CDC's HIV prevention grant applications in 1999 listed people living with HIV as a key population, that figure increased to 58 percent by 2001.[18] Thus, the CDC announcement clearly was not just lip service; it had the effect of prompting new research and new interventions targeting people living with HIV.

CDC funding streams did more than just generate new lines of academic research on positive prevention; that money directly supported the development of new HIV prevention interventions targeting HIV-positive people. While it is not possible to analyze the broad array of HIV

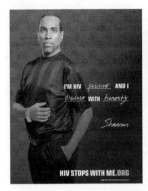  

FIGURE 3 *(Left)*. HIV Stops with Me ad: "I disclose with honesty." Source: Better World Advertising.

FIGURE 4 *(Middle)*. HIV Stops with Me ad: "I am the cure." Source: Better World Advertising.

FIGURE 5 *(Right)*. HIV Stops with Me ad: "I believe in responsibility." Source: Better World Advertising.

prevention campaigns across the country enacted under these policies, one social marketing campaign has achieved dominance. Initially launched in San Francisco in 1999, HIV Stops with Me has since been adopted in various forms by over a dozen state and local health departments across the country, from Los Angeles to New York City to Alaska.[19] Each iteration is typically funded by city or state health departments. It uses posters, billboards, and other media featuring "real HIV-positive people" speaking openly about the realities they face in managing HIV and its transmission. As perhaps the most widely disseminated and longest-running prevention campaign targeting HIV-positive people, it provides a useful case study for examining how positive prevention has been applied in the field.[20]

Figures 3, 4, and 5 feature three emblematic examples of the HIV Stops with Me campaign. Each takes a slightly different tack in representing how its HIV-positive subject takes responsibility for his disease. In the image depicted in figure 3 from a 2012 campaign targeting New York, Boston, Virginia, and Alaska, the message from "Shannon" is that "I'm HIV positive and I disclose with honesty." By tying disclosure to a value—honesty—the 2012 campaign is intended to provide a moral context for the practice of disclosing one's HIV-positive status: disclosure is not just a strategy for managing HIV risk; it is the right thing to do.

The poster depicted in figure 5 takes a similar approach. Used in eleven metropolitan areas in 2003, the spokesperson declares: "I believe in responsibility" and "I feel good knowing that I care enough to make sure I don't infect anyone. I value other guys and my community." The ad thus suggests that taking measures to prevent transmission means one is a responsible community member who cares for others and one's community.

Finally, in the image depicted in figure 4, which was used in 2006 in Boston, Los Angeles, Long Beach, San Francisco, and Oregon, "Gerardo" declares himself to be "the cure"—suggesting that, while they cannot cure themselves, HIV-positive people can provide a "cure" by taking care not to infect others. The president of the advertising firm that designs and manages the HIV Stops With Me brand proclaimed in a press release announcing the I Am the Cure campaign that "HIV positive individuals have the power to prevent new infections and they can be the cure."[21]

Each of these ads promotes responsibility in different ways. Figure 3 depicts taking responsibility as a *behavior,* the act of disclosing one's HIV-positive status to one's partner. Figure 4 does not promote a specific behavior; rather, it promotes responsibility by suggesting that HIV-positive people can "be the cure" for HIV by playing their part in ending HIV. Figure 5 picks up a similar thread, promoting the idea that HIV-positive people should not infect anyone else. In this ad, taking responsibility for HIV is an expression of caring for one's partner and community.

Yet, while each ad takes a slightly different approach to promoting responsibility, each construes the responsible party as "me"—an individual who should take action to prevent HIV transmission. The campaign's slogan is, after all, HIV Stops with Me, *not* HIV Stops with We. HIV-negative partners and their role in preventing HIV are not represented. While the third ad does make reference to a need to value "other guys and my community," the job of protecting that community from HIV is depicted as solely that of the HIV-positive spokesperson.

In short, HIV Stops with Me promotes a notion of individualized responsibility that resembles an approach cautioned against by many public health scholars.

TREATMENT AS PREVENTION: HIV-POSITIVE BODIES AS THE NEW FRONTIER

As the decade wore on, more and more HIV prevention advocates became exasperated with what seemed like signs of failure. In the first half of the 2000s, researchers designed dozens (if not hundreds) of studies to measure how many people were not using condoms. They repeatedly published the same finding: across the country, many men who have sex with men (MSM) reported having sex without condoms.[22] While gay men had always been having sex without condoms, these studies seemed to suggest that rates of condomless sex were on the rise.

As *barebacking* (intentionally engaging in condomless sex) became a common term in HIV prevention circles, public health advocates expressed frustration that—thirty years into the epidemic—condoms remained the only tool in their toolbox.[23] In the pages of the *American Journal of Public Health,* one public health scholar ominously wrote:

> Behavioral interventions to promote condom use—the only strategy currently available to stem the MSM epidemic—are failing. Under the best of circumstances, when proven effective, they are not promptly and easily disseminated, and certainly not straightforwardly translatable across the age spectrum, ethnic groups, and subcultures. Without sustained but costly quality assurance procedures, they drift.[24]

Among the potential alternatives to condom promotion, authors typically cited vaginal and rectal microbicides or gels that would be applied to the genitals to reduce the risk of infection. In putting all their eggs in the condom basket, had public health missed opportunities to develop other options?

In trying to decide what public health should do next, advocates and scholars often drew a line in the sand between behavioral interventions (condoms) and biomedical interventions (such as microbicides). Although studies demonstrated that a handful of interventions could get people to use condoms for a few months, none was highly effective in the long run. Faith that public health could do much to change behavior was eroding. But what if we could develop a medical technology—a "silver bullet"—that could stop HIV in its tracks? Biomedicine became HIV prevention's great hope.

Unfortunately, findings from the first published studies testing biomedical interventions were sometimes underwhelming. Data from the most promising vaccine trial in years suggested that the vaccine was, at best, only partially effective.[25] While clinical trials evaluating the efficacy of male circumcision demonstrated up to a 60 percent reduction in the risk of contracting HIV among African men,[26] results from microbicide trials have yielded more mixed results. An initial trial failed to show that the gel had any effect,[27] and a later trial with a different gel demonstrated only a 30 percent efficacy among women.[28] A third candidate was thought promising after initial results suggested it could reduce risk up to 54 percent among "high adherence" patients.[29] However, the National Institutes of Health prematurely halted a follow-up study that was unable to replicate these findings.[30]

In the eyes of many public health authorities, none of these interventions were blockbusters. Many suffered from conflicting scientific data. Others seemed too costly with too little return. While male circumcision was cheap and highly effective at preventing heterosexual HIV transmission, many in the West viewed promoting circumcision to African men as unethical—especially as circumcision directly protected only men from infection, not women (who are disproportionately impacted by HIV in many African countries).[31]

Scientists instead placed their bets on the growing body of science that suggested treating HIV could also help to prevent it—an idea called "treatment as prevention." Anti-HIV medications lower the amount of virus present in the bodily fluids of HIV-positive individuals. At such low levels, HIV becomes scientifically undetectable, making it difficult or even impossible to transmit. Many HIV advocates and researchers had suspected this was true since the first treatments had been rolled out in the mid-1990s. Indeed, a 1998 Australian AIDS campaign targeting gay men featured the message "While we are still in the dark about viral load, use a condom."[32] Despite these suspicions, however, science had yet to weigh in on the matter.

The Australian viral load campaign reveals that some communities had long believed that treatment could be a form of prevention. Yet it took at least a decade for any established HIV scientist to publicly give credence to this idea. That moment came in 2008 when a group of Swiss scientists issued a report that became known as the Swiss Statement. Their report shocked many because it argued that there was *zero risk* of sexual transmission for HIV-positive individuals under three conditions:

1. if they were on treatment;

2. if their viral load was undetectable; and

3. if they did not have another sexually transmitted co-infection.[33]

American HIV prevention experts did not warmly embrace the Swiss Statement. The director of the CDC's Division on HIV/AIDS Prevention, Robert Janssen, argued that the Swiss scientists' conclusion was "premature."[34] Epidemiologist Myron Cohen (ironically, the very scientist whose findings would later validate the Swiss claims) argued similarly that there was not yet sufficient evidence to support the Swiss claims:

> We have every reason to pause and reflect. The protection provided from [antiretroviral therapy] is not absolute and is not absolutely predictable. In a study involving discordant couples in Africa, Sullivan et al. reported that 4 (2.3 percent) of 175 transmission events among a group of 2,993 discordant couples occurred when the index patient was receiving therapy. In a very recent evaluation of discordant couples in Henan, China, 84 HIV transmission events were noted among a group of 1,927 couples who were followed up from 2006 through 2008, and these transmission events were equally distributed among patients who were receiving and those who were not receiving ART.[35]

If these debates sound familiar to readers, it may be because they closely parallel debates over the initial promotion of *condoms* by gay health advocates in the United States in the early 1980s. When New Yorkers Richard Berkowitz and Michael Callen famously distributed their pamphlet promoting condom use, "How to Have Sex in an Epidemic: One Approach," in May 1983 on the heels of HIV's discovery, they did so without a scientific consensus on condom efficacy to back up their recommendations.[36] At the time, many scientists wrung their hands over whether it was appropriate to promote condom use without conclusive evidence. To this day, condoms are not yet FDA-approved for anal sex.[37]

In a scientific analysis of condom studies published *ten years* after Berkowitz and Callen's pamphlet, epidemiologist Susan Weller argued in 1993:

> Until more is known about condom effectiveness, condom use promotion may have both positive and negative effects. . . . Condoms will not eliminate risk of sexual transmission and, in fact, may only lower risk somewhat. . . . Empirical data (reviewed in this report) indicate that a 90 percent reduction in risk due to condom use may be overly optimistic. The protective effect as estimated from human studies, regardless of use definitions, indicates a possible 69 percent reduction in risk.[38]

Well over one hundred thousand Americans died of AIDS in the ten years between Berkowitz and Callen's pamphlet and Weller's waffling statement on condoms. Communities could not (and did not) wait for scientific consensus. While less urgent, the need to promote *anything* to help prevent HIV in 1983 was not entirely dissimilar from the need twenty-five years later to find alternatives to condoms.

Public health's collective anxiety about the Swiss Statement reveals the gap—or rather, the *chasm*—separating community-based and scientific expertise. While many gay men were well aware as early as the late 1990s that treating HIV had a preventive effect, public health policy required cold, hard evidence. Despite their initially frigid response to the Swiss Statement, public health scholars and practitioners quickly warmed up to the concept as study after study validated its arguments in the 2010s. While studies of couples in which one person is HIV positive and the other is HIV negative had already shown that providing HIV-positive people with access to treatment reduced the risk of infection to their HIV-negative partners,[39] the results published in 2011 from a randomized control trial (HPTN 052) of early treatment sent tidal waves through the world of prevention science and public health practice.[40] In a cover story, the prestigious journal *Science* declared "Treatment as Prevention" was 2011's "Breakthrough of the Year." The author describes how the trial's results "stunned" the lead researchers behind it:

> The researchers planned to compare the groups until 2015. But on 28 April, an independent monitoring board that periodically reviewed the data stunned Cohen and his collaborators when it recommended that the results of the trial be made public as soon as possible. Of the 28 people who become infected with HIV that genetically matched the viruses in their long-term partners, only one was in the early treatment group—which also experienced 41 percent fewer serious health problems associated with HIV. Infected people in the delayed arm of the study were offered ARVs immediately.[41]

At a conference in early 2014, preliminary results were announced from a study monitoring 767 heterosexual and same-sex serodiscordant couples in which one partner was HIV positive, on treatment, and had a suppressed viral load, and the other was HIV negative. In order to participate, couples had to report having sex without condoms at least some of the time. After a two-year period, the study found that no transmissions had occurred between partners after an estimated 44,400 sexual encounters.[42] When a conference participant asked the researchers in the Q&A what the findings revealed about the risk of an HIV-positive person with a treatment-suppressed viral load transmitting the virus, the lead researcher responded: "Our best estimate is it's zero."[43] Final results from the PARTNER study released in 2016 confirmed the preliminary results: After over 58,000 reported condomless sexual encounters (representing 1,238 couple-years), the study observed *zero* linked transmissions.[44] In light of these stark findings, AIDS activists have now begun trumpeting a new message: "Undetectable = Untransmittable."[45]

In the scientific equivalent of a blink of an eye, treatment as prevention (TasP) went from being a dubious European theory to one of the

Un/Detectability

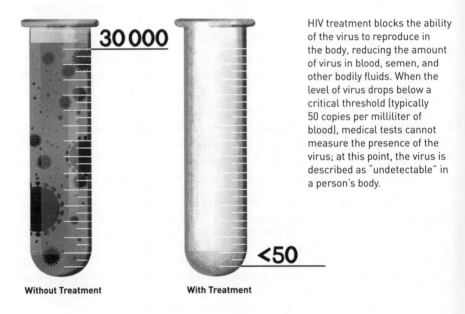

30 000

<50

Without Treatment   **With Treatment**

HIV treatment blocks the ability of the virus to reproduce in the body, reducing the amount of virus in blood, semen, and other bodily fluids. When the level of virus drops below a critical threshold (typically 50 copies per milliliter of blood), medical tests cannot measure the presence of the virus; at this point, the virus is described as "undetectable" in a person's body.

-96%

It is much harder to transmit HIV sexually when a person's bodily fluids contain very few copies of the virus. In 2011, scientists published the results of a study evaluating whether initiating early treatment reduced the risk of transmission in couples in which one partner is HIV positive and the other is HIV negative. The study found that starting treatment reduced the risk of transmission by 96 percent.

FIGURE 6. Undetectable = Uninfectious. Design: Jonathan Lefrançois. Illustration: Justin Karas for Pulp & Pixel.

PARTNER Study

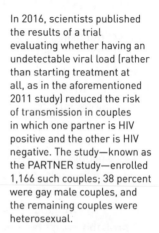

In 2016, scientists published the results of a trial evaluating whether having an undetectable viral load (rather than starting treatment at all, as in the aforementioned 2011 study) reduced the risk of transmission in couples in which one partner is HIV positive and the other is HIV negative. The study—known as the PARTNER study—enrolled 1,166 such couples; 38 percent were gay male couples, and the remaining couples were heterosexual.

One important condition of enrollment in the PARTNER study was that partners had to be having sex without condoms at least some of the time. This condition allowed scientists to isolate the effects of having an undetectable viral load from the protective effect of condoms. In total, scientists estimate that the couples enrolled engaged in 58,000 condomless sexual encounters during the study.

After nearly four years of following enrolled couples, scientists reported zero linked transmissions between HIV-positive and HIV-negative partners. While eleven HIV-negative partners did contract HIV during the study period, genetic testing revealed that they were not infected by their primary partner. This finding has led advocates to declare that "undetectable = uninfectious."

most prestigious science journals' breakthrough of the year. Scientists suddenly agreed that treatment was, indeed, prevention. The number of scientific papers referencing TasP followed in kind, from virtually no references to the subject in academic papers catalogued by Google Scholar published in 2008 to nearly one thousand published in 2014.[46]

The CDC responded to these ongoing advances by announcing its latest plan for controlling the epidemic, high-impact prevention (HIP), in 2011.[47] HIP aimed to combine "scientifically proven, cost-effective, and scalable interventions targeted to the right populations in the right geographic areas."[48] Although HIP includes interventions targeting HIV-negative individuals at least on paper, the emphasis is on identifying and treating HIV-positive people. Indeed, the first two prevention strategies in the announcement were "testing and linkage to care" and "antiretroviral therapy." In a 2012 presentation from a public health consulting firm advising agencies adapting to HIP guidelines, the authors note that the "standard proposal . . . probably won't be fundable next CDC round" and that interventions "must primarily target PwP [prevention with positives]."[49]

The implications of this new framework for HIV prevention were important. Because HIV medications were reframed as a tool for prevention, treatment was no longer just an intervention done solely for the benefit of the HIV-positive patient. Under TasP, HIV therapy also became an intervention for the sake of future (or current) HIV-negative partners. It was perhaps no coincidence that this new justification for HIV treatment emerged at precisely the same time that a global recession had hampered massive, multibillion dollar campaigns to treat every person infected with HIV globally. The largest of these efforts, the U.S. President's Emergency Plan for AIDS Relief (PEPFAR), allocated over three-quarters of its budget to the treatment and care of HIV-positive individuals.[50] Reframing their work as both treatment and prevention provided a new rationale for funders looking to get more done with fewer dollars.

On the ground, public health agencies had taken their marching orders and reorganized their work. "Use a condom" was no longer their mantra; under TasP, "test and treat" became the rallying cry of agencies across the world. Unlike previous HIV prevention strategies that emphasized behavior change and condom use, test-and-treat emphasized biomedical technologies such as rapid HIV-antibody tests and antiretrovirals. This message carried significant political appeal: HIV tests and pills were far less politically contentious than the tools of the behavioral HIV prevention programs of yore: namely, condoms and clean needles.[51] In foregrounding concerns over access to health care and compliance

FIGURE 7 *(Left)*. HIV testing campaign: "Testing makes us stronger." Source: Centers for Disease Control and Prevention.

FIGURE 8 *(Middle)*. HIV testing campaign: "My reasons for getting an HIV test." Source: Centers for Disease Control and Prevention.

FIGURE 9 *(Right)*. HIV testing campaign: "Get a free HIV test." Source: Centers for Disease Control and Prevention.

with treatment regimens, test-and-treat effectively relocated challenging conversations about sex and drugs to the back burner. Given the cycle of moral outrage from elected officials that frequently threatened public health budgets, health authorities may have viewed the shift to test-and-treat as particularly welcome.

The approach quickly caught on. At time of writing, of the five CDC-developed HIV prevention campaigns aimed at at-risk populations, four encourage people at risk to get tested and one raises general awareness about HIV. None focus primarily on encouraging safer sex practices for HIV-negative people, nor do any promote treatment for HIV-positive people.[52] Figures 7, 8 and 9 illustrate three of the campaigns encouraging people at risk to get tested. The first, "Testing makes us stronger," targets African American MSM. The second ad, "My reasons," is similar, except that it targets Latino MSM. The third ad targets African American women.

Most of these ads promote a collective version of responsibility that resembles the public health recommendations examined earlier in this chapter. The third ad could be interpreted as promoting an individualistic form of responsibility similar to that depicted in the HIV Stops with Me campaign, in that the woman is depicted as making a decision on her own to get tested. It is not immediately obvious whether she is motivated to get tested for her sake or her partner's—or for both. The ad implies that she may have been unknowingly exposed to HIV by her male partner. Although it does not plainly state that he knew he was infected and did not tell her, it does not foreclose suspicion of that possibility. In fact, it seems to be *promoting* suspicion as a primary motivating factor for getting HIV tested.

It is notable that the "Take Charge. Take the Test" campaign depicts an African American woman's decision to get tested in different terms from those depicted in the campaigns targeting Latino and Black MSM. The campaign necessarily walks a tightrope of political sensibilities between race, gender, and sexuality. On the one hand, while the ad is opaque about what knowing "everything" might entail, popular discourse on African American men is rife with racist narratives about their "down-low" sexual practices and untrustworthiness that facilitate readers coming to their own conclusion: get tested because you cannot know what your man does in his free time.[53] On the other hand, in a condom-focused HIV prevention context, women do report frustration with having to rely on men to truthfully report whether or not they have been faithful or recently tested.[54] In such a context, promoting suspicion may be a useful strategy for navigating this gendered uncertainty.[55]

Taken together, these HIV testing campaigns would seem to be placing responsibility on HIV-negative individuals. But what does that responsibility entail? Under test-and-treat, the only explicit obligation assigned to HIV-negative people is to get tested; protective behaviors that would explicitly implicate their responsibility for preventing their own infection are no longer emphasized. Indeed, the only HIV-negative individuals of interest under the test-and treat model are those who are *not*, in fact, HIV negative, but undiagnosed *HIV positive*. On the other hand, the potential infectiousness of HIV-positive bodies comes into focus, implicating their responsibility for preventing infecting others. Thus, the notion of responsibility that comes out of the test-and-treat model seems to relieve HIV-negative individuals of much of their responsibility for protecting themselves.

Notably, CDC did not develop a treatment-focused social marketing campaign targeting HIV-positive people until 2016, when it introduced the HIV Treatment Works campaign.[56] The campaign presents HIV-positive people living happy, productive lives, unencumbered by their diagnosis. However, in the dozens of posters and materials produced for the campaign, the preventive benefits of treatment are barely mentioned, suggesting the CDC remains uncertain over how to best promote treatment as prevention. This uncertainty was further evidenced when the CDC announced new recommendations the following year for HIV-negative women wishing to become pregnant with a male partner who is HIV-positive; many AIDS activists and experts promptly criticized those guidelines for continuing to support expensive techniques like "sperm-washing" instead of recommending that couples combine the preventative benefits of treatment (for the HIV-positive man) and pre-exposure prophylaxis (for the HIV-negative woman).[57]

The CDC's tepid embrace of treatment's prevention-oriented benefits may be in part due to the private nature of the doctor-patient relationship in which treatment decisions are made. Rather than investing in billboards or radio ads, some recent CDC-developed HIV prevention campaigns aimed at HIV-positive people target them indirectly through their health care providers. Included in the materials of one such intervention—Prevention Is Care—is a patient brochure targeting HIV-positive patients in serodiscordant relationships (or relationships in which one partner is living with HIV and one is HIV-negative). The brochure's tips for how you can stop the spread of HIV are broken into two parts. The first, "Do tell," encourages patients to disclose their HIV-positive status to their partners so "he or she will know it's important to be safe during all sexual activity and to be tested often for HIV."[58] The second part, "Don't take risks," which is on preventing transmission, states that "abstinence (not having sex) is the best way to prevent the spread of HIV. But if abstinence is not possible, use condoms."[59] In regard to whether lower viral loads might reduce or eliminate the risk of transmission, the brochure states definitively:

> Don't think you have "safe" times. Even when tests show that your viral load (the amount of HIV in your blood) is very low or undetectable, you can give HIV to your partner because the virus is still in your body. HIV can be high enough in other body fluids to be spread to your partner.[60]

Forgetting, for a moment, that the CDC brochure promotes abstinence as the "best way" to prevent HIV (despite its high failure rates observed throughout human history), recent studies show that having an undetectable viral load reduces the risk of HIV transmission by somewhere between 99.9 and 100 percent. Of course, when this brochure was published in 2011, these figures were not yet available to the CDC. Nonetheless, the brochure's claim that an HIV-positive person with an undetectable viral load "can give your partner HIV" appears to have become quickly outdated.

More broadly, the brochure again implies a host of individual responsibilities for HIV-positive people for managing HIV. Despite targeting HIV-serodiscordant relationships, the brochure does very little to acknowledge what the HIV-negative person might do to share the responsibility of managing that risk. HIV-positive partners are instructed to disclose their status so that that their partners "will know it's important to be safe," which presumes that the HIV-negative partners would not otherwise know that they should protect themselves against infection. Despite studies showing that partners can play an important role in helping HIV-positive people adhere to their medication regimen, the brochure does not advise HIV-positive people how or why they might discuss their treatment with their partners.[61] Although the brochure does note that anal sex is much riskier than oral sex, studies have long demonstrated that there is a wide range of harm-reduction strategies beyond using a condom that both HIV-negative and HIV-positive people can employ to reduce the risk of transmitting HIV.[62] These practices—sometimes referred to as *seroadaptation*—are not discussed. In short, the brochure provides a wide array of responsibilities for HIV-positive people, while mostly ignoring their partners.

Yet, while CDC-developed prevention materials indirectly targeted HIV-positive people to encourage them to go on treatment, outside agencies funded with CDC dollars had already begun developing more explicit social marketing campaigns. A new iteration of the HIV Stops with Me campaign was announced in 2014 that depicted its spokesmodels before and after suppressing their viral load (see figure 10). The campaign's tagline plainly stated its intended effect: "Find doctor / Keep appointments / Take meds / Check lab results." In this series, the spokesmodel's portrait was divided. On the left side, having a "detectable" viral load was described in negative, shameful terms. On the right side, having an "undetectable" viral load was depicted in positive terms. The ad's central message was reinforced by visual cues: having a detectable viral load was depicted in black and white, suggesting an old-fashioned or antiquated way of being. Having an undetectable viral load was depicted in full color, suggesting progress and a happier, modern way of living.

According to the campaign, suppressing one's viral load was only a matter of accepting one's HIV-positive status and feeling in control of one's life. But surely there are many reasons why HIV-positive people are not linked to care, many of which are not merely psychological and that are outside an individual's control. These could include housing instability, an inability or fear of navigating a complex health care bureaucracy, negative experiences with stigmatizing health care providers, or a fear that showing up at the local health clinic for HIV treatment might spark hurtful gossip. These obstacles are not reducible to "wishing away" one's HIV-status: they are social problems, not personal issues.

More than a decade has passed since public health experts warned against individualistic positive prevention campaigns. At time of publication, no widely distributed campaign targeting HIV-positive people has done much to connect that personal responsibility to wider institutions and social problems. This problem is not limited to HIV prevention, of course. Critics of modern public health campaigns have long argued that health marketing tends to focus solely on the individual and do little to consider the broader social context in which those individuals live.[63] Consider, for a moment, the most recent public health campaign you can remember—whether anti obesity, anti teen pregnancy, or some other health issue. The tagline most likely had something to do with encouraging you (the individual) to make a "smarter" or "healthier" (personal) choice. The problem is more systemic and has to do with the way we conceive of "health" as the cumulative result of a series of individual choices. But while the promotion of individual responsibility is common in public health campaigns, in later chapters we will see that the stakes are considerably higher when it comes to HIV: if you are HIV positive, being labeled irresponsible can land you in prison.

THE PROMISE OF PREP?

Although the condom is not yet extinct, HIV prevention campaigns targeting HIV-positive people have reshaped notions of responsibility in public health practice. Prevention with positives repolarized the field, switching its focus from HIV-negative people to people living with HIV. In doing so, it turned our assumptions about who should be responsible for preventing future HIV infections on their head.

But the field is never static. A new technology appears poised to push back against this trend. In July 2012, the Food and Drug Administration (FDA) approved an antiretroviral already used for treating HIV for use by HIV-negative individuals in order to protect against infection. Pre exposure prophylaxis—PrEP, for short—is a prevention strategy that involves taking a pill daily to protect against infection. Some gay activists have likened the approach to a kind of gay "birth control."[64] PrEP was approved on the heels of remarkable clinical trial data that showed it could reduce an HIV-negative person's risk of contracting the virus by 96 percent when taken daily.[65] Although critics were initially

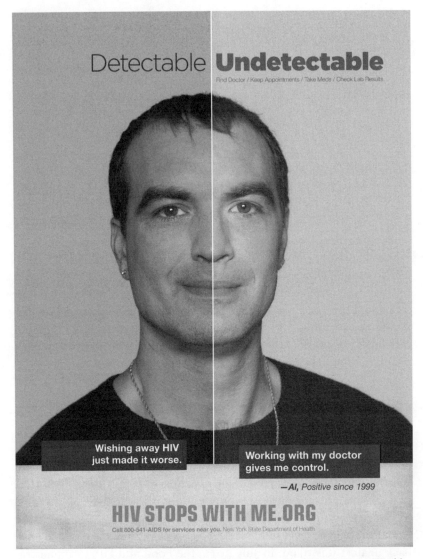

FIGURE 10. HIV Stops with Me ad: "Detectable/Undetectable." Source: Better World Advertising.

concerned that PrEP's remarkable success might be limited to the clinical trial environment where patients are monitored closely, data from Britain's PrEP demonstration project measuring the pill's effectiveness in the real world, announced in 2015, show it to be just as effective in practice.[66] In short, taking a pill a day can protect against HIV infection.

There is just one problem: not enough of the people who need it most are taking it. A recent study estimated that only 49,158 started PrEP in the United States between January 2012 and September 2015.[67] While that study estimates that the number of PrEP prescriptions is increasing year over year at a fast clip, its authors also estimate that 74 percent of PrEP prescriptions went to White patients, 12 percent to Latino patients, and 10 percent to Black patients. These figures stand in stark contrast to today's epidemic, however: the CDC estimates that 45 percent and 24 percent of new HIV diagnoses in 2015 were among Black and Latino people respectively.[68] Moreover, the same report estimates that Black and Latino women had roughly four times lower rates of PrEP initiation than White women, yet they made up 61 percent and 15 percent of new HIV infections among women in 2015.[69] In short, while the number of people taking PrEP has accelerated, it has not yet reached the populations hardest hit by the epidemic. If this course holds, PrEP may even further exacerbate the racially disparate impact of the epidemic.

Given that PrEP is so highly effective when taken daily, how can we make sense of its molasses-paced uptake among communities hardest hit by the epidemic? Perhaps ironically, the answer may be a mix of stigma and science. In terms of stigma, despite PrEP's high effectiveness and few side effects, its use has been a polarizing subject in public discourse.[70] Tense debates have pitted AIDS activists against one another, with some describing those who take the drug as irresponsible "Truvada whores."[71] Despite the millions or perhaps even *billions* of dollars at stake, even the pharmaceutical company that manufactures the drug has been at times reluctant to market the drug for PrEP.[72]

In terms of science, HIV is no longer a terminal illness. By transforming HIV into a chronic illness, antiretroviral treatment eliminated a gruesome outcome that motivated many people to protect themselves against infection. The public face of HIV was eventually transformed from a disfigured person dying in a hospital bed to a happy, healthy person whose once-a-day medication regimen seems almost like a multivitamin. In this context, some may perceive PrEP as taking a pill a day to prevent having to take a pill a day. A recent study estimating life expectancy for HIV-positive people diagnosed today demonstrates the dramatic improvement in recent years for people living with HIV: while life expectancy for newly diagnosed HIV-positive patients overall was reduced, the study estimated that a twenty-year-old gay man diagnosed with HIV today will live an additional 69.3 years—*several years longer than men in the general population* (although the study in question did not speculate as to what might be driving this surprising finding, it may be related to the average man's habitual avoidance of doctors; in this study, HIV-positive men were presumed to regularly see a physician).[73] The remarkably healthy prognosis for HIV-positive people today will almost certainly make promoting HIV prevention more challenging.

But if HIV-negative people *are* called to take responsibility for protecting themselves against HIV infection, how will that responsibility be represented? Will it be presented as an individual choice made for one's own personal health? For the love of a partner? Or will it be sold as a way to come together as a community to fight the epidemic? Only time will tell. At the time of writing, PrEP's lackluster adoption in nonwhite communities means that identifying HIV-positive people and getting them linked consistently to care remains a key strategy of twenty-first-century HIV prevention.

THE POLITICS OF RESPONSIBILITY

Individualistic positive prevention campaigns like HIV Stops with Me fall into many of the traps experts caution against. Their HIV-positive spokespeople proudly proclaim disclosing and caring for their communities. However, the social context for these efforts to prevent HIV is largely absent. For example, HIV Stops with Me does not connect disclosure to emotional well-being or structural problems that many HIV-positive people face, such as housing insecurity, financial instability, and domestic violence. Yet we know that the decision to disclose one's HIV-positive status can be influenced by many such factors. Not accounting for these broader issues facing HIV-positive people leaves the viewer with the impression that HIV-positive people could stop HIV if they would only choose to do so: the perfect recipe for blame and shame.

On the other hand, the HIV testing campaigns targeting HIV-negative individuals promote a different, more collective kind of responsibility. In the ads in figures 7 and 8, the decision to get tested is situated within a particular social context: a relationship, a family, a group of friends. Whereas the responsibilities promoted for HIV-positive people by the HIV Stops with Me campaign were largely individualistic ("I disclose with honesty"; "I am the cure"; "I believe in responsibility"), HIV-negative MSM are depicted as taking on a socially embedded responsibility alongside family, friends, and romantic partners. If they fail to get tested, presumably the blame extends beyond the individual.

Why was their community not more supportive? Was their partner judgmental about HIV testing? These are the kind of questions asked when a collective responsibility is not met.

When individual responsibility is not met, however, the questions are markedly different. As described earlier in the chapter, researchers justified the need for developing prevention strategies targeting HIV-positive people by citing a criminal case against a New York man, Nushawn Williams, accused of infecting nearly a dozen women. As the second half of this book will reveal in greater detail, criminal laws punishing HIV-positive people have spread during the very same time as the repolarization of HIV prevention analyzed in this chapter. To date, more than thirty U.S. states have enacted HIV-specific criminal statutes that generally make it a crime for HIV-positive people to have sex without first disclosing their HIV-positive status.[74]

It is no coincidence that public health scholars directly invoked Williams's criminal case as a justification for targeting HIV-positive people for prevention. HIV-specific criminal laws depend on the same notion of individual responsibility for people living with HIV promoted in the HIV Stops with Me campaign. Although unintentional, the repolarization of HIV prevention may have inadvertently contributed to the criminalization of HIV.

The next chapter examines this relationship more closely. How do the big-picture policies and rhetoric explored in this chapter play out on the ground? In the age of test-and-treat, local health departments are ramping up their surveillance programs targeting HIV-positive people. These programs are not only useful for public health purposes; they also happen to be useful for enforcing the law.

CHAPTER 3

The Public Health Police

As the HIV epidemic wore on in the 2000s, the scientific evidence demonstrating that antiretroviral treatment could virtually eliminate the risk of sexual transmission grew steadily into a mountain. In the midst of widespread pessimism that a vaccine or cure would ever be found, public health authorities focused on a target they viewed as more pragmatic: ending AIDS. Of course, ending AIDS did not imply eliminating new HIV infections; instead, it referred to the hope that HIV infection could be halted from progressing to AIDS by putting every newly infected person immediately on antiretroviral therapy. To succeed, however, health authorities would need to find a way to get HIV-positive people to take their pills. The age of condoms was over. The age of positive prevention had begun.

For decades, AIDS activists resisted public health efforts to track HIV-positive people more closely on civil liberties grounds. Because of the disease's highly stigmatized nature, advocates worried that the standard intrusions into patient privacy in the name of public health were likely to drive the epidemic underground. For these reasons, they lobbied for an approach that came to be known as "AIDS exceptionalism," or treating HIV differently from other infectious diseases. Instead of the standard, more invasive approach, activists proposed that protecting civil rights and squashing discrimination would be a much more effective strategy for containing the epidemic. These arguments prevailed in the early years, when an HIV-positive diagnosis was terminal and effective treatment was nonexistent. However, as this chapter will demonstrate, a series of medical advances in the late 1980s and 1990s shifted the terms of the debate. Was there still a legitimate rationale for treating AIDS differently than other diseases? For many in public health, the short answer was no; it was time for the gloves to come off.

The previous chapter illustrated how HIV prevention was repolarized to target HIV-positive people. In this new era of positive prevention, people living with HIV were no longer thought of as tragic "AIDS victims"; they were expected to take care of themselves and their partners. This chapter draws on interviews with local health officials in Michigan to explore how local health authorities ensure that HIV-positive clients behave in a manner officials deem responsible—and how they catch and punish those who do not.

While the last chapter explored the shift toward promoting individual responsibility among people living with HIV, this chapter looks at how punitive disease control emerges at the local level through police-like investigations and public health policies explicitly designed to hold people living with HIV legally responsible for their behaviors.

THE END OF AIDS EXCEPTIONALISM

Thirteen-year-old Ryan White was an unexpected AIDS activist, propelled to the national spotlight after he was expelled from his Kokomo, Indiana, middle school in 1984. The petition for his expulsion was signed by both parents of his classmates and teachers. White was one of the estimated 50 percent of hemophiliacs who contracted HIV through tainted blood products during the early years of the epidemic. He was young, White, and had a sympathetic story—the perfect poster child for a campaign against HIV stigma.

When AIDS was first reported in the early 1980s, the public was most sympathetic to individuals infected with HIV through tainted blood products or through childbirth—causes out of one's control. Many Americans had little sympathy for the other members of the "4-H club" (hemophiliacs, homosexuals, heroin users, and Haitians), who were most at risk of contracting the disease. Members of the religious Right proclaimed AIDS to be the "cure" for homosexuality, and they fought tirelessly to block efforts to fund HIV prevention in the name of helping gay men or junkies. In such a moralistic political context, a child like Ryan White was the perfect spokesperson for HIV funding. Even the most blackhearted member of Congress would find it hard to go on television to tell a dying child that he did not deserve public assistance. It is no coincidence that the major piece of federal legislation that continues to fund HIV treatment to this day—the Ryan White CARE Act of 1990—is titled in White's memory.

AIDS activists cited discrimination against people living with HIV, such as White's expulsion from his school, as evidence against calls for more invasive public health measures to track and control HIV-positive people. Activists argued that although other diseases were stigmatized, HIV stigma was exceptionally potent in the way that it fostered discrimination and exclusion in American society. For these reasons, they lobbied for treating HIV differently from other infectious diseases.

Campaigns to treat HIV differently were often successful in the early years of the epidemic. However, a series of scientific advances over the next decade would take the wind out of the sails of AIDS exceptionalism arguments. First, heating experiments published in 1984 demonstrated that HIV could be eliminated from tainted blood products used by hemophiliacs, ending the epidemic in that population nearly overnight.[1] Second, scientists developed an accurate HIV test in 1985, and screening was immediately implemented for all donated blood. Third, scientists discovered that an experimental drug, azidothymidine (AZT), worked against HIV and that it was particularly good at preventing mother-to-child transmission during childbirth; the number of babies born with HIV in the United States peaked in 1992 and declined by an estimated 67 percent through 1997.[2] In short, the two most sympathetic faces of HIV, children and medical patients, were no longer being infected with the disease in large numbers. Mercifully, there would never be another American AIDS activist like Ryan White.

However, if the inventions of safe blood products and AZT were flesh wounds to AIDS exceptionalism, the introduction of effective HIV treatment in 1996 was the coup de grâce. As HIV was transformed from a terminal illness to a chronic disease, the logic of affording special protections to people living with HIV was gravely undercut. Many in public health began to argue for a return to more invasive surveillance practices. In a *New England Journal of Medicine* essay published in 2005, then-commissioner of New York City's health department Thomas Frieden and colleagues argued that the time for treating HIV differently had passed. Frieden—whom President Obama would later tap to become director of the Centers for Disease Control in 2009—argued that it was time public health implemented "traditional disease-control principles and proven interventions that can identify infected persons, interrupt transmission, ensure treatment and case management, and monitor infection and control efforts throughout the population."[3] With HIV-positive people living normal lives instead of dying soon after infection, controlling the behavior of people living with HIV became a top priority for prevention efforts.

At the center of many such debates was whether health departments should collect the names of people newly diagnosed as HIV positive in order to track the epidemic in each state. Proponents argued that name-based systems were critical to collecting and maintaining accurate surveillance data; without names, they argued, it would be much more difficult to ensure that anyone diagnosed as HIV positive was not later counted again as a new infection. AIDS activists countered that the privacy pitfalls that came with amassing the names of people living with HIV in a single data set were unacceptable.[4] These concerns were inflamed by egregious examples in which those pitfalls were exposed, such as a Florida health department staff member being accused in 1996 of using a health department list of over four thousand HIV-positive people to screen potential sexual partners—and inviting his friends to do the same.[5]

Instead of adopting name-based systems, activists proposed that states adopt anonymous, code-based systems. They argued that systems based on sufficiently unique codes could achieve similar results to name-based systems without compromising the privacy of such a marginalized population. Health officials argued that the risks associated with name-based systems were minimal and that the public health value of good surveillance data outweighed them. Moreover, collecting names not only produced better surveillance data, they argued, but it also enabled health department staff to follow up with newly diagnosed patients in order to offer them additional services such as counseling and, in later years, treatment.

Without the ability to follow up with HIV-positive clients, health officials could not universally implement additional surveillance programs targeting those diagnosed as HIV positive—programs such as universal contact tracing. Developed in the early twentieth century for managing syphilis outbreaks, contact tracing involves asking diagnosed individuals to reveal the names of their sexual partners so that they might be tested and treated, if necessary.[6] The practice is best suited to diseases that are curable and highly contagious—two things that HIV is not. Despite questions over its effectiveness (not to mention its potential threat to privacy), the practice was widely implemented in HIV testing clinics around the country.[7]

By 2005, debates over privacy and HIV surveillance programs had quieted. Forty-three state and local health departments had adopted name-based reporting and, for the most part, the proverbial sky had not fallen. The CDC leveraged this momentum by issuing a dear colleague letter to encourage the fourteen state and local health departments still using code- or name-to-code-based systems to transition to name-based systems.[8] The next year, CDC officials pushed even further by issuing new guidelines recommending that all Americans between 13 and 64 should be tested for HIV and that providers should abandon the practice of requiring informed consent for HIV testing. Instead, they proposed that clinics implement a practice of "presumed consent" in which HIV testing is performed unless the individual explicitly and proactively objects. By 2008, every health department in the United States had implemented name-based HIV case reporting.

This chapter explores how local health officials in one state have put these tools to work in their efforts to control HIV-positive people. Michigan was an early adopter of many of these policies, moving to implement name-based reporting in 1988 when less than a dozen states were using such systems. The Michigan legislature provided the legal basis for its surveillance practices in a sweeping omnibus legislation package passed in December 1988. This wide-ranging set of bills dealing with HIV was "tie-barred" together, requiring that they all pass in order for any of them to go into effect. It included a little-debated legislative package aimed at controlling "recalcitrant" HIV-positive people deemed a "health threat to others" (HTTO).

This bundle of statutes is most well-known for its criminal provision making it a felony crime for HIV-positive individuals to engage in a wide range of sexual practices without first disclosing their status (chapter 5 explores how Michigan criminal courts enforce this law). But the bulk of the "health threat" legislation outlines civil law procedures for controlling HIV-positive clients labeled "recalcitrant"—procedures such as forcing individuals to undergo counseling, treatment, and/or quarantine.

This chapter explores how twenty-five Michigan health officials tasked with managing HTTO cases interpret and apply both the criminal and civil portions of this law. These officials hail from fourteen of the seventeen local health departments in Michigan with staff specifically assigned to handle HIV in their community. Eleven manage their jurisdiction's HIV program; eleven serve as "disease intervention specialists," who are responsible for tracking down newly diagnosed people's prior sexual partners for contact tracing; and three serve both functions. While the state maintains that the work of local health officials is done solely in the interests of promoting public health, many of the strategies they employ suggest they are also engaged in policing and law enforcement.

Why Michigan? When it adopted these policies in 1988, its combination of epidemiological surveillance technologies, civil law, and criminal penalties was pioneering.[9] Others states had name-based reporting, health-threat laws, and criminal disclosure laws, but few had all three. Today, most states have similar public health practices in place and similar laws on the books. Consequently, Michigan provides a useful test case for understanding the social implications that these policies and practices have for public health, social justice, and inequality. All the participant names used in this chapter are pseudonyms chosen solely at the discretion of the interviewee in order to protect confidentiality.

POLICING PUBLIC HEALTH

When clients visit one of the many publicly funded health clinics in Michigan to be tested for HIV, they can expect more than just a finger prick. HIV testing counselors sit down with clients, reviewing their sexual history with a fine-tooth comb. How many times have you engaged in anal sex in the last six months? Did any of your partners ejaculate inside you? How many times in the past six months have you used narcotics when having sex? Clients' responses are often catalogued and collectively analyzed. Considered by health experts as an opportunity for clients to reflect on their sexual lives and perhaps commit to taking more care to prevent acquiring HIV in the future (if they test negative), pre- or post-test HIV counseling has long been one of the cornerstones of HIV prevention.

If a client tests positive for HIV or any other reportable sexually transmitted infection (STI), the testing counselor will not only provide counseling and referrals for treatment but is also legally required to conduct contact tracing and ask the client to report the names of sexual partners. Health officials later attempt to contact those individuals to recommend that they be tested for HIV and other infections—a program known as "partner services." However, health officials use the information gathered through HIV testing and partner services to do more than just inform partners and facilitate their testing. In some jurisdictions, health officials use these surveillance data as a mechanism for identifying potential health-threat lawbreakers.

Mitch (HIV/AIDS coordinator, jurisdiction 2) paints a clear picture of how this works in her jurisdiction, where she coordinates the local health department's HIV/AIDS programs. The process begins when a person is newly diagnosed with an STI like HIV or gonorrhea and is asked to disclose partners' names. But a very pointed question is tacked on: "Did any of the named partners disclose that they were HIV positive?"

> We make sure that we say everything very confidentially. So the one question that we have that we always ask somebody when they're giving us names is . . . if that person gave me four names, I would say, "Did any of these four people ever tell you that they were HIV positive?"

Tacking on this question is not standard practice. Indeed, it is specifically added in order to catch people who are not disclosing their HIV-positive status.

The state health department—the Michigan Department of Community Health (MDCH)—describes the following as goals of partner services:

- "Counseling HIV/STD-infected clients on disease state and need to identify their sex and/or needle-sharing partners at risk for HIV/STD;
- Locating partners, and notifying them of exposure and offering testing and treatment, prevention, education, and referral to medical and support services."[10]

The state health department positions the work of partner services solely in the terms of public health and medicine. However, despite these claims, some local health departments have clearly modified partner services for law enforcement purposes.

Notably, partner services is not limited to HIV testing; public health staff attempt to collect the names of past sexual partners for anyone newly diagnosed with other STIs such as gonorrhea, chlamydia, and syphilis. For example, although a client may be diagnosed with, say, syphilis rather than HIV, health officials are still required to provide partner services. And despite the fact that the client did not test for HIV, health department staff can still use the occasion to seek out HIV-positive partners. Donna (disease intervention specialist, jurisdiction 13) describes this process:

> Let's say they come in and they have a secondary infection. Let's say they have chlamydia and gonorrhea. Okay, by law—or by our duty, basically—

gonorrhea cases are reportable to us. . . . Part of our investigation process is to ask, "Who's your partner?" In this instance, this person mentioned, "So-and-so is my partner." So when we pulled up the file looking for the other person, we realized at that time that the person was HIV-infected also . . . so that tells us, "You're having unprotected sex."

There are several "files" that Donna might refer to in order to identify a reported partner as HIV positive. Mitch describes the two likely possibilities:

I may not know any of those people on that list, but the next step that I do is I'm going to go back to *my files* and see if I have a file on any of these people. I will then go to *the state* and see if any of these people have already been reported as positive. And when that report comes back or when we have a file that one of those four people is positive, that becomes a flag. (emphasis added)

When Mitch refers to "my files," she is referring to the local health department's records on HIV-positive clients. However, these files are only likely to include people who live in the county and have visited the health department for services. In order to refer to a much broader data set, Mitch goes to "the state" in order to cross-check the name against the state's name-based reporting data that describe everyone in the state ever diagnosed as HIV positive. If a person named as a partner by a client who did not report having sex with any HIV-positive people turns out to be listed in that database, an investigation is launched.

Under this system, HIV-positive clients—typically the poor—who are forced to rely on the public health infrastructure to assist in (or in some cases provide) their medical care and other services are more likely to be noticed. By visiting the local health department more frequently, their names are more likely to be recognized if they are ever named as a prior sexual partner. For example, Charlie, who coordinates the HIV/AIDS programs in a different jurisdiction (9) explains:

I was actually testing another individual who [was] testing for everything. I tested; they were [HIV] positive. . . . After they gave me one of their partner names, I knew the name immediately. . . . I didn't say anything at that time. I just said *[sighing]*, "Oh, I know that name." Went back, sure enough, confirmed that this person was already positive.

When health officials such as Charlie report cross-referencing the names of past partners against the state's confidential name-based database, this is not an automated process. It requires picking up the phone and making a call to a state health official, an extra effort that jurisdiction officials may be more likely to take when their suspicions are aroused.

Of course, many HIV-positive people disclose to their HIV-negative partners. Even so, some health officials regard HIV-positive people with a certain level of suspicion when they report a relationship with an HIV-negative partner. Cash (HIV/AIDS coordinator, jurisdiction 8) was concerned after an HIV-positive man came to the health department for regular STI testing and tested positive for gonorrhea. The client assured Cash that he had disclosed his status to all his partners, including his HIV-negative girlfriend. But Cash was not convinced:

> So I'm thinking, okay, it's possible maybe he didn't do disclosure. I'm going to call [his partner] in for regular STD, and then when she reports that she's never had anybody who's been a sex partner who's HIV positive . . . then there will be that whole question.

But when his partner came in to get tested, she named him as a partner and said that he had, in fact, disclosed his HIV-positive status. "It's like all the pieces fit together. He did tell her."

The pieces do not always fit together, however. When they do not, policing public health requires carefully navigating the numerous health privacy regulations that limit what health officials can and cannot do to intervene. For example, health officials often described immediately recognizing a named partner as someone they already knew to be HIV positive in the community. But strict patient confidentiality laws forbid them from revealing that information, which is protected by laws such as the federal Health Insurance Portability and Accountability Act of 1996 (HIPAA). In addition, Michigan law makes it a misdemeanor for someone to reveal another person's HIV-positive status without his or her express permission, a provision included in the same set of laws as the HTTO regulations.

These regulations are the reasons behind Mitch's efforts to word her questions to clients during partner services interviews "carefully." For example, let's say that a newly diagnosed client reports having had sex with two people: John and Bob. Even if Mitch were to recognize Bob's name as that of an HIV-positive client, she cannot directly ask the client whether he knew that Bob was HIV positive. That would be tipping her hand. To prevent revealing more than she is legally allowed, Mitch says, "We just make it very generic: 'Did any of these people ever tell you that they were HIV positive?'"

While health officials never described breaking patient privacy laws outright, they did describe navigating them in ways that might be described as bending the law. For example, Shirley (HIV/AIDS coordinator, jurisdiction 4) describes one case in which a public health nurse struggled to get an HIV-positive client who had recently been released from prison to disclose to his new girlfriend:

> The nurse asked the new positive man, "Have you told your partner about your HIV status?" The new HIV guy said that he hadn't told his partner yet, and [the nurse] . . . told him, "You need to tell her. If you don't tell her I will." So [the nurse] gave him two weeks, made both of them an appointment in two weeks' time, and told him that "when you come to that appointment, if she hasn't been told about your status yet by you, then I'm going to tell her."

In this case, the nurse did not actually reveal the client's HIV-status to the partner—the nurse merely threatened to do so. When the couple returned two weeks later, things did not go well:

> It was kind of interesting how he told her, because he waited until they were in the waiting room, waiting for the appointment. They were waiting in the waiting room with families, with their children waiting for immunizations. It became physical.

That the situation described by Shirley became physical is not particularly surprising; disclosing one's HIV-positive status to a partner is rife with emotional volatility. HIV-positive women are particularly vulnerable in these situations; reports of violent reactions from male partners are common. In 2012 and 2014, for example, two HIV-positive women were murdered in Texas by their male partners when the women's HIV-positive status was discovered.[11] And as the instance described by Shirley demonstrates, even heterosexual men can risk physical retaliation from their partners when disclosing.

Although the nurse did not, in fact, disclose the partner's status, reports suggest that this sometimes happens—and that such reports can directly result in criminal charges being filed under Michigan's felony HIV disclosure law. A man in Kent County pleaded guilty in 2000 to charges that he did not disclose his status to a woman with whom he had a sexual relationship. According to a newspaper report, "Authorities have said the woman had no idea [the defendant] was infected with AIDS until contacted by a health worker who knew about [his] condition. The victim then went to police."[12]

THE CONDOM QUESTION

Partner services programs are not the only tools health officials have for catching potential health threats. Local health officials in Michigan repeatedly described using the test results of other sexually transmitted infection—such as syphilis, chlamydia, and gonorrhea—as evidence of "recalcitrant" behavior. CT (disease investigation specialist, jurisdiction 10) describes a recent case involving a local HIV-positive man:

> He then had picked up actually gonorrhea and syphilis in one occasion. . . . It became obvious that the person picking up these diseases was likely not using the appropriate protection. Bacterial STD is probably the most objective thing to look at as far as the person being in an unsafe sexual activity. The people who are actually picking up those STDs are probably not using protection. What we find is that they are oftentimes too not disclosing their HIV status. It's almost a given in that regard.

CT viewed a diagnosis with an STI as evidence that individuals were having sex without protection—referring presumably to the use of condoms during anal or vaginal sex. Many health officials agreed, frequently citing positive STI results as a common way that health threats are identified. When I asked Fern (disease intervention specialist, jurisdiction 11) how most health-threat cases came to her attention, she replied:

> Well, usually it's all of a sudden their name appears with another STD . . . All the STDs have to be reported on the [Michigan Disease Surveillance System]. So . . . if the [syphilis coordinator] has any syphilis cases where they're also showing that they're HIV positive, then she and I work together, and . . . if I've got a case report, then it goes to a "health threat to others," more or less. Because if they come up with syphilis, they're having unprotected sex.

The logic inherent in this perspective is that sexually transmitted bacterial infections such as gonorrhea are necessarily the result of sex without condoms. But this is not necessarily true. While latex condoms can *reduce* the risk of transmission of STIs such as gonorrhea, they do not eliminate it.[13]

In a letter written to me after these findings were originally reported, Michigan's state health department explicitly denied that an STI diagnosis is sufficient grounds for classifying someone as a health threat. But reports from local health officials suggest otherwise: in many jurisdictions, local health department staff described STI screening as a primary technique for identifying health-threat cases.

Although many people reported viewing STI results as evidence of a health threat, it is important to note that not everyone agreed. Mark, a disease investigation specialist in a large, urban jurisdiction (3), says he differs from others on this point:

> A client comes here—and they are HIV positive—and to the STD clinic, and the doctors see there was syphilis; they just made it a health threat. Me,

myself, I don't consider them a health threat, because they could have had sex with their partner and told them they are positive, so you never know.

That there is disagreement on the issue suggests that where a person lives and who manages their case file may play an important role in shaping whether they are labeled as a health threat.

Mark's comments illustrate the complicated logic of interpreting STI tests as evidence of health-threat behaviors. How did Fern make sense of this connection?

> *Hoppe:* A positive STI test result . . . you all see as evidence of nondisclosure. . . . Why is that interpreted as a potential health threat?
>
> *Fern:* Well, they're having unprotected sex. But, again too, sometimes what I come up against is when I do get there, they'll say, "Well, I did tell them." You know, "They're positive also." I say, "Well, that doesn't matter." You know, "Just because they're positive also, you still need to be using protection."

Fern's concern in this case was not that the client might not be disclosing HIV-positive status but that the client was not using condoms. Even in cases where their partners are also HIV positive, Fern insists that HIV-positive clients are required to use condoms. Contracting an STI is evidence that they failed to do so and is used as evidence to label an HIV-positive client a health threat. This raises the question of whether HIV-positive people can legally have sex without condoms in Michigan.

In a 2008 e-mail obtained through a Freedom of Information Act request by journalist Todd Heywood, the state health department's legal director, Denise Chrysler, clearly describes how she interprets Michigan's health-threat statute:

> Would an HIV-infected individual who has unprotected sex be a health threat to his/her sex partner? Are there any circumstances where unprotected sex not be a health threat? . . . It sounds like the individual would always be a health threat, even if the individual's partner is also HIV positive. An HIV-infected individual is not relieved of all responsibility to prevent transmission simply because he/she has warned their sex partner of the HIV-infection. We (in public health) and the infected person still have responsibilities to prevent the spread of serious communicable disease even if the infected individual's sexual partner consents to the risky behavior. In fact, under section 5203, the local health officer *shall* issue a warning notice against such an individual.[14] (emphasis added)

The state health department maintains that Chrysler's statement was not an official legal opinion.[15] However, the fact that its legal director believed that an HIV-positive person engaging in sex without condoms "would always be a health threat" suggests that the law is open to interpretation—contradicting the state's assertion that the law is unambiguous.

In many cases, local health department policies reflect an interpretation of the health-threat statute as requiring HIV-positive people always to use condoms. Five jurisdictions have developed "client acknowledgement forms" that newly diagnosed HIV-positive clients are asked to sign immediately after learning that they have tested HIV positive.[16] While there are various versions of the form, the most controversial language was found in forms that asked clients to place their initials beside the following statement (quoted from the form used in Macomb County, shown in figure 11): "You are required to inform individual/s of your HIV infected status before sexual contact. You and your sexual partner/s must use a barrier protection such as latex condoms, dental dams, and/or female condoms in a correct and consistent manner."[17] While most forms were more ambiguous and simply referred to a requirement that clients engage in "safe behaviors" and/or "risk reduction," the language used in some of these forms suggests that at least some health officials believe their HIV-positive clients must use condoms at all times.

These forms are not just a way to inform clients of their legal responsibilities. They serve as a means of holding HIV-positive clients legally responsible for not disclosing their HIV status at a later date. As Mitch reports, these forms were developed after clients suspected of not disclosing simply denied knowing they were HIV positive in the first place:

> Sometimes, they'll try and say, "Well, nobody ever told me I was positive. I tested but I didn't get my results. They didn't tell me I was positive." And that's why—we do a lot of paperwork now about, a lot of the education that we do, we actually have to have the people sign, anytime we have a positive, we go through felony law and do all of this education: what you need to do and what you don't need to do. Get them hooked up with support services and then we make them sign a paper that basically says, "I've been educated. I know that I can't do this without disclosing my status. I've been warned of that and I could potentially have charges brought against me if I don't do that." We make everybody sign that, so that when we have that piece of paper and the name, say this person were to come up again all of the sudden, we've got that on file and we would say, "You can't tell me that you didn't know that you were positive, because we've got this on file."

These forms have already played a role in prosecuting HIV-positive people in Michigan. For example, a news report on the 2007 sentencing of a man to 5–15 years in prison for failing to disclose his HIV-positive

MACOMB COUNTY HEALTH DEPARTMENT
SOUTHWEST HEALTH CENTER
27690 VAN DYKE AVENUE
WARREN, MICHIGAN 48093
(586) 465-9127   FAX (586) 573-2019
macombcountymi.gov/publichealth

CLIENT NOTIFICATION OF POSITIVE HIV ANTIBODY STATUS AND MICHIGAN LAW

Client Name _____	Date of Birth _____
Client ID Number _____	☐ Male ☐ Female
Date of Pre-test Counseling and Testing _____	
Date of Post-test Counseling & Notification of Test Results _____	
HIV Antibody Test Result: Elisa = Reactive Western Blot = Reactive	

You have just been informed your test result for HIV Antibodies is reactive. This means you are infected with the Human Immunodeficiency Virus (HIV) and you have the potential to be infectious to others. It is important that you understand this test result and the HIV/AIDS laws in Michigan. You have the option to decline signature of this form, but you must follow the law and statements below:

☐ 1. You are required to inform individual/s of your HIV infected status **BEFORE** sexual contact. You and your sexual partner/s must use a barrier protection such as latex condoms, dental dams and/or female condoms in a correct and consistent manner.

☐ 2. **MICHIGAN LAW STATES THAT IT IS ILLEGAL FOR AN HIV-INFECTED INDIVIDUAL, WHO KNOWS HE/SHE IS INFECTED, TO ENGAGE IN SEXUAL PENETRATION WITHOUT FIRST INFORMING THE OTHER PERSON OF THE HIV INFECTION. FAILURE TO DISCLOSE PRIOR TO PENETRATION IS A FELONY.**

☐ 3. You must not attempt to sell or donate blood, plasma, semen, ovum (eggs), or any other body tissue or organ.

☐ 4. You must notify current and past partners (sexual or needle-sharing) of your infected status. Health Department staff can assist you with a *confidential* notification process (call Ms. Fern @ 586-465-8434).

☐ 5. You are strongly advised to notify all of your health care providers (i.e. doctors, dentist, first aid responders) of your HIV infected status to allow them to provide appropriate care.

☐ 6. You have been given, read, and understand the meaning of the Health Infection Notification and **WILL NOT ENGAGE IN BEHAVIORS THAT ARE KNOWN TO TRANSMIT HIV, SPECIFICALLY, UNPROTECTED ORAL, ANAL OR VAGINAL SEXUAL INTERCOURSE AND THE SHARING OF DRUG INJECTION EQUIPMENT.**

_____   _____
Client's Signature   Date

_____   _____
Witness   Date

☐ Client declined to sign form
                                                          _____   _____
                                                          Date   Counselor Initials

▪ Macomb County Health Department keeps this information *confidential*, except when disclosure is allowable per Michigan law. You should keep this Health Infection Notification in a place that is safe and private.

FIGURE 11. Sample client acknowledgment form. Source: Macomb County Health Department.

status to two sexual partners noted, "Police say [the defendant] knew what he did was illegal because he had signed a disclosure form with [a neighboring county's] Department of Public Health."[18] Other reports show these forms have been used to help prosecute HIV-positive defendants in three additional counties.[19]

As data were being collected for this project, journalist Todd Heywood obtained several of these forms and published a series of articles highlighting their use.[20] AIDS activists around the country expressed outrage. One of the nation's leading organizations working on HIV and the law, the Center for HIV Law and Policy, spoke out against the forms. Its executive director, Catherine Hanssens, told one media outlet:

> The form . . . treats all types of sex as equally risky, and all persons with HIV as equally infectious. . . . This is a level of medical inaccuracy that is unacceptable from a state Department of Health. Lawyers who think that banning only unprotected sex is legal might want to acquaint themselves with the U.S. Constitution and legal opinions which have long since established the decision to conceive children as a Constitutionally-protected, fundamental right.[21]

In my interviews, some local health officials echoed these concerns. Mac (HIV/AIDS coordinator, jurisdiction 6) criticized client acknowledgment forms because "it takes that right away from them":

> *Mac:* There are some agencies that actually have them sign that they are aware of that law. We don't have anything at the health department stating that. And I don't know . . . I kind of feel . . . I guess I have mixed feelings on that.
>
> *Hoppe:* In what way?
>
> *Mac:* In the way that it was stated in the form that was sent to us. It was basically . . . I just feel like it doesn't . . . it takes that right away from them almost. I don't know how to explain it. Some of the wording just didn't sound—I don't want to say *good* to me. I don't know. It was just something about the wording of it. I don't know how to explain it. . . . But basically saying, "You"—and I'm not saying that they don't have to follow it, they do. But it's more strong and stern and to the point where it's like "Oh my gosh. You *have* to do this." And I know they have to, but it just didn't sound right to me.

Mac's comments suggest that the controversy over the use of these client acknowledgement forms reached within health departments themselves.

In the wake of these articles, the Michigan Civil Rights Commission expressed interest in investigating the use of these forms, raising the stakes of the debate considerably.[22] The state health department issued a carefully worded statement, saying that it was changing its position by advising "local health departments that if they are going to use client acknowledgment forms . . . —and there is nothing saying they must use such forms—they need to quote the law."[23] However, state health officials did not require that local health departments discontinue their use.

"LIVING IN THE SALEM WITCH TRIALS"

Health officials are not the only ones in the community keeping tabs on people living with HIV. Community members are also actively engaged in policing their HIV-positive neighbors. In five health department jurisdictions, officials reported regularly receiving what they bureaucratically term "third-party phone reports." These calls typically involve a resident phoning the health department to report that someone they believe to be HIV positive is having sex without disclosing his or her HIV status. These callers do not report actually having sex with the accused; instead, they offer a variety of explanations for how they know an individual is not disclosing his or her status (usually word-of-mouth rumor).

These calls are so common that the state health department developed guidelines for handling them. According to guidelines distributed to local health departments by the MDCH in 2006, officials should "determine if the information has merit" by

1. Securing the full name, address, and if available, the telephone number of the third party.
2. Requesting that the third party submit a written statement that describes the behavior/s of the suspected carrier, and supports the allegations.
3. Requesting that the third party provide the local health department with the suspected carrier's name and other information such as an address or telephone number to locate the suspected individual.[24]

These instructions turn out to be flexible. The standards for determining the merit of third-party denunciations may be relaxed where (1) the reported individual has previously been identified as an at-risk partner during contact tracing, or (2) there have been repeated allegations concerning the same individual by different parties.

Health officials were often ambivalent about relying on this kind of rumor mill to identify health-threat cases. For example, Therese (disease intervention specialist, jurisdiction 5) acknowledged that most phone calls she received were "bogus claims" that were sometimes maliciously motivated. To illustrate this, she recounted a case in which the health department received a series of coordinated phone calls all reporting the same individual:

> [People around here are] very judgmental and just angry. And they don't like to talk about controversial subjects. It's an older population that was calling in. It wasn't like I had somebody young calling in. I had somebody in their sixties calling in, and [they were all older]. And it turns out they all actually belong to the same church. As you may know, it's very big around here too in our Black churches—in our African American churches here. They do express . . . um . . . not good things about people who are gay and homosexual and people who have HIV and AIDS and so on and so forth. . . . [The person they were calling in about] was a female who had male partners, however . . . that doesn't . . . you know, it . . . they were Black and so . . . in the churches around here, somebody told their business and everybody just kind of ganged up. A lot of people around here . . . you think you're . . . living in the Salem witch trials, basically, and it's terrible.

After investigating these claims, she discovered that the callers were all members of the same church. Linking the local church's negative views about homosexuality to its prejudices against HIV, Therese speculates that it was the churchgoers' judgmental attitudes that resulted in callers "ganging up" on one person—a coordinated attempt that exemplifies how communities can police their HIV-positive neighbors.

Notably, race and gender played a significant role in the way that health-threat cases were described by health officials in several jurisdictions in which third-party phone reports were common. In the incident above, Therese notes the influence of Black church leaders in stigmatizing HIV and nonnormative sexuality more generally. That the church leaders were orchestrating an effort against a Black woman (rather than a man) reflects the higher stakes women face in navigating HIV stigma. Indeed, that Therese referred to a campaign against women—the Salem witch trials—suggests that Black women who are HIV positive in this community may face a particularly noxious stigma. Gossip and rumor thrive and fester in this context, helping to feed hostility in the community against HIV-positive Black women who step out of line.

Indeed, in jurisdictions where health officials discussed race explicitly, Black women featured prominently in their comments. For instance, in another jurisdiction across the state, an HIV/AIDS coordinator in jurisdiction 3, who chose the pseudonym Sentient, reported that third-party phone reports were a common way that health-threat cases were identified. However, Sentient also noted a peculiar annual trend: During the holiday season, the health department received numerous prank calls:

Hoppe: Can you walk me through—point A to point B—in terms of how those [health-threat] cases come onto your radar screen?

Sentient: Usually, they come in the form of a phone call. If they call the health department's general number, they usually go to the administrative floor for HIV . . . and then they take down the person's information and they call me and give it to me and I call the person back. And usually the person will say, "I know someone who's HIV infected and they're having unprotected sex." Or "I was infected by this particular person, and I want to know how to report them or what I should do." During the holiday season, we usually have unusual claims. Like, they're a star and—Aretha Franklin seems to be a very common one. Diana Ross. And they have been infected and they're infecting all these people in the area.

Though it could well be a coincidence that both celebrities Sentient named were African American women, it is also plausible that this pattern is the result of community members perceiving Black women's sexuality as threatening—a pattern reflected in the scientific literature.[25]

In the remaining jurisdictions in which third-party phone reports were common, health officials gave few clues about the race or gender of the individuals involved. Because of the delicate confidentiality issues involved in these interviews, officials sometimes chose to talk neutrally about individuals—avoiding male or female pronouns or other demographic markers. While there were scant indications about the person doing the calling or about whom the caller was reporting, it was clear in one instance that a concerted effort had been made against a specific individual. Following up about a recent case that Lucy (one of the two disease intervention specialists in jurisdiction 10) had described, I asked how that case came to her attention:

It was just a community person—somebody from the community concerned about somebody in their neighborhood who they were thinking had HIV. And I guess they just felt that they needed to report it to the health department as a concern. Preliminary record search, nothing was found on this individual. The caller was unwilling to give their information—and it was a situation where there were other people in the background, kind of egging the person on the phone on. So in that case, after I briefed my supervisor about it, no further follow-up was done.

The presence of "other people in the background" whom Lucy suspected of egging on the caller suggests a collective community policing effort. In this case, Lucy attempted to verify whether the accused person was known to the state to be HIV positive. The person was not, and thus the case was closed. However, the fact that Lucy took the call, recorded the information about the person being accused, and conducted a record search suggests that she nonetheless determined the anonymous group report deserved further inquiry. She did not speculate about what she might have done had the accused person been found to be HIV positive.

This kind of community policing takes several forms. In one county, HIV stigma took on a life of its own in the form of a legendary "book down by the river," a near-mythical object that allegedly contains the names of everyone in the area who is HIV positive. Therese describes this book:

> You know, the big thing we have here is people talk. And that's how most things are done around here, how most complaints are filed. In fact, it all usually starts with the same phone call. They're like, *[impersonating stereotypical Black female voice]* "Well . . . I'm calling because I know . . ." And they'll go on this whole rampage, like "my cousin's baby's daddy's uncle who watches TV and they produce for the show"—all these weird things! They find every string to connect this person to them. "And I just want to verify if that's true." [And I ask,] "Well, why do you want to do that?" "Well, because I know . . . I can't find it today, but I know that there's a book." Oh my God, this whole county swears to God that there's a book that's down by some railroad tracks in [name of town] by the river. There's a book that has all the HIV-positive people's names in it.

During our interview, Therese gestured to a map on the wall to identify the general area in town where people say the book can be found. Emphasizing that it was "*not* a good area," she noted that she usually brings along a male coworker whose physicality resembles his nickname, "Muscles," when her job requires her to visit this particular area. The neighborhood in question is almost entirely African American, plagued by widespread poverty and high rates of unemployment. Like countless towns across the state, the manufacturing jobs that once provided the lifeline for this neighborhood are long gone.

In all likelihood, the book probably does not exist as a real object to be found and consulted. Assuming that the book is more legend than reality, what social purposes might this mythical volume serve? Through years of gossip and rumor, "the book" has become a way for people to trade, seek, and reveal information about others in the community without anyone being held responsible for doing the telling. Therese explains that people who move into the county visit the health department and demand to see the book: "They will say the same exact thing: 'Yeah, I just moved here and I heard that there's a book here. And I wanna see the book of all the positive people.'" As described in the beginning of this chapter, it is illegal in Michigan for anyone to disclose another person's HIV-positive status without their express written permission. The book, then, may well provide the perfect alibi for community members looking to trade information without being held legally liable.

The rumor of a list of everyone in the county who is HIV positive was not idiosyncratic to this jurisdiction. Health officials in another jurisdiction told a similar tale of people asking to see "the list." Doctor Q (disease intervention specialist, jurisdiction 14) laments:

> Well, and you'd be surprised too . . . the people that come in and want to see the list of HIV-positive people *[laughs]*. . . . They think it's just like the post office, where you've got your "Ten Most Wanted"—well, we got the HIV-positive list here! I had some woman here, God, it was probably six months ago; she came in with her two teenage daughters. She wanted to see the list. And I said, "We don't keep a list of HIV-positive people." "Oh, come on now, I know you got a list of HIV"—and I said, "And if we did, why would you want to see that list?" "'Cause I want my daughters to look at it, so they know who not to have sex with." I wanted to reach across there and slap her. "You stupid bitch, is that how you teach [your daughters]: 'Here's the list. Don't fuck any of these guys'"?

After years of working in the same job at the health department, Doctor Q was secretly planning to call it quits. His frustration with his job and his clients was, to say the least, palpable.

However, Doctor Q's frustrations may have unintentionally revealed much about the contradictions of disclosure as public health imperative. As he points out, his client was seeking the identities of everyone in the area known to be HIV positive so that her daughters could avoid having sex with them. The state actually *does* possess that information, even if the county does not keep a list available for the public to consult. So the client was not as "stupid" as Doctor Q inferred. Obviously, the client's desire to gain access to such information was in direct conflict with medical confidentiality. However, her desire to know the identities of HIV-positive people in the community makes sense given that health officials promote HIV status disclosure as a public health strategy. Promoting disclosure implies that knowledge is prevention: if an HIV-negative person knows who is HIV positive and who is HIV negative, then he or she can make informed decisions that will reduce the risk of contracting HIV. If this is your primary HIV prevention strategy, then having a list of HIV-positive people is the equivalent of a crib sheet for a college exam.

"SCARE TACTICS"

So what happens after someone is flagged for investigation? Health departments have a range of options for handling potential health-threat cases. Most departments described a tiered approach to managing these cases. First, the person is issued a tersely worded warning letter telling them that they have been identified as putting others at risk; reminding them of their legal obligations; and warning them that if they are identified again, they will be formally labeled a health threat and legal action against them will be taken. Figure 12 is an example of the model warning letter distributed by the Michigan Department of Community Health to local health departments as guidance in 2006.

Along with the warning letter, health officials meet with the client to offer counseling and other services. If the client does not comply with health department demands, officials then move to petition the probate court to intervene. The entire process is painstakingly depicted in policy documents obtained from local health departments. Figure 13 illustrates a condensed version of the typical process as it was reported to me by local health officials. The process begins with a report of "recalcitrant" behavior either as a result of a positive STI test or from first-party witnesses (prior sexual partners) or third-party complainants (neighbors, friends, etc.). Officials consider a number of factors in their assessment of each case, including whether a client has a mental illness; whether health officials believe the allegations have merit; and whether the complaining witness is willing to testify in court.

If the complaint came from a third party, health officials reported treating it with a great deal of skepticism. Mitch, the HIV/AIDS coordinator from jurisdiction 2, reported having serious doubts about the validity of information obtained from informants over the phone. Despite these doubts, Mitch indicated that if the accused person was in fact determined to be HIV positive, someone from the health department would "make an appearance":

> We get a lot of phone calls: "I know that so-and-so's positive and I know that they're sleeping around with a whole bunch of people and not telling their status." If that person is not willing to come in and write out a statement, then we may look for that name and see if there is actually a report on that name. And then we may try and make contact and go, "Hey, how's things going? You remember that felony law thing that we talked about? You doing okay with that?" *[laughs]* Kind of just make an appearance with them. But we don't put a whole lot of . . . a whole lot of . . . what do I wanna say? We have a lot of people that call us and complain about other people, and a lot

Page 1 of 2   **Attachment B**
Logo of Health Department Issuing Warning Notice For Recalcitrant individual In   Person.

Name and Address of Recipient

MODEL WARNING NOTICE

Dear ____(Subject's Name)____ :

The (Health Department) has determined that you are infected with the Human Immunodeficiency Virus, a serious infection that is spread from person to person through contact with certain body fluids (blood, semen, vaginal secretions). Based upon information supplied to our department, it is believed that you represent a health threat to others by putting others at danger because of the behaviors indicated:

In compliance with Michigan's Public Health Code, Part 52, Hazardous Communicable Diseases, you are required to cooperate with the (Health Department) in its efforts to prevent or control the spread of this infection. You are required to:

(1) CEASE and DESIST any activity which puts others at risk of infection including, but not limited to: 1) the misrepresentation of your infectious status to future sexual or needle-sharing partners; 2) engaging in sexual intercourse or needle-sharing activity without first notifying the individual of your HIV status; and/or, 3) the donation of blood or body tissue.

(2) Present yourself to the (Health Department) at (time) on (mth/dav/yr) to receive HIV prevention, risk reduction and behavior modification counseling. The health department is . located at ____(Address/City____).

If you are unable to keep this appointment, you must contact (name of contact individual) at (telephone number) to reschedule.

(3) Possibly undergo testing for Sexually Transmitted Diseases (Syphilis, Gonorrhea, Chlamydia), and/or the presence of other serious communicable diseases, to the satisfaction of the health officer to verify your status as a carrier.

Failure to comply with the conditions set forth within this notice will result in the health department's petition to the probate court of this county to implement enforcement procedures as defined by Michigan's Public Health Code, Part 52.

Except in the case of emergency, you have the right to a notice and hearing before the probate court issues an order in your case.

Copy 1: Client Copy 2: Serving Agent

FIGURE 12. Model warning letter. Source: Michigan Department of Community Health.

Determining a Health Threat to Others

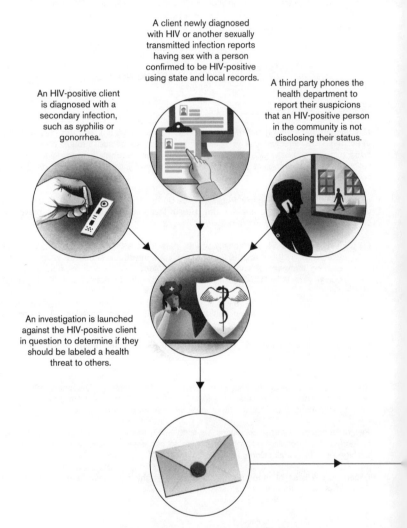

A client newly diagnosed with HIV or another sexually transmitted infection reports having sex with a person confirmed to be HIV-positive using state and local records.

An HIV-positive client is diagnosed with a secondary infection, such as syphilis or gonorrhea.

A third party phones the health department to report their suspicions that an HIV-positive person in the community is not disclosing their status.

An investigation is launched against the HIV-positive client in question to determine if they should be labeled a health threat to others.

If they are determined to be a health threat, the local health department sends a "cease and desist" letter through certified mail.

FIGURE 13. HTTO identification. Design: Jonathan Lefrançois. Illustration: Justin Karas for Pulp & Pixel.

Another certified letter may be issued or civil
proceedings may be brought against the client to
force them to be quarantined or (more likely) undergo
counseling and testing.

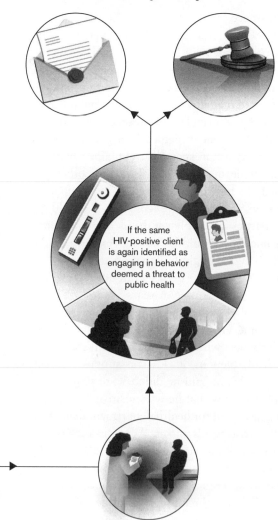

If the same
HIV-positive client
is again identified as
engaging in behavior
deemed a threat to
public health

Once labeled a "health threat," the HIV-positive client
may be required to undergo testing or counseling
through the health department.

of the time it ends up being a he-said-she-said type of thing, because so-and-so is mad at so-and-so because they slept with so-and-so.

Mitch stressed that this "appearance" would be more akin to a check-in than a serious investigation. However, while these meetings may be nothing more than a check-in on paper, having a health official show up on your doorstep asking questions about your knowledge of the HIV disclosure law is likely to have a chilling effect: We've got eyes in the community, don't do anything stupid. And that effect is presumably intended.

Whether they are delivered by informal "appearance" or certified cease-and-desist letter, health department demands are not always heeded. Doctor Q, a disease intervention specialist, explained his particular frustration with a client deemed a health threat to others in 2008. The client was identified as a health threat after "showing up here every 3 to 5 months with a new STD. . . . His excuse was 'I would go down to [the city], just these parties, probably get drunk and high, pass out, and I'd wake up and somebody would be having sex with me.'" But Doctor Q believed he was lying. "I might buy that once or twice . . . But hey, after the twelfth time you've had a disease, I'm not buying it." After "probably the eighth time over a couple of years" of testing positive for a secondary STI, Doctor Q called the state's partner services director to discuss his case. After a certified warning letter was delivered to his home, the client agreed to meet with health department staff. "He came the first time, then basically blew us off. He was supposed to get into a group for positives . . . which he said he didn't want to get into, because he didn't want people to know that he was positive."

Frustrated with the client's disregard for health department demands, Doctor Q called the county prosecutor's office. An assistant county prosecutor met with health department staff but informed Doctor Q that the county could not pursue criminal charges without testimony from a partner. "That's basically where I became disillusioned with the system," Doctor Q lamented. Echoing the punitive attitudes of American social conservatives in the early years of the HIV epidemic, Doctor Q reported that he told the client he wished he could have his status tattooed on his body: "I told this guy . . . if it was up to me, if I was king [of the county], I would have a tattoo across his pubic hair: 'I'm HIV positive.' Where if somebody rips your pants down while you are passed out, then at least they can read, they can see that you are HIV positive."

Policy documents obtained from several health departments refer to the need for testimony from previous sexual partners in order to proceed with criminal legal intervention. Even before the warning letter is issued, health department staff are instructed to advise the complaining witnesses that they could meet with law enforcement personnel to discuss their complaints if they so choose. Health privacy laws sometimes make this difficult, however, in cases where health department staff discover a reported partner is HIV positive but the original client did not report knowing that any of their partners were HIV positive. How do you tell someone to call the cops if they do not know what to report? In Mitch's words, handling such cases requires a bit of "tiptoeing":

> There's a lot of "Well, we'd like you to come back into the office and talk to you a little bit more about your situation." That's when we'll try and say, "Have you had any other partners? Have any of your other partners ever said anything about being HIV positive?" At that point, sometimes we might say, "We'd like you to report this to the police. We'd like you to contact the police." Recently we had somebody we had called back to come in and do that, and then the person never showed. We were going tell them to contact the police because we have a person who is being a "health threat to others." But the person never showed up.

Policies for interacting with the police may vary by county. But in at least some jurisdictions in Michigan, health department staff encourage clients to report their complaints to law enforcement.

Rather than personally appealing to the police or to the prosecutor, most health officials use the threat of legal intervention in order to frighten clients into compliance. When asked what it means for clients that are labeled a health threat, Debra, an HIV/AIDS coordinator in jurisdiction 13, responded that it's mostly a "scare tactic":

> I let the [disease intervention specialist] build the relationship, get the information, try to see if our tactics on changing behavior work, and if they don't work, then I will go through the process of getting the HTTO, or try to bring in the law. But I think we just use it as a scare tactic. The fact is we can send people to jail. That is a fact. But at the same time, we don't want the community to stigmatize testing, or the health department, or that sort of thing. But my thing is that I can recognize when someone is being malicious versus somebody just having difficulty disclosing.

Debra's scare-tactic approach reflects how most Michigan health officials viewed the value of the HTTO law in their own work. Ninety-six percent of health officials I interviewed believed that health departments should strive to use public health interventions before calling the prosecutor's office (see table 1). However, even if most health department staff try to avoid immediately involving law enforcement, the strategies

TABLE 1 WHAT DO HEALTH OFFICIALS THINK ABOUT MICHIGAN'S "HEALTH
THREAT" LAWS?

Survey Item	Agree	Disagree	Neutral
In any given "health threat to others" case, the HIV-positive person should not be charged with a crime unless one of their partners tests HIV-positive as a result of having sex with them.	12%	80%	8%
Laws that mandate HIV-status disclosure for HIV-positive people should be repealed.	0%	76%	24%
If an HIV-positive person was known to have used condoms consistently with their partners, they should not be criminally charged for failing to disclose their HIV status to their partners before having sex.	8%	64%	28%
An HIV-positive person should only be criminally charged for failing to disclose their HIV status if there is evidence that they were engaging in high-risk sexual behaviors with their partners.	28%	56%	16%
Laws requiring that HIV-positive people disclose their HIV status before having sex help to reduce the number of new HIV infections each year.	44%	20%	36%
Public health officials should first attempt to intervene in "health threat to others" cases by attempting behavioral counseling and/or other health interventions before referring a person for prosecution.	96%	0%	4%

NOTE: In 2012, I asked every health department official I interviewed to complete a survey regarding their attitudes towards "health threat" laws and HIV/AIDS more generally. These are their responses to questions about the law and cases brought under it. They are ordered from the statements most disagreed with to the statements agreed with by the most officials.

and techniques health officials employ to identify health-threat cases can have grave legal consequences for HIV-positive clients.

Three cases help to illustrate these consequences. First, in 1992, a woman in Muskegon County, Michigan, became one of a handful of people living with HIV known to be legally quarantined in the United States. The media widely reported the case of Brenda J. (discussed more extensively in chapter 5), which was made particularly controversial by her IQ of 72—just two points above the medical threshold for an intellectual disability diagnosis.[26] After reports surfaced again that she was having sex without disclosing her HIV-positive status, the Muskegon county prosecutor charged her under Michigan's felony HIV disclosure law. She was convicted in 1995 and sentenced to thirty-two months in prison.[27]

In another case in Muskegon County, in 2003, news reports revealed that a police investigation explicitly began when the health department contacted police. According to a May 22, 2003, news report, "An investigation by police was started last week after the Muskegon County Health Department contacted the prosecutor's office."[28] That investigation was triggered by an HTTO notice issued by the health department. "Prosecutor Tony Tague said that a 'warning notice' had been sent to the woman by the health department on May 7. . . . The investigation revealed that [the defendant] had sex on May 9 and 12 with the victim without telling him she was HIV positive."[29]

This appears to not have been the only time Michigan health officials have forwarded cases to law enforcement for investigation. Documents obtained by a Michigan-based journalist reveal that the Grand Traverse County Health Department wrote to the county prosecutor about complaints against a local HIV-positive man in February 2009. The recently unearthed memo was prompted by allegations to health department staff that the man—referred to as Mr. X in the redacted memo—was engaging in "unprotected" sex with partners he met online and in public restrooms. In the memo, the health department director writes:

> I suggest three options: 1. This Mr. X be warned by you and/or prosecuted for failure to inform his sex partners of his HIV status. 2. There be a "sting" operation by the police at the public bathroom where this person is reported to have had his encounters. 3. That I go public and inform the public via the media that this activity is happening and that anyone who has engaged in this behavior should get tested for HIV and other STI. I would not divulge the name of the person or the public bathrooms. 4. All or two of these options.[30]

Despite these efforts, follow-up requests to the prosecutor's office suggest that Mr. X was not criminally charged.

Of course, these cases are atypical examples. The first case involves the only person known to have been placed under quarantine for HIV in Michigan. And although the following cases suggest some coordination between health departments and prosecutors, health departments did not routinely send memos to county prosecutors recommending sting operations. Nonetheless, these cases illustrate the high stakes involved when health departments become arms of the police.

WHY DISCLOSURE?

Reports from around the country reveal that the tactics employed in Michigan to control HIV-positive people are not unique. A North Carolina court found an HIV-positive man guilty of violating his probation in 2008 when he tested positive for an undisclosed sexually transmitted infection at a local health clinic. He had been arrested "after Wake County Public Health officials contacted his probation officer with information that he had possibly violated court orders by having sex without a condom. . . . Health officials became aware of the DJ's violation after he contracted another sexually transmitted disease that could have been prevented by the use of a condom."[31]

In Indiana, a county health department administrator went on local television news in April 2015 to report that the health department was pursuing criminal charges against an HIV-positive client that it determined "has infected eight people with HIV, one with AIDS." (As it is not possible to infect someone with AIDS, presumably the health department staff person meant that one of the partners' HIV infections had progressed to AIDS.) The health department reportedly knew the person was aware of the legal obligations because "the person in question signed a document saying that person 'would' warn others." In Tennessee, a judge cited a similar information form designed by a local health department as a basis for enhancing the sentence of a criminal defendant.[32] Reports suggest that health departments in additional states, including Mississippi, North Carolina, and Florida, currently or have recently employed such forms.[33]

In other cases, local health departments appear to have violated confidentiality laws in ways that facilitated the prosecution of people living with HIV. In a criminal case reviewed for the analysis in chapter 5 of this book, for example, a Tennessee prosecutor revealed that a woman pressed felony HIV exposure charges in 2002 after the local health department informed her that a man she reported as a partner during a partner services interview was HIV positive—echoing several of the statements made by local Michigan health department staff earlier in this chapter.[34] This report resembles a previously mentioned case from Kent County, Michigan, in 2000 in which court reports revealed that the complainant learned of the defendant's HIV-positive status directly from a "health worker."

What are the consequences of a local health department that begins to act like the police? At the most basic level, one likely outcome is that people will think twice before speaking candidly to health officials. Studies since 1996 have shown that marginalized communities often fear disclosing sensitive information to medical providers because they do not know how that information will be used.[35] In this chapter, we have seen that Michigan health officials engaged in surveillance practices that they did not disclose to their clients. For example, when they asked newly diagnosed clients if any of their partners disclosed to them that they were HIV positive, they did not preface that question with an explanation that they were trying to catch lawbreakers. This lack of transparency directly conflicts with the public health ethical principle that "where government authorizes or mandates the collection of identifiable health data, both the data to be collected and the reason for collection should be a matter of public record."[36]

But policing public health and punitive disease control more broadly may have other, even more harmful effects that are difficult to predict. Clearly, some people viewed the health department in much the same way that they viewed the police. If there is a person in your neighborhood causing trouble, who are you going to call? At least in some cases, the answer appears to be your local health department. By accepting their phone calls and collecting their information, health officials are inviting community members to participate in the naming, shaming, and blaming of their HIV-positive neighbors. This may encourage community members (like the "stupid" client described by Doctor Q) to seek out and trade in the HIV statuses of people in their communities, intensifying stigma and prejudice while ramping up the everyday surveillance of HIV-positive people.

Health officials participate in this network of gossip in the name of promoting disclosure. But community members may interpret this emphasis on disclosure as a license to know who is and who is not HIV positive. Public health promotes a model of disclosure that resembles informed consent in medicine, where an HIV-positive person discloses his or her status to potential partners so that they can weigh the risks and benefits of having sex with him or her. Community members, however, trade in the disclosure of other people's HIV statuses without their permission—using a mythical book as an alibi for their illegal behavior. While the two forms of disclosure seem unrelated, they both rely on the assumption that knowing another person's HIV-positive status is an effective tool for reducing HIV risk.

But does disclosure actually work as an HIV prevention strategy? Health officials did not think so. While none of the officials believed the felony HIV disclosure law should be repealed, fewer than half (44 percent) believed that the law actually helps to reduce the number of new HIV infections (see table 1). Rather than a tool for HIV prevention, the law's utility seems to be that it reinforces the belief that HIV-positive people have an ethical duty to inform their partners of their HIV status. But the new science of HIV begs the question of why HIV-positive people should be compelled to tell others about their infection if it is impossible for HIV-positive people on treatment to transmit the virus sexually. Why do HIV-negative people have a right to know?

This book cannot directly answer these ethical questions. However, what it can do is to explain the consequences that flow from punishing disease. The next three chapters explore this more closely by analyzing the criminal justice system. Who is being punished? Why? By better understanding how HIV-specific criminal laws are being applied across the United States, the stakes involved in these ethical debates become clearer.

PART TWO

The Criminalization of Sickness

CHAPTER 4

Making HIV a Crime

On October 15, 1982, a White House reporter asked President Ronald Reagan's press secretary Larry Speakes about the AIDS epidemic for the first time. More than a year had passed since the June 1981 report from the Centers for Disease Control (CDC) documenting a handful of pneumonia cases involving young gay men in Los Angeles. The CDC had recently termed the disease "acquired immune deficiency syndrome," but the president had remained silent, even as the disease claimed the lives of hundreds of Americans. In an almost-casual act of callous indifference, Speakes feigned ignorance, asking, "What's AIDS?" When the reporter replied, "It's known as the gay plague," the entire room erupted in laughter. "I don't have it," Speakes replied. "Do you?"

For several years, the Reagan administration's official response to AIDS would be no response at all. AIDS had become political fodder for religious conservatives who characterized the disease as the "cure for homosexuality." Any legislation introduced to fund AIDS research, treatment, or prevention became mired in moralizing debates over whether these efforts might have the effect of "promoting homosexuality"—a view summarized neatly in a 1983 Oklahoma newspaper editorial criticizing calls for increased federal AIDS funding:

> Any human being is entitled to compassion. And any American citizen deserves the best medical care he can afford. But the public is under no moral obligation to provide a disproportionate share of its wealth to deal with a problem that, at least for 75 percent or more of the victims, results from their

own pursuit of a lifestyle that the vast majority considers to be perverted, abnormal and immoral.[1]

By 1985, over one hundred thousand Americans had contracted the disease. Many of them had died—including America's one-time heart-throb, actor Rock Hudson. With so many Americans affected by the epidemic, it became increasingly indefensible for the government to remain indifferent, even in the face of sharp criticism like the editorial above. Yet, even as legislators across the country finally began to mount a response to the disease, fear and stigma continued to guide their approach. When the U.S. House considered $189.7 million in funding for AIDS research and prevention in the fall of 1985, Republican legislators tacked on a provision allowing the surgeon general to close gay bathhouses. Representative William Dannemeyer (R-CA) justified the effort to crack down on gay establishments, arguing that "God's plan for man was Adam and Eve, not Adam and Steve."[2]

Beyond just a question of funding, however, the legal and regulatory problems posed by AIDS were systemic. Basic bureaucratic concerns such as what agencies were responsible for managing which aspects of the government's response to AIDS needed to be sorted. Monitoring the epidemic also required clarifying technical public health surveillance issues such as how newly diagnosed cases were to be reported to health authorities. And with so much misinformation and stigma circulating among Americans, there was an urgent need to clarify whether existing civil rights legislation protected HIV-positive children from being barred from enrolling in school and dying tenants from being evicted by their landlords.

While the federal government had a role to play in providing funding, instituting regulations, and designing guidelines, much of the day-to-day work of prevention, treatment, and surveillance was not done at the federal level. As is the case in most areas of public health practice, the bulk of the responsibility for managing the response to HIV lay instead with state departments of public health and their county- and city-run counterparts.[3] In most states, basic provisions for public health practice are housed in state public health codes enacted by the state legislature—meaning that adapting each state's public health infrastructure to HIV generally required action by lawmakers.[4]

In many states, this was a daunting task: most states had adapted their disease control laws piecemeal over time in response to the specific epidemics of the day. As legal experts Lawrence Gostin, Scott Burris, and

Zita Lazzarini put it, these laws "tell the history of disease control in America much as geologic strata tell the history of the earth":

> In the eighteenth century, communicable disease statutes focused primarily on smallpox, though quarantine regulations were generally applied to any identified disease or "fever" that might be perceived as a threat. . . . In the nineteenth century, states and municipalities enacted regulations in response to periodic epidemics of yellow fever and cholera. . . . Increasing attention was also paid to tuberculosis, which was one of the leading causes of death. . . . Continuing efforts to control syphilis in the first half of twentieth century led to statutes authorizing premarital screening, reporting, contact tracing, and involuntary treatment.[5]

Each new disease brought a new layer of legal regulation and control. However, rather than overhauling the entire public health code when new threats emerged, lawmakers tended to either draft new provisions specific to the new illness or simply tack it on to antiquated statutes.

Although AIDS bore similarities to diseases that came before it, three key differences set it apart from epidemics of the past. First, while HIV was transmitted sexually like syphilis and gonorrhea, it was also frequently transmitted through nonsexual *blood-to-blood contact*. Regulating injection drug use was not quite the same as regulating sexual behavior. This made HIV somewhat ill suited for the "venereal disease" statutes enacted during the syphilis panics of World War II.

Second, although AIDS could be deadly like tuberculosis (TB), it was *untreatable and incurable*—meaning that inserting AIDS into long-standing TB quarantine statutes would have entailed locking up people living with HIV for the rest of their lives; the human rights implications were perilous, not to mention the cost to the state of such a program. HIV is also different from TB in that it is not highly contagious. For these reasons, quarantine has never been widely regarded by public health experts as a sensible approach to HIV prevention.[6]

Third, because the disease was sexually transmitted, deadly, and primarily associated with gay men and drug users, the *stigma* attached to HIV was considerable: HIV-positive children were kicked out of their schools;[7] prominent conservatives promoted conspiracy theories that the government was lying about the contagiousness of AIDS;[8] and some funeral homes even turned away people who died of AIDS-related illness out of an unfounded fear of contracting the disease.[9] Consequently, many in public health argued that lawmakers needed to codify exceptionally stringent privacy safeguards to help promote HIV testing—an approach that came to be known as AIDS exceptionalism.[10]

These complexities made it all but impossible for legislators to simply tack HIV onto existing public health law; they needed to draft entirely new, HIV-specific legislation. Over the next five years, legislators across the country introduced a flurry of legislative proposals for testing, treating, and preventing HIV.

At the heart of many of these legislative efforts was a debate over whether to restrict the civil liberties of people diagnosed with the disease—often positioned as necessary to protect the "general population" (a category that presumably excluded gay men and other minorities). Conservatives called for invasive and punitive measures to curtail the rights of people living with HIV, and polling data suggests that support for such proposals grew over time. A 1987 *Los Angeles Times* poll found that 42 percent of Americans believed that "civil liberties must be suspended in the war on AIDS," and 68 percent favored "criminal sanctions against people with acquired immune deficiency syndrome who remain sexually active."[11] Perhaps even more troubling, the *Times* poll found that the number of people supporting conservative columnist William F. Buckley's proposal to tattoo newly diagnosed patients had doubled from 15 percent in 1985 to 29 percent in just two years.

AIDS emerged in this punitive culture of fear, which directly shaped how legislators in the United States responded to the disease and sought to manage it. By harnessing AIDS stigma, lawmakers stoked Americans' fears in order to justify new punitive policies that explicitly and implicitly targeted gay men, sex workers, and injection drug users—a tactic lifted straight out of the war on drugs playbook.[12]

This chapter analyzes how HIV-specific criminal legislation spread throughout American state legislatures between 1985 and 2014. Historically, scholars have suggested that federal policies were responsible for prompting states to enact HIV-specific criminal penalties. Specifically, they point to Ronald Reagan's presidential commission, described in more detail later in the chapter, which recommended enacting HIV-specific criminal laws in its 1988 report. They also point to the Ryan White CARE Act of 1990, which included a provision that required states to certify that their criminal laws were "adequate to prosecute any HIV infected individual" who knowingly exposes a person to HIV.[13] However, as this chapter shows, by the time the commission issued its report in the spring of 1988, lawmakers in sixteen states had already introduced over two dozen bills that would impose some form of criminal sanction against HIV-positive people during the 1985, 1986, and 1987 legislative sessions. This chapter argues that rather than being the spark that ignited a wave of criminalization, these federal policies played a diminished, institutionalizing role, legitimizing the moves toward criminalization that were already well under way.

This chapter explains four factors that actually did motivate states to enact HIV-specific criminal laws. First, *prosecutors attempted and failed to use general criminal laws* such as assault and attempted murder to punish HIV-positive defendants, but a series of high-profile acquittals and dismissals drove many prosecutors and members of law enforcement to conclude that HIV-specific criminal laws were necessary.

Second, numerous news reports from the mid-1980s reveal an *organized aggravation* among police and prosecutors confronted with sex workers who had tested positive for HIV; police, prosecutors, and media organizations cried out for HIV-specific felony prostitution penalties.

Third, some states began to consider criminalizing HIV as a necessary measure in response to the *decriminalization of sodomy*—a move that some believed would lead to an explosion of new HIV cases.

Fourth, a Republican state representative from Illinois and member of Reagan's presidential commission—wryly referred to in this book as "Lawmaker Zero"—worked with an influential lobbying organization to leverage her institutional networks, helping to disseminate a model statute to dozens of states around the country.

Rather than a singular top-down story of federal influence, these four factors reveal a far more complex origin story of the movement to criminalize HIV.

PROSECUTION, INTERRUPTED: WHY LAW ENFORCEMENT DEMANDED HIV-SPECIFIC CRIMINAL LAWS

In October 1985, the San Antonio Health Department took an unprecedented step in its effort to control HIV: department staff hand-delivered letters to the homes of fourteen of the seventeen city residents known to have contracted HIV. These letters were not intended to console or provide counsel for the terminally ill patients, but rather to warn them: if they engaged in any sexual activity whatsoever with an HIV-negative person, they would face felony criminal charges.[14]

The letters were reportedly sparked by warnings from an area physician that "at least three" people living with the disease "had not limited their sexual activities."[15] San Antonio's health director, Dr. Courand Rothe, reassured the public at a news conference organized to respond to criticism over the letters. "I'm not interested in putting people in jail. I just want to control this disease," he said. Nonetheless, the hand-delivered letters threatened the recipients with third-degree felony charges carrying a maximum penalty of ten years in prison and a $5,000 fine under the Texas Communicable Disease and Control Act. The letter specifically instructed:

> You must not engage in sexual intercourse with anyone not having a confirmed diagnosis of AIDS. You must not share the use of needles with another. You must not donate blood, blood products, semen, body organs or other tissues. You must make the fact that you are a diagnosed AIDS patient known to physicians, dentists, and others whom you consult as a patient on a professional basis.[16]

The National Gay Task Force (one of the nation's leading gay rights organizations) called the response "hysterical" and criticized health authorities for making "people think gays with AIDS are being irresponsible."[17] The organization argued that the best way to control the disease was not punishment but education and the use of condoms.

The health department director's threat of criminal charges represents one of the first systematic attempts in the United States to criminalize the behavior of people living with HIV. At the time, it was not specifically a crime for HIV-positive people to engage in sexual activity under Texas law—or anywhere else in the country, for that matter. Rather, the director was creatively deploying a provision in a 1983 Texas statute providing for felony charges against any person who "knowingly refuses to perform or to allow the performance of certain control measures ordered by a health authority or the department."[18] The health director did not wait for a particular person to demonstrate behavior that might put others at a risk of transmission. Instead, he simply delivered his orders to almost every single person diagnosed as living with HIV in the city of San Antonio, effectively writing a city-level, HIV-specific felony into law.[19] This provision gave local health departments in Texas the unilateral power to classify as felonious any actions they deemed a threat to public health.[20]

San Antonio turned out to be an aberrant case; few health departments took such strident actions. Much more typical were efforts by prosecutors to devise creative strategies for using other statutes not specifically designed to punish people living with HIV. For example, on October 6, 1985, police arrested Blaine Prairie Chicken "during a disturbance at a laundromat" in El Cajon, California.[21]

"Chicken is accused of biting one of the officers through his uniform, drawing blood, and then telling the officer that he was a homosexual who had AIDS and that he hoped the officer contracted the disease," reported the *San Diego Union-Tribune*.[22] Prosecutors charged Chicken initially with resisting arrest and battery on a peace officer but fought to keep him behind bars while they could determine what charges to seek in the case. After effectively denying Chicken bail, municipal court judge Victor Bianchini told the media: "This is such a novel case. . . . We could have a homicide or an attempted homicide case."[23]

Despite the fact that HIV was not known to be transmitted through biting, Chicken's case dragged on for nearly a year as prosecutors waited to determine if Chicken did, in fact, have the disease. His defense attorney and the prosecutor came to a plea agreement that was contingent on the outcome of those tests: "Prairie Chicken will be sentenced for misdemeanor assault if the officer is determined not to have been exposed to AIDS. If the officer has been exposed, however, Prairie Chicken will receive a felony sentence."[24] Ultimately, testing showed Chicken to be HIV negative; he pled guilty to misdemeanor offenses and was sentenced to ninety days in jail.

Several miles away in San Diego County, authorities were simultaneously trying to determine the HIV status of a man who was arrested during the city's twelfth annual gay pride festivities after he reportedly "squirted water" at antigay demonstrators.[25] As he was being arrested, Brian Barlow allegedly bit two officers on the hand and shoulder. After taking Barlow to the hospital to be treated for injuries sustained during the arrest, police officers asked him if he was gay and HIV positive.[26] He said that he was gay, but denied being HIV positive twice before finally stating that "for the officers' sake, you better take it that I do." After refusing to voluntarily submit to a blood test for HIV, police forcibly drew his blood and booked him on charges of battery on a police officer. The officers planned to test the sample for HIV, and, if the tests came back positive, prosecutors intended to increase the charges against Barlow to felony assault with a deadly weapon. State law, however, prohibited the results of an HIV test from being shared, barring authorities from accessing vital records. Officers appealed a lower court's ruling that prohibited them from accessing the results, but the California Supreme Court ultimately ruled against them. A jury ultimately acquitted Barlow of the lesser criminal charges.[27]

Across the country, police and prosecutors were often thwarted in their attempts to apply general criminal statutes against people living with HIV. In cases like Chicken's and Barlow's, medical privacy laws prevented accessing defendants' HIV-test results. In other cases, however, prosecutors struggled to fit HIV-related prosecutions into legal structures that were not designed for punishing disease. Like the judge assigned to Chicken's case, authorities often boasted of their goals to charge defendants with attempted murder. However, their efforts to do so were almost never successful, as homicide statutes require that prosecutors prove that the defendant specifically intended to kill.

In 1987, for example, Fresno, California, prosecutors dropped attempted murder charges against a woman sex worker and a man described as her "pimp." The prosecutor told the media that murder charges were deemed inappropriate "because California law requires proof of a specific intent to kill in order for the charges to be made."[28] Later that year, a Los Angeles judge dismissed attempted murder charges against a gay man accused of selling his blood to a plasma bank because "the prosecution failed to show the defendant intended to kill anyone."[29] These widely reported cases came on the heels of similar cases in which homicide-related charges were dismissed or failed to stick in Florida and Michigan in 1986.[30]

In the face of these failed prosecutions, media outlets demanded that legislators introduce HIV-specific criminal laws. An *Orlando Sentinel* editorial specifically argued that stiff penalties were necessary to discourage "case-by-case experimenting" in which authorities "dream up novel ways to prosecute today's version of Typhoid Mary."[31] But nowhere in the country was the discussion as heated as in California, where conservative extremist Lyndon LaRouche had stoked the fears of Americans through repeated ballot initiatives aimed at restricting the civil rights of people living with HIV.[32] In a 1987 editorial titled "There Ought to Be a Law," *Daily News of Los Angeles* staff wrote that "it is time for Sacramento to exercise the political will needed to prevent unstable AIDS victims from passing on a death sentence to others."[33]

Although some were skeptical, public health experts had different opinions as to whether criminalization was a good idea. Some did expressly oppose criminalization, such as public health law expert Lawrence Gostin, who frequently argued against imposing criminal sanctions on the grounds that they "would make it more difficult to combat the disease."[34] In a 1987 address to a joint session of the California legislature, Nobel laureate and AIDS researcher Dr. David Baltimore implored lawmakers to "hold in check the instinct to punish the infected."[35] Other experts were more ambivalent, such as Surgeon General C. Everett Koop, who questioned whether such laws were enforceable: "There are people who say you should make it [a] felony for [people living with HIV] . . . to 'exchange bodily fluids.' How are you going to do that? Are you going to monitor every bedroom?"[36]

Other public health experts, however, were explicitly in favor of criminalization. In an *American Journal of Public Health* article published in 1989, Dr. Victor E. Archer proposed a six-point HIV control plan that included implementing a quarantine system he termed "HIV parole" as well as a call for public health officials to sponsor "uniform laws throughout the United States making it a felony . . . to infect someone else with HIV."[37] Findings from a 1994 survey of state health departments reflect this diversity of opinion: one-third supported the use of criminal laws to punish people living with HIV; one-third were opposed; and one-third were uncertain or did not respond.[38] In short, there was no consensus on the matter among public health practitioners, leaving the professionals with the most expertise largely relegated to the sidelines as these debates unfolded.

Although initially dismissive, President Ronald Reagan's administration did eventually put together a commission tasked with making policy recommendations for addressing the HIV epidemic in the United States. When Reagan's Presidential Commission on the HIV Epidemic issued its final report in 1988, the authors did not equivocate on the subject of the criminal law. They argued that "HIV-infected individuals who knowingly conduct themselves in ways that pose a significant risk of transmission to others must be held accountable."[39] However, they recognized the problems facing authorities hoping to do so:

> Use of traditional crimes such as murder or attempted murder to prosecute an individual for HIV transmission presents such difficulties as proving that the intent of the HIV-infected individual . . . and proving that the act of transmission was the actual cause of death. Although the assault model provides a more useful tool for criminal prosecution of HIV transmission, the penalties for assault would prove too lenient in those cases where the transmission was intentional.[40]

In this passage, the presidential commission's report zeroes in on a key problem facing prosecutors hoping to press charges against HIV-positive defendants. Under criminal statutes such as assault with a deadly weapon and attempted murder, the prosecutor must show that the defendant acted with criminal intent, or mens rea. A string of high-profile acquittals and dismissals for failure to prove intent and/or to legally secure the defendant's medical records fueled a belief among some in law enforcement that general statutes were insufficient. While it did not explicitly say that general statutes were insufficient, the presidential commission nonetheless spoke to this concern by encouraging states to review their statutes and determine whether HIV-specific laws were necessary.[41]

"SELLING DEATH": ORGANIZED AGGRAVATION AND THE FIGHT FOR FELONY PROSTITUTION PENALTIES

During the early 1980s, there was considerable anxiety among public health professionals and the public that prostitution might provide a "bridge" for HIV to jump from urban centers to American suburbs. These fears were inflamed by a series of small studies that found high levels of HIV prevalence among female sex workers in several African countries.[42] In 1985, a team of researchers examining the heterosexual transmission of HIV warned that "prostitutes could serve as a reservoir for [HIV] infection for heterosexually active individuals."[43] Based on these findings, health authorities worried that HIV in the United States could become what epidemiologists call a "generalized epidemic"—diffuse throughout the American population instead of concentrated in specific subpopulations.

But as a 1989 article in the *San Francisco Chronicle* describes, the impending heterosexual epidemic driven by prostitution never came:

> In 1985, public health officials—particularly in New York City, where as many as half of all prostitutes are estimated to be HIV-infected—predicted that it was only a matter of time before the businessman from Cleveland was spreading around viral souvenirs to his wife or girlfriend. At the CDC, the epidemiologists waited for evidence that this would happen. And they waited. Several years into their watch, however, it hasn't.[44]

A CDC researcher told the *Chronicle*, "There isn't any evidence that I'm aware of that clearly indicates prostitutes as a transmitter of HIV infection."[45] As most sex workers are women, this was likely due to the fact that it is much more difficult for HIV to be transmitted from women to men than the reverse. This was not uncommon knowledge. For example, a legal expert reported in a 1988–1989 law review article: "Current statistics reveal that prostitutes are an unremarkable source of AIDS infection. . . . Nor is the virus spread effectively from the female prostitute to the customer."[46]

Numerous news reports from the mid-1980s had described a sense of aggravation among law enforcement authorities confronted with sex workers who had tested positive for HIV. Prostitution was generally a misdemeanor offense in most states, which meant that anyone arrested for prostitution would likely be free from jail in a matter of months or even days. Police were upset that there was little they could do to keep these individuals behind bars. In a criminal justice context, *aggravation* typically refers to factors that make an individual crime more egregious and, thus, deserving of a more severe punishment. As the next chapter reveals, HIV is frequently viewed by judges and prosecutors as an aggravating factor in a court of law. But as this section reveals, a similar phenomenon can be observed on a broader scale when members of law enforcement organize to label a set of practices as especially egregious and deserving of increased punishment—what this book terms *organized aggravation*.

In Georgia, the Fulton County prosecutor declared his intent to charge HIV-positive sex workers with felony assault.[47] He relied on a newly implemented regulation issued by the Georgia Department of Human Services that allowed that agency to report the HIV-test results of convicted sex workers to local judges.[48] In Rhode Island, Chief Judge Albert E. DeRobbie invoked a new state law that allowed the health department to involuntarily test a person deemed to be a threat to public health, demanding that district court judges relay the names of individuals convicted of prostitution to local health departments for testing; Judge DeRobbie justified these efforts by labeling AIDS as deadly and anyone who infects someone else as an executioner. "If you give someone AIDS, you sentence them to death."[49] In Minnesota, prosecutors sought to revoke the probation of a woman suspected of being HIV positive after she was entrapped by an undercover police officer for soliciting. The prosecutor did not mince words in defending his efforts: "It is akin to someone walking down the streets carrying a bomb."[50]

In the face of these legal challenges, lawmakers in several states sought to enact legislation that would aid the efforts of prosecutors and the police to put sex workers living with HIV behind bars for far longer. They did not rely on scientific studies to justify their efforts; instead, they sensationalized individual arrests of HIV-positive sex workers. These widely publicized cases represent one type of what crime policy scholars call "triggering events," which include sensationally reported crimes, court decisions, interest-group lobbying, and other factors that trigger lawmakers to devise new criminal sanctions.[51] Police lobbied for new laws on the basis that these individual sex workers were just the tip of the iceberg, representing a much larger problem that they believed needed to be addressed through legislative action.

In fact, the practice of pointing to specific HIV-positive sex workers dates back to the first known attempt to pass HIV-specific criminal legislation. On May 6, 1985, New Jersey legislators introduced the first HIV-specific crime bill in the United States. Assembly Bill 3577 was broadly construed so as to impose penalties on any person living with HIV who, "knowing that he is infected by acquired immune deficiency syndrome, transmits the disease to another person through sexual contact."[52] Nonetheless, the bill's sponsor, New Jersey state senator Gerald Stockman, told media outlets that he drafted the bill "at the request of Trenton police," who were reportedly concerned that "a 25-year-old AIDS victim who has two young children with the disease had been working as a prostitute on city streets."[53] (The bill did not pass.)

Notably, it was police who brought the issue to the attention of New Jersey lawmakers. Throughout the 1980s, law enforcement frequently lobbied for legislation that would impose criminal sanctions against people living with HIV—far more than any other interest organization. Although police representatives occasionally made their case in public to the media, they also lobbied lawmakers behind closed doors—evidence of their influence remains only in lawmakers' public statements such as Stockman's. Although New Jersey's bill failed, police continued to press lawmakers in several states to enact specific legislation that would enable prosecutors to charge HIV-positive sex workers with what is sometimes termed *aggravated prostitution*—a felony offense targeting HIV-positive sex workers.

In Nevada, the only state in the country that allows local jurisdictions to permit prostitution, lawmakers led the way in enacting such legislation when they passed a landmark bill in 1986 requiring anyone convicted of prostitution to be tested for HIV; those who tested HIV positive would face felony charges if they were ever again caught selling sex. According to Nevada state legislator John DuBois, the bill was supported by law enforcement. He told the media that "law enforcement was particularly for this because it fills a void. . . . They have no law on the books to really do anything about these people except something that makes spreading an infectious disease a misdemeanor."[54]

In other states, aggravated-prostitution legislation was influenced by partisan politics as legislators jockeyed to position themselves as tough on crime to their constituents. In 1988, for example, California representative Bruce Bronzan introduced a felony bill targeting sex workers living with HIV. Bronzan, a Democrat, had voted against punitive AIDS bills in the past, but in 1988, he was up for reelection in conservative

Fresno. His Republican opponent promptly criticized his sponsoring the bill as an attempt to play party politics during an election year.[55] Bronzan, on the other hand, said he was motivated to introduce the bill in the wake of the 1987 Fresno case discussed earlier in this chapter in which prosecutors failed to secure a felony attempted murder conviction against an HIV-positive sex worker.[56] Although the Bronzan bill was approved by the legislature, the governor ultimately vetoed it in favor of a broader proposal (enacting stiffer penalties for a range of sex crimes, not just prostitution) sponsored by one of the most conservative members of the state senate, John Doolittle.[57]

In Florida, law enforcement, legislators, and even the media spoke out as a chorus of "moral entrepreneurs," or individuals or organizations who advocate for a particular behavior or phenomenon to be labeled as crime.[58] Collectively, they rallied to label sex work for people living with HIV as homicidal and to demand new laws to combat the phenomenon. Orange County prosecutors charged an HIV-positive sex worker with felony attempted manslaughter in the winter of 1987. Despite the fact that the woman used condoms, State Representative Rich Crotty declared that the woman's actions were "tantamount to murder."[59] Days later, another HIV-positive female sex worker was arrested in Fort Lauderdale; instead of being charged with manslaughter, she was convicted of misdemeanor prostitution and sentenced to ninety days in jail. Both the city police chief and the prosecutor labeled the sentence as inadequate and spoke out publicly to demand the legislature enact stiffer criminal penalties for sex workers living with HIV. Despite the fact that no one was known to have been infected by the woman, Fort Lauderdale prosecutor Scott Walker complained that "it should be a felony. It's like a slow murder."[60]

In the wake of these cases, the editorial board of Fort Lauderdale's largest newspaper, the *Sun Sentinel,* took on the role of bully pulpit to argue in an op-ed for legislators to take action. According to the editorial board, the women arrested were "living proof that . . . 'prostitution is a victimless crime' is a vicious lie."[61] Citing a police-reported figure that over two hundred sex workers in Fort Lauderdale were living with HIV (as well as Walker's "slow murder" comment), the paper's editorial board declared: "New state laws are needed, to provide longer felony sentences for prostitutes infected with AIDS and even for possible quarantines."[62]

The Florida House of Representatives had voted down felony charges targeting sex workers living with HIV in 1987, but the pressure had mounted considerably in the wake of the two highly publicized cases.[63]

Two Republican representatives, Rich Crotty and Javier Souto, introduced a felony prostitution bill a mere nine days after the *Sun Sentinel* editorial went to print. The American Civil Liberties Union lobbied against the bill, arguing that the issue should be labeled as a problem for doctors instead of the criminal justice system: "These people are a medical problem, not a criminal problem."[64] Souto defended the stiffer penalties by again invoking the homicide label, arguing that "60 days is a very short period of time when we're dealing with a killer."[65] Ultimately, the felony prostitution penalty was folded into a much larger bill relating to public health and HIV—House Bill 1519—and was voted into law.[66]

Over the next several years, familiar stories played out in more states—such as Colorado two years later. News broke in early January that a woman living with HIV named Avis had been arrested for prostitution for the twenty-sixth time in Denver.[67] But while medical privacy laws prevented health authorities from publicly discussing Avis's case, city prosecutors and the police publicly expressed their frustration with her case to the media. City attorney Steve Kaplan complained, "Yea, we're frustrated. . . . We're real frustrated. We're the ones who have to deal with her."[68] The police did more than just complain, however; reports reveal that they reacted to Avis's case by actively organizing to label sex work for people living with HIV as a felony, launching a media campaign and sending lobbyists to the Denver capitol building to advocate for an HIV-specific felony prostitution bill. On January 31, 1990, a *Rocky Mountain News* article opened with the following lede: "Denver police say AIDS is spreading among the city's prostitutes, many of whom continue to work the streets despite knowing they are dying of the disease and passing it on to their clients."[69] Mostly informed by police sources, the story does not cite a specific case of transmission from a sex worker to a client; instead, it relies on police representatives' claims that a group of women sex workers were exposing countless Denver residents to the disease.

Less than a week later, the *Denver Post* ran a story picking up where the *Rocky Mountain News* story left off, dedicating much of the story to Avis's case.[70] In this story, however, police explicitly label the woman's actions as homicidal—not just to her clients, but to her family. Sergeant David Watts told the *Post* that "Avis and others like her are selling death. . . . People say that the john (solicitor of prostitutes) gets what he deserves. Well, it goes further than that. AIDS is transmitted to his wife and to their baby." In Watts's view, prostitutes were not just killing their clients, they were endangering the lives of innocent women and children. However, no incidents in which HIV was transmitted along such a route were identified.

In previous cases, police had frequently pointed to isolated cases rather than scientific data to justify their calls for criminalization. This is likely due to the fact that scientific studies conducted in the United States largely contradicted their claims that sex workers posed a significant health threat. While sex workers often had elevated HIV prevalence rates, studies concluded that prostitution was not likely to drive a heterosexual epidemic in the United States.[71] Rather than relying on published figures, however, Denver police made up their own statistics, telling the *Post* that 75 percent of male sex workers and 50 percent of female sex workers were HIV positive. These figures were outrageously high and stood in stark contrast to scientific findings published at the time that less than 7 percent of women sex workers in American urban areas were living with HIV.[72] Police representatives told the *Post* that they had "no way of verifying our statistics." However, the *Post* story suggests that this was not true: Apparently police could have obtained more reliable figures had they picked up the phone and called the state health department: The director of Colorado's HIV control problem informed the *Post* that only 1 percent of sex workers tested *by order of the police* had tested HIV positive. "It's not like it's a widespread problem. I don't know where they are getting their figures," he added.[73]

In an editorial published days later, the *Rocky Mountain News* relied on those health department figures to argue for a more well-informed debate on the issue.[74] Police and prosecutors, it argued, were identifying the wrong cause driving the epidemic: injection drug use, not prostitution, was the deserving culprit. "While we don't necessarily object to such a law," said the editorial,

> we do dissent from pointless fear-mongering. The fact is that female prostitutes are not spreading AIDS willy-nilly. . . . Between 1986 and '88, Denver General Hospital tested 372 prostitutes picked up by Denver police. Only four tested positive. . . . True, of 538 other people tested last year who admitted several "high risk factors" at some time in their lives, including IV drug use and prostitution, 51 tested positive. But this says little or nothing about the risk of getting AIDS for either non-drug-using prostitutes or their customers, since needle-sharing is a great way to transmit the virus.[75]

However, the engines of criminalization already in motion were not fueled by statistics or science; the organized aggravation of police was instead based on emotions and stigmatizing views of HIV and its transmission. Denver police assigned Detective John Schnittgrund to lobby lawmakers for an HIV-specific felony bill targeting sex work, even going as far as drafting statutory language for lawmakers, specifically modeled on Nevada's felony law.[76] Although police initially struggled to find a sponsor for their proposed bill, the repeated high-profile media stories may have helped to pressure lawmakers to take up the police bill. Two weeks after the *Rocky Mountain News* urged caution, House Bill 1255 was introduced and ultimately approved by the legislature.

By 1995, ten states had enacted felony HIV-specific penalties targeting sex workers. In many cases, those laws paved the way for broader statutes that criminalized any form of "exposure," or any sexual activity by an HIV-positive person who did not disclose his or her HIV status—HIV exposure and nondisclosure laws, for short. Among the seven states that enacted both laws targeting HIV-positive prostitutes and more general HIV disclosure or exposure statutes, four enacted prostitution penalties in advance of broader statutes. Many more states would go on to pass much broader HIV-specific criminal laws, which are discussed in the following section; however, the prostitution panic of the mid-1980s provided the kindling for the wave of criminalization to come.

"A CESSPOOL FOR DISEASE": PUBLIC HEALTH AS PRETENSE FOR PUNISHING GAY SEX

In May 1985, a three-judge panel of the United States Court of Appeals for the Eleventh Circuit struck down Georgia's sodomy law, ruling that it had violated Michael Hardwick's right to privacy when he was arrested for engaging in oral sex with another man in 1982. The court ruled that Georgia could not justify such an invasion into the private lives of American citizens without demonstrating a compelling state interest. "The Constitution prevents the states from unduly interfering in certain individual decisions critical to personal autonomy because those decisions are essentially private and beyond the reach of a civilized society," the justices ruled.[77]

By the time the appeals court ruled in 1985, much had changed since Michael Hardwick's arrest. Some observers wondered whether states might pivot to argue that the need to control AIDS—rather than simply a bigoted view of homosexuality—provided a renewed justification for sodomy laws. Frederick Allen, a columnist for the *Atlanta Journal and Constitution,* proposed such a strategy for Georgia's legal team:

The court's challenge to Georgia officials to find a rationale for regulating sexual behavior has a distinctly defiant tone, as if no rationale could possibly exist—but the 11th Circuit panel has opened precisely that door. The state of Georgia is free to argue, for instance, that promiscuous homosexual contact encourages the spread of AIDS, and that the public at large thus has a compelling interest in closing down gay bathhouses or policing the interstate rest stops that have become gay gathering places.[78]

The problem with that approach, Allen continued, was that "the state would be defending a severe, sweeping, unenforceable law that was written with morality, not AIDS, in mind." A more sensible solution would be "for the General Assembly to rewrite Georgia's statute so that it adopts the limited goal of outlawing the public practice of acts that are known to spread a fatal disease."[79]

Georgia ultimately appealed the decision to the Supreme Court of the United States, which heard oral arguments in *Bowers v. Hardwick* in late March 1986. Most of the arguments centered on whether American citizens have a right to engage in whatever forms of consensual sexual behaviors in private that they choose. But at the very end of the hour-long hearing, Justice Sandra Day O'Connor asked the lawyer for the Georgia man arrested under the state's sodomy ban, Laurence Tribe, a curious question: "You suggested that if the state were to assert its desire to promote traditional families instead of homosexual relationships would not suffice in your view. . . . Perhaps the state can say its desire [sic] to deter the spread of a communicable disease or something of that sort?"[80] In other words, if promoting the heterosexual family was not a sufficient justification for enforcing anti-sodomy laws, then perhaps the state might instead argue that these laws serve a public health interest. In his response to Justice O'Connor, Tribe cites an amicus brief submitted by the American Public Health Association in which it argued that sodomy laws are more harmful than helpful when it comes to public health.[81] However, he suggested that a more specific law might pass muster: "Surely, if a narrowly tailored law could be shown necessary to protect the public health, that would be a compelling justification, but Georgia offers no such justification here."[82]

As the court deliberated for the next several months, lawmakers across the country braced for its decision. Dozens of state legislatures by then had repealed their anti-sodomy laws. However, so-called buggery laws—which had the effect of criminalizing homosexuality—were still on the books in nearly half of U.S. states when the court decided

Bowers in 1986.[83] In the end, the court reversed the Eleventh Circuit's decision, ruling that homosexuals did not have a fundamental right to privacy; it made no mention of AIDS or public health in its ruling. Nonetheless, the notion that a "narrowly tailored law" might replace or buttress the state's effort to criminalize homosexuality persisted.

In the summer of 1993, for example, Nevada lawmakers took up Senate Bill 466. The bill would repeal sections of the state's sodomy law that criminalized private, consensual sex between members of the same sex, while adding more severe penalties for anyone who engaged in the "infamous crime against nature" with a minor.[84] The bill also implemented mandatory HIV screening for prisoners admitted to the Department of Corrections, a provision that one lawyer argued was necessary to protect prisoners in the wake of the anti-sodomy law's repeal (presumably because prisoners were now vulnerable to being legally sodomized by HIV-positive inmates).[85]

At the May 24, 1993, Senate Judiciary Committee hearing on the bill, AIDS loomed large in the debates over whether to repeal the state sodomy law. Of the eighteen individuals who testified in support of the bill, three specifically argued that repealing the anti-sodomy law would help to promote HIV prevention by easing relationships between medical providers and gay patients, who sometimes feared reporting illegal sexual practices. Of the thirteen critics who testified in opposition to the bill, however, eight specifically argued that repealing the anti-sodomy law would *encourage* the spread of AIDS. Echoing pamphlets distributed to legislators by antigay crusader Paul Cameron, one local woman, Carolyn Nelson, argued that "garden variety sexual practices of homosexuals are a medical horror story. . . . This population of gays and lesbians is a cesspool for disease."[86] Another woman, Lynn Chapman, argued that "she has had acquaintances who have died of AIDS, is acquainted with homosexuals, and . . . did not understand how the behavior which spreads the disease could be condoned." Lobbyist Andy Anderson later held up a book about AIDS to the committee members and argued that "the book shows the result of the private lovemaking referred to in the law at issue. . . . Therefore, there is no such thing as a private affair, and what is done by homosexuals does affect the rest of the public." Finally, a lobbyist for the Nevada Coalition for Concerned Citizens, Lucille Lusk, asked Senator Mark James whether "a law could be written which would assure the protection from the various possible effects spoken of by her and other opponents of S.B. 466." Senator James asked Ms. Lusk what law she might have in mind, but she declined to elaborate.[87]

Four days later, the Senate convened and read the bill for the third time.[88] Two Republican senators—Ann O'Connell and Ray Rawson—spoke in favor of the adoption of Amendment No. 679, which would have added felony penalties to the sodomy decriminalization bill for any person who tested HIV positive to "willfully, wantonly or negligently [engage] in conduct in a manner that is intended or likely to transmit the disease."[89] At least on paper, the amendment was defended purely as a strategy for promoting public health. To make this noble goal explicit, the amendment authors penned a lengthy—if convoluted—preamble justifying the need for the anti-sodomy law (which would remain on the books to punish public sex, prostitution, and statutory rape) entirely on public health grounds:

> WHEREAS, It is in the interest of the residents of this state to encourage the control, prevention and treatment of communicable diseases; and
>
> WHEREAS, The state has a vital interest in protecting the welfare of the public by restricting behavior that increases the risk of transmitting such diseases; and . . .
>
> WHEREAS, It is recognized that certain private behavior is beyond the scope of the state's interest in protecting the health and welfare of its residents; and
>
> WHEREAS, It is the public policy of the State of Nevada and the purpose of this act to balance the interest of the state in protecting the health, welfare and safety of its residents with each resident's legitimate right to privacy; now, therefore . . .

However, while the language of the amendment may have been painstakingly neutral, the authors' remarks on the senate floor reveal the anti-gay bias that at least in part inspired them. Asking his fellow senators to vote yes on the amendment, coauthor Senator Ray Rawson declared: "The fact is, and this is fact, that much of the activity associated with homosexual sex is dangerous. We can forget all of the moral arguments. We can forget all of the religious arguments. But there is a danger that is associated with the practice of this sexual activity." One senator expressed sympathy with the author's intentions but vowed to reject the amendment on the grounds that it would "muddy the waters" on an otherwise narrowly drafted piece of legislation.[90] Chairman of the Senate Committee on Judiciary Mark James warned his fellow lawmakers that, "if this amendment is defeated, the Senate Judiciary Committee will introduce a bill which handles Section 2 of the amendment on Tuesday morning.[91]

The amendment was voted down by a vote of 4–16. Senator Rawson lamented, "This is the most disappointing day that I have ever had in the Senate." He went on to cite pseudoscientific materials produced by Paul Cameron's Family Research Institute, an antigay organization the Southern Poverty Law Center classifies today as a hate group: "Eighty percent of the heterosexual men, in this country, will die of old age. Two percent of the homosexual men will die of old age." Despite these highly stigmatizing and wildly inaccurate claims, Senator Rawson insisted "I am not talking about morality."[92]

The amendment's failure did not stop legislators who intended to enact the HIV-specific criminal language in a separate bill. Senator Ernest Adler declared that he intended to have the chairman of the Senate Judiciary Committee "amend one of my bill drafts to place language in it [that would criminalize willful HIV transmission]. . . . I would like to say that I, for one, do take the whole idea of transmittable diseases very seriously."[93] Even local newspapers urged the legislature to act. In an editorial published just days after the amendment's failure, the *Reno Gazette-Journal* notes, "There is one amendment, though, that merits approval as a separate measure. This is the proposal . . . that would make the willful transmission of AIDS a felony."[94]

Senate Judiciary Committee chairman Mark James made good on his promise to act, introducing a bill containing identical language to Amendment 679, Senate Bill 514, on June 1, 1993—just two business days after the senate rejected the amendment. Although it received far less debate than the sodomy repeal bill, many of the same organizations and interest groups turned up to argue the issue. Although one prominent AIDS services provider argued against singling out HIV among other diseases, no one staunchly opposed the legislation; rather, they debated the specific wording of the statute, prompting lawmakers to amend the law to provide for a defense if the person disclosed his or her status.[95] It passed unanimously in the senate and the house and was signed by the governor on July 9, 1993.

The notion that enacting HIV-specific criminal legislation was tied to state sodomy laws persisted right up until the Supreme Court again revisited the issue in 2003, when it decided *Lawrence v. Texas*. In 2000, for example, Virginia lawmakers had introduced House Bill 141, the latest in a string of bills introduced since 1989 that would have made it a misdemeanor for someone living with HIV to expose someone else to the disease. While bills had failed to move out of committee in previous legislative sessions, the 2000 effort finally made it to the floor of the senate after the language was modified to require proof of intent for prosecution, a provision not included in previous legislation.

Whereas Nevada lawmakers argued that decriminalizing sodomy would have the unintended effect of legalizing HIV exposure, Virginia lawmakers worried instead that criminalizing HIV might have the unintended effect of legalizing sodomy. The reason, they argued, was that the laws effectively criminalized the same practices—but under the HIV law the practices would be misdemeanors, whereas under the sodomy statute, they were felonies. When the bill came up for debate in the General Assembly, Virginia delegate Brian Moran explained this argument:

> Another objectionable provision of this bill is that these behaviors that you have to engage in to be guilty of this are in fact felonies in the Code of Virginia 18.23621, "Crimes against Nature." There is already felony punishment to engage in such behaviors. When I asked the Patron in the Courts and Justice Committee how a victim of this law could possibly incriminate themselves in testifying as to this behavior. He said that some sort of deal would be made with the prosecutor. It's objectionable to me and I hope it would be objectionable to you that we would be asking the prosecutor to absolve felony behavior so that he or she may prosecute misdemeanor behavior.[96]

Virginia delegate and Democrat minority leader C. Richard Cranwell took the floor later in the day to again highlight this concern: "I suggest to you that what you're fixing to do is to legalize sodomy and a lot of other crimes between consenting adults where one may have HIV."[97]

Although the bill passed the house 71–26, a senate committee subsequently amended the bill to classify HIV exposure as a felony rather than a misdemeanor. It is not known precisely what motivated the Virginia senate to modify the penalty provisions of the bill. However, it may have been motivated by the concerns expressed by delegates Moran and Cranwell that the HIV bill would exonerate felony sodomy crimes in favor of punishing misdemeanor HIV exposure. By raising the HIV-related penalties to the same felony level as sodomy statutes, the senate may have sought to neutralize this criticism. This suggests that, at least in part, the heightened felony penalty for HIV exposure in Virginia may be a vestige of the state's commitment to punishing sodomy.

In the United States, the interplay between sodomy laws and HIV-specific criminal laws largely ended in 2003 when the Supreme Court ruled that American adults had a right to engage in whatever kinds of consensual sex they wished—at least in private and not for money—in its *Lawrence v. Texas* ruling. However, evidence that efforts to criminalize HIV are interwoven with a desire to punish sodomy and gay sex continue to be found abroad. In 2009, for example, lawmakers in

Uganda famously debated a bill critically labeled by Western LGBT activists as the "kill the gays" bill.[98] In fact, the bill would have criminalized "the offense of homosexuality" (punishable by life in prison) and introduced a set of "aggravating" factors under which that offense could be punishable by death. These factors included seven possible scenarios, including sex with a minor, sex with a person living with a disability, and any homosexual act committed by a person living with HIV.[99] The death penalty clause was ultimately removed from the bill when it was finally signed into law in 2014 and was replaced by life imprisonment; it was soon thereafter struck down by the country's Constitutional Court.[100]

These cases illustrate how the logic of criminalizing HIV has been propelled at least in part by homophobia. For legislators who held antigay beliefs such as those expressed on the Nevada Senate floor by Senator Rawson, AIDS provided a scientific glaze for their efforts to crack down on gay sex—a cover that allowed Senator Rawson to insist that he was not motivated by antigay morality but instead by a desire to promote public health. These strategies echo those of early twentieth-century eugenicists, who used pseudoscience to argue for racist policies in the name of promoting population health.[101] In this case, however, they resulted in a set of still-standing policies that criminalize people living with HIV.

AN EPIDEMIC OF LEGISLATION: "LAWMAKER ZERO" AND THE INSTITUTIONALIZATION OF HIV CRIMINALIZATION

When Ronald Reagan's Presidential Commission on the HIV Epidemic issued its final report in 1988, it issued a forceful call for criminalization. In the commission's view, HIV-specific criminal laws "would provide clear notice of socially unacceptable standards of behavior specific to the HIV epidemic and tailor punishment to the specific crime of HIV transmission."[102] The commission was made up of thirteen experts and leaders, including doctors, policy makers, and other authority figures. Only one elected official joined them: Illinois representative Penny Pullen, a conservative lawmaker who would go on to become a champion of the antiabortion movement.

Before Representative Pullen joined the antiabortion movement, she cut her teeth fighting for punitive policies against people living with HIV. In 1988, her influence was even noted by one Missouri newspaper, which reported that "Illinois Rep. Penny Pullen, R-Park Ridge and a member of President Ronald Reagan's AIDS task force, led the forces in the Illinois Legislature seeking mandatory contact tracing, quarantines and other coercive measures to combat the deadly disease."[103] In addition to serving on the presidential commission, Representative Pullen also contributed to a 1989 report on AIDS policy from the American Legislative Exchange Council (ALEC), a conservative think tank that drafts and disseminates model legislation to state lawmakers.

Evidence suggests that Representative Pullen was a key figure behind mobilizing both the presidential commission and ALEC to take a strong stance in favor of criminalization. By the time both reports were issued in 1988, the evidence already presented in this chapter clearly showed that the path to criminalization had been well laid: state governments from Florida to Nevada had already approved HIV-specific criminal legislation. Yet, these influential reports helped to institutionalize the argument in favor of criminalization and served to disseminate the concept to lawmakers across the country.

It would be impossible to trace the criminalization of HIV back to one lawmaker, state, or interest group, as Randy Shilts tried to do with HIV in his "Patient Zero" narrative that drove his dramatized account of the early years of AIDS, *And The Band Played On*. In that book, Shilts famously laid the epidemic at the feet of one promiscuous French Canadian gay male flight attendant who was said to have helped catapult the epidemic across the Americas. As discussed in chapter 1, we now know that the concept of a Patient Zero was a fantasy invented by the book's publisher to drive sales. But this chapter concludes with an effort to rehabilitate Shilts's concept by using it to analyze how one state and one lawmaker played an outsize role in sparking a different kind of epidemic—not of contagion, but of legislation.

In 1989, ALEC issued its final report on AIDS policy, *The Politics of Health: A State Response to the AIDS Crisis*.[104] The working group behind the report included over two dozen members of both the private sector (pharmaceutical and insurance companies) and the public sector (mostly conservative state legislators). The 161-page report included model legislation on a range of HIV-related issues, including public education, insurance regulations, partner notification, and the mandatory screening of prisoners. One section of the report titled "Extraordinary Situations" included two coercive proposals: the "Model HIV Assault Act" and the "Model Emergency Public Safety Measures Act." The latter related to quarantine and isolation procedures for people living with HIV. The former presented states with a model statute for criminalizing the actions of people living with HIV.

In a 2013 report, investigative journalist Todd Heywood interviewed the author of the 1989 ALEC report, Michael Tanner, to understand what had prompted ALEC to include this model statute proposal.[105] The author recalled that it was Representative Penny Pullen who first proposed the idea; although she had not served on the working group that drafted the report, she was invited to testify before the working group (presumably given her experience as a member of the presidential commission). According to Heywood, "Tanner said he recalls that former Presidential Commission member Pullen, who testified before the ALEC working group, introduced the Model HIV Assault Act during her testimony." Pullen declined to comment on the story.

Representative Pullen would have had experience in drafting such legislation. Earlier that year, she had acted as lead house sponsor for Illinois Senate Bill 1180 of 1989, a bill that would have enacted HIV-specific criminal penalties. On June 8, 1989, she introduced an amendment in the House Committee on the Judiciary that gutted the entire bill and replaced its contents with the following language:

> Sec. 12–16.2. Criminal Transmission of HIV. A person commits criminal transmission of HIV when he or she, knowing that he or she is infected with HIV:
>
> 1) engages in intimate contact with another;
> 2) transfers, donates, or provides his or her blood, tissue, semen, organs, or other potentially infectious body fluids for transfusion, transplantation, insemination, or other administration to another; dispenses, delivers, exchanges, sells, or in any other way transfers to another any nonsterile intravenous or intramuscular drug paraphernalia.
>
> For purposes of this Section,
>
> a) "HIV" means the human immunodeficiency virus or any other identified causative agent of acquired immune deficiency syndrome.
> b) "Intimate contact with another" means the exposure of a mucous membrane of one person to a bodily fluid of another person.
> c) "Intravenous or intramuscular drug paraphernalia" means any equipment, products, or material of any kind which are peculiar to and marketed for use in injecting a substance into the human body.
>
> Nothing in this Section shall be construed to require that an infection with HIV has occurred in order for a person to have committed criminal transmission of HIV. It shall be an affirmative defense that the person exposed knew that the infected person was infected with HIV, knew that the action could result in infection with HIV, and consented to the action with that knowledge.

A person who commits criminal transmission of I IV commits a Class 2 felony.

Section 2. This Act shall take effect upon becoming a law.[106]

She did not invent this language specifically for Senate Bill 1180. Instead, she lifted it directly from her bill in the house, House Bill 1871. That bill was amended slightly, resulting in the following language when it was finally approved by both legislative bodies (differences from Senate Bill 1180 are highlighted in bold):

Sec. 12–16.2. Criminal Transmission of HIV. (a) A person commits criminal transmission of HIV when he or she, knowing that he or she is infected with HIV:

(1) engages in intimate contact with another;

(2) transfers, donates, or provides his or her blood, tissue, semen, organs, or other potentially infectious body fluids for transfusion, transplantation, insemination, or other administration to another; **or**

(3) dispenses, delivers, exchanges, sells, or in any other way transfers to another any nonsterile intravenous or intramuscular drug paraphernalia.

(b) For purposes of this Section:

"HIV" means the human immunodeficiency virus or any other identified causative agent of acquired immunodeficiency syndrome.

"Intimate contact with another" means the **exposure of the body of one person to a bodily fluid of another person in a manner that could result in the transmission of HIV.**

"Intravenous or intramuscular drug paraphernalia" means any equipment, product, or material of any kind, which is peculiar to and marketed for use in injecting a substance into the human body.

(c) Nothing in this Section shall be construed to require that an infection with HIV has occurred in order for a person to have committed criminal transmission of HIV.

(d) It shall be an affirmative defense that the person exposed knew that the infected person was infected with HIV, knew that the action could result in infection with HIV, and consented to the action with that knowledge.

(e) A person who commits criminal transmission of HIV commits a Class 2 felony.

Both bills were ultimately approved by the Illinois legislature, but the governor vetoed the senate version due to their redundancy.

Representative Pullen's legislation bears a striking resemblance to the Model HIV Assault Act disseminated to state lawmakers by ALEC in its report issued later that year.[107] That model legislation reads as follows (differences from House Bill 1871 are highlighted in bold):

> Section 2. **(A) A male or female commits the crime of HIV Assault if,** knowing that he or she **is infected with the Human Immunodeficiency Virus (HIV), he or she:**
>
> (1) engages in intimate contact with another;
> (2) transfers, donates, or provides his or her blood, tissue, semen, organs, or other infectious body fluids for transfusion, transplantation, insemination, or other administration to another; or
> (3) dispenses, delivers, exchanges, sells, or in any other way transfers to another any nonsterile intravenous or intramuscular drug paraphernalia used by said person.
>
> **(B) HIV Assault is a felony and shall be punished by a fine of not more than $20,000, or imprisonment in a state correctional institution for not less than one year or more than several years, or both.**
>
> (C) Nothing in this section shall be construed to require that an infection with HIV has occurred in order for a person to have committed HIV assault.
>
> **Section 3. Any individual who commits the crime of HIV Assault under Section 2 of this Act shall be civilly liable for damages if another individual becomes infected with the human immunodeficiency virus as a result of such violation.**
>
> Section 4. If shall be an affirmative defense that the person exposed knew that the infected person was infected with HIV, knew that the action could result in infection with HIV, and consented to the action with that knowledge.
>
> Section 5. For purposes of the Act:
>
> **(A)** "HIV" means any human immunodeficiency virus **(HIV)** or any other identified causative agent of acquired immune deficiency syndrome **(AIDS).**
> **(B)** "Intimate contact" means the exposure of the body of one person to the bodily fluid of another person in a manner that **can transmit the HIV virus.**
> (C) "Intravenous or intramuscular drug paraphernalia" means any equipment, products, or material of any kind **that** is peculiar to **and used for** injecting a **controlled** substance into the human body.

Apart from the penalties outlined (civil liability and the specified term of imprisonment), Illinois House Bill 1871 and ALEC's Model HIV Assault Statute are nearly identical. Notably, of the eight states that had enacted HIV exposure or nondisclosure laws before 1989 (Florida, Georgia, Idaho, Michigan, Missouri, Oklahoma, South Carolina, and

Washington), none enacted legislation that bears any resemblance to the ALEC model law. Representative Pullen's legislation appears to be the only plausible source of inspiration.

In the wake of the ALEC report, legislators in seven states would go on to introduce twenty-two bills between 1990 and 2004 that use a structure similar to ALEC's model statute—suggesting that it helped to plant the seed of criminalizing HIV in state legislatures across the country.[108] However, as all but one of the twenty-two bills that use language similar to the ALEC model statute failed or was vetoed, the legacy of Representative Pullen's efforts is not that her bill's language was perfectly adopted by states across the country. Instead, her legacy lives on in the inspiration her efforts provided for other lawmakers around the country. This was especially true for Illinois's southwestern neighbor, Missouri. Even *before* Illinois passed its felony HIV-specific criminal bill in 1989, officials in Missouri were citing Representative Pullen's efforts to enact punitive measures against people living with HIV. As previously noted, the *St. Louis-Dispatch* specifically cited Representative Pullen's efforts to enact coercive policies against people living with HIV, such as mandatory contact tracing and quarantines.[109] Those measures are credited with inspiring Missouri lawmakers to enact similar efforts in Missouri, including an criminal HIV disclosure law later that year.

Further, even though Representative Pullen's statute was not widely adopted verbatim, it was cited frequently by other state lawmakers in their debates over whether and how to criminalize HIV. When Nevada lawmakers considered Senate Bill 514 in 1993, committee records reveal that they looked to Illinois for clarification regarding what language to use to describe the offense. Nevada lawmakers were concerned that "married couples or people in a relationship . . . [should] not be made to be committing criminal conduct."[110] They noted that the language devised by Illinois lawmakers regarding an affirmative defense for individuals who have disclosed their status "would take care of one of the major concerns of the committee."[111] The Nevada lawmakers repeatedly turned to Illinois's statute during committee meetings to help them consider the issue and draft amendments to their own bill.[112] Thus, although the Nevada statute does not perfectly mirror Illinois's HIV-specific criminal law, aspects of the Illinois law did directly inform Nevada lawmakers as they drafted their own bill.

A similar story played out in 1995 when Alaska lawmakers considered Senate Bill 91. Although the language of the bill is not identical to

Illinois's statute, it does rely on a highly similar structure that outlines the prohibition of intimate contact, the transfer of bodily fluids or organs, and the sharing of drug paraphernalia. Committee records reveal that the legislative aide to Republican representative Scott Ogan—the bill's sponsor –made repeated calls to Illinois officials to seek counsel in drafting the legislation:

> [Rep. Ogan's aide] informed the committee that he had contacted numerous staff attorneys in the Attorney General's office in Illinois for information. He spoke to people at the policy making level, and he spoke with actual prosecutors who tried cases like this. Illinois law is similar to Alaska's. He asked for input about any problems that we could address in our law and they brought up two concerns. One was that there was a challenge that went all the way to the Supreme Court; it was challenged because of the lack of definition to intimate contact. They said it should be defined further. Still, the Illinois Supreme Court upheld their looser language with less definition.

The fact that the Illinois law had survived a constitutional challenge—in spite of its "looser language"—was later cited as an important justification for Alaska lawmakers to use it as a model. After the 1995 bill failed, lawmakers introduced similar legislation in 1997. Senate Bill 17 was virtually identical to the Illinois statute. Indeed, at a committee hearing of the bill, a staff member for the bill's sponsor, Republican senator Robin Taylor, noted that "in drafting S.B. 17, the Illinois statute was used almost verbatim."[113]

The bill read as follows (differences from Illinois House Bill 1871 are highlighted in bold):

> Sec. 11.66.160. Criminal transmission of HIV. (a) A person commits **the crime of** criminal transmission of **human immunodeficiency virus (HIV) if the person,** knowing that **the person** is infected with HIV,
>   (1) **voluntarily** engages in intimate contact with another person;
>   (2) transfers, donates, or provides **the person's** blood, tissue, semen, organs, or other potentially infectious body fluids for transfusion, transplantation, insemination, or other administration to another, **excluding perinatal transmission**; or
>   (3) dispenses, delivers, exchanges, sells, or in **any manner** transfers to another **person** any nonsterile intravenous or intramuscular drug paraphernalia.
> **(b) In a prosecution under this section,**
>   (1) **it is** an affirmative defense that the person exposed **to HIV by the intimate contact, the transfusion, transplantation, insemination, or other administration or the transfer,** knew that the **defendant** was

infected with HIV, knew that the action could result in infection with HIV, and consented to the action with that knowledge;

(2) **it is not necessary to show that the victim has been actually infected with HIV for the defendant to be convicted.**

(c) **In this** section,

(1) "HIV" means the human immunodeficiency virus or **another** identified causative agent of acquired immunodeficiency syndrome;

(2) "intimate contact" means **sexual penetration or any contact in which** the body of one person **is exposed to a body fluid of another person** in a manner that could result in the transmission of HIV;

(3) "intravenous or intramuscular drug paraphernalia" means any equipment, product, or material of any kind that is peculiar to and marketed for use in injecting a substance into the human body.

(d) Criminal transmission of HIV is a class B felony.[114]

But the language of Illinois's statute was not the only source of inspiration for Alaska lawmakers. In committee records for Senate Bill 17, lawmakers reference the Illinois statute in some way thirty-two times. For example, they cite figures from the Illinois Department of Health regarding the annual number of HIV tests before and after the bill's passage. To refute the common charge that criminalizing HIV will negatively impact the number of people seeking HIV tests, Alaskan lawmakers cited figures from Illinois, noting that the number of tests had not changed in the six years since the Illinois law had been passed.[115]

Senate Bill 17 went on to be approved by the Alaska legislature, but Governor Tony Knowles used his veto power to block the bill's passage. Nonetheless, the debate over its passage is one end of a thread of Illinois influence and Representative Pullen's legacy that is woven into the history of HIV criminalization. No other state is cited as frequently in the archives obtained for this research project, nor does any legislative leader have such a lasting influence as Representative Pullen. Indeed, she is as close to "Lawmaker Zero" as one could find in the history of HIV criminalization in the United States. Her efforts as a moral entrepreneur helped influence both the presidential commission and ALEC to use their resources to push for HIV-specific criminal laws—prompting almost two dozen states to consider legislation directly modeled on the Illinois statute.

AN EPIDEMIC OF CRIMINALIZATION

As this chapter has demonstrated, AIDS is not just a viral epidemic—it is also an epidemic of laws, bills, committee hearings, legislative debates,

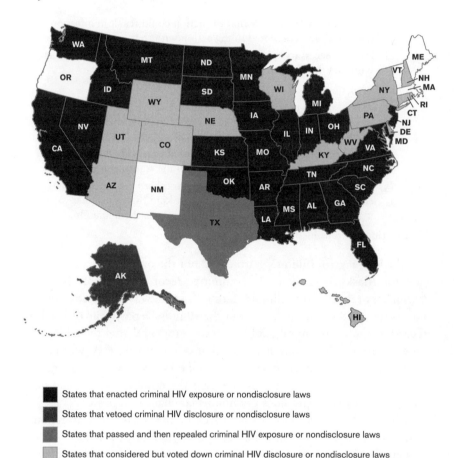

States that enacted criminal HIV exposure or nondisclosure laws

States that vetoed criminal HIV disclosure or nondisclosure laws

States that passed and then repealed criminal HIV exposure or nondisclosure laws

States that considered but voted down criminal HIV disclosure or nondisclosure laws

States that have not attempted to enact criminal HIV disclosure or nondisclosure laws

FIGURE 14. HIV-specific criminal legislation, by state. Design: Jonathan Lefrançois. Illustration: Justin Karas for Pulp & Pixel.

and bureaucratic administration. Today, twenty-eight states have misdemeanor or felony laws on the books that make it a crime for people living with HIV to have sex without disclosing their HIV status or to more generally "expose" another to the disease. In forty-five states across the country, lawmakers considered over 150 criminal bills between 1985 and 2014 targeting HIV (for a list of bills identified and studied for this chapter, see appendix 2). Figure 14 illustrates where bills that would have criminalized HIV exposure or nondisclosure in the United States were considered and enacted, and where they failed.

To continue the epidemiological metaphor, the epidemic of HIV-specific criminal laws has spread throughout the country, but what are its root causes? This chapter identified four broad trends that facilitated the spread of HIV-specific criminal laws: high-profile failures to apply general statutes, organized aggravation by police against sex workers, the decriminalization of sodomy, and the institutionalizing influence of Lawmaker Zero. Looking at these trends collectively, we can identify four underlying drivers of criminalization that cut across them:

1. *social stigma,* including HIV stigma, homophobia, and stigma against sex work;

2. *sensational media reports* of arrests of HIV-positive defendants and failed prosecutions;

3. *moral entrepreneurs* such as Lawmaker Zero who campaigned to label HIV as a criminal problem; and

4. *interest-group lobbying* by organizations such as police departments and ALEC.

Any one of these factors was not sufficient. Many states that did not pass HIV-specific criminal legislation presumably had legislators who held antigay attitudes, or prominent public officials who called for criminalization but did not find support in the legislature. In combination, however, the four factors frequently resulted in states enacting HIV-specific criminal laws.

Of course, the fact that homophobia and fear of sex work drove legislators to enact HIV-specific criminal laws does not mean that these laws went on to be used specifically against these groups. As the next two chapters reveal, the application of these laws has not followed predictable patterns. The factors that drove the epidemic of criminal legislation are not necessarily the same as those that drive how those laws are enforced.

CHAPTER 5

HIV on Trial

Stigma and the Illusion of Harm in American Courtrooms

On June 24, 1991, Michigan governor John Engel signed extradition papers to request that officials in New York State remand Jeffrey H.[1] to Michigan law enforcement custody.[2] Jeffrey was the first person charged in Michigan under a 1988 law that made it a felony for people living with HIV to engage in "sexual penetration" without first disclosing their HIV status. Despite going into effect in 1988, the law had not yet been tried in court when a young man came to Lake County prosecutor Michael Riley to report that he had had oral sex with Jeffrey once and that he did not disclose being HIV positive.

By the time the complainant had stepped forward, however, Jeffrey had moved back home to Dutchess County, New York, to live with his family. Riley told the press that he was aggressively pursuing the case because "I'd like to see that [Jeffrey] does not give any more death notices out. . . . He knew it was criminal activity and he did it anyway."[3] Jeffrey fought the extradition on the grounds that New York did not have an HIV disclosure law on the books at the time; a judge rejected his arguments and New York governor Mario Cuomo signed extradition papers to send Jeffrey back to Michigan. He was arrested at work on June 15, 1991.[4]

The case immediately became fodder for sensational media coverage, landing on the pages of *USA Today*, the *San Francisco Chronicle*, gay and lesbian publications such as the *Advocate*, and dozens of newspapers across the country. The fact that it involved HIV, extradition hearings, and a gay man accused of cheating on his male lover with another man helped propel the coverage for nearly a year between Jeffrey's arrest in June 1991 and sentencing in May 1992. According to testimony in court, Kevin, the complainant, had become aware of Jeffrey's HIV-positive status only months later when he telephoned Jeffrey's former residence. Jeffrey did not answer, however, because he had moved to New York; instead, his ex-lover of several years, Patrick, picked up the phone. Kevin testified that Patrick (illegally) informed him of Jeffrey's HIV-positive status, advising him that he "needed to be checked."[5]

AIDS activists protested the case, characterizing Patrick as a "jilted lover" who was "looking to make a name for himself."[6] Patrick testified in court that he had split up with Jeffrey in December 1990 after Jeffrey had repeatedly cheated on him with other men: "[Jeffrey] couldn't stay in a monogamous relationship, and we both agreed that he should go."[7] Once the case had gained national media exposure, Patrick appeared on the nationally syndicated talk show *Donahue* to discuss it and gave numerous press interviews.[8] After the prosecution bungled its efforts to legally secure medical evidence that would prove Jeffrey's HIV status, Patrick stepped in to aid the prosecutor by providing a doctor's billing statement found at home that documented Jeffrey's treatment for "HIV Sinusitis."[9]

Notably, precise estimates of the risk of oral transmission did not exist in 1991. There were case reports involving newly diagnosed gay men who reported engaging in only oral sex in the months preceding their infection.[10] However, labeling the practice "risky" remained controversial because quantitative studies found that oral sex was *not* statistically associated with infection.[11] Jeffrey's defense attorney argued that his client should not be held liable under the law because Jeffrey had been counseled at an HIV support group "that protection was not needed for oral sex."[12] In a written brief, the judge squashed any plans the defense may have had for using the risk of oral sex to rebut the charges. The judge ruled that although Jeffrey might have "been of the opinion" that oral sex was less dangerous than anal sex, "that does not mean that the statute was not violated."[13]

Despite ruling that the level of risk was immaterial to the case, the judge would go on to defend the law as necessary to protect society from the homicidal behavior of HIV-positive people like Jeffrey. Responding to defense arguments that its client was being discriminatorily prosecuted because he was gay, the judge argued in a written brief that the prosecutor was simply interested in ensuring that Jeffrey should "not be allowed to kill others":

> Evidently the Defendant feels he is being focused upon because of his homo-
> sexual status, but the Prosecutor's concern as revealed by the news articles
> submitted by Defendant that persons not be allowed to kill others reflects a
> societal concern which situationally involves [Jeffrey], but does not reflect
> that the Prosecutor is convinced all gays should be punished or that the
> problem is limited to the gay community.[14]

Presumably being "allowed to kill" would entail putting another person
in harm's way. But neither the wording of Michigan's disclosure law nor
the judge's interpretation of that statute required the prosecution to
prove that such harm existed—or that the defendant acted with criminal intent. As discussed in chapter 4, most states with HIV-specific criminal laws, Michigan included, do not require proof that the defendant
intentionally infected his or her partner, or even that a sexual partner
was put at risk of acquiring HIV infection; the law merely requires the
prosecution to prove that an HIV-positive person failed to inform a
sexual partner of his or her infection. Words—or rather their absence—
constitute the offense.

In the face of these rulings, Jeffrey had little recourse for presenting a
compelling defense. He accepted a deal brokered with the prosecutor,
pleaded no contest, and was sentenced to one year in jail and five years'
probation.

Although Jeffrey was not the first person in America to be charged
under an HIV-specific criminal law, his case was by far the most widely
publicized when news of his prosecution broke in 1991.[15] In Michigan,
he was the sole defendant convicted during the first four years that
state's law was in effect, but fourteen defendants were convicted during
the four-year period following his conviction. A prescient media report
published the day Jeffrey was convicted cited a number of investigations
across the state that "have proceeded quietly in the wings as authorities
carefully followed the progress of the AIDS disclosure case in Lake
County."[16] That report quoted Prosecutor Michael Riley saying, "I
don't have any doubt this will make it easier for [other prosecutors]. . . .
They now know what worked and what mistakes to avoid."[17] Nation-
wide, cases had been scattered and rare before Jeffrey's conviction, but
convictions became commonplace in the wake of his case. As such, his
conviction marks the beginning of a new era of HIV criminalization in
the United States.

As this chapter will show, prosecutors and judges adopt stigmatizing
views of HIV in their arguments against HIV-positive defendants. State
laws do not require them to prove that the defendant put anyone in

harm's away or that they intended to do so, yet the explosive rhetoric that characterizes HIV as a death sentence and defendants as killers creates the *illusion of harm*. These assertions might have been more understandable in the days when an HIV diagnosis was largely terminal. But treatment introduced in 1996 radically transformed the lives of people living with HIV, reshaping HIV from a terminal illness into a chronic, manageable disease and rendering those who are on treatment virtually noninfectious (as discussed in chapter 2). Despite these advances, even in cases in which defendants could not have plausibly infected their partner, judges scold defendants for being a deadly threat to society.

In many ways, the treatment of HIV under the law mirrors broader trends in how prosecutors and judges harness stigma to advance their arguments in American courtrooms. This chapter is titled "HIV on Trial" to highlight the ways in which prosecutors and judges often wield outdated, inaccurate, and stigmatizing assertions about HIV and the alleged crimes in order to justify incredibly harsh sentences. The title borrows from the work of criminologists Charis Kubrin and Erik Neilson, who have examined how rap music lyrics are introduced as evidence in criminal cases against amateur rappers—a trend they describe as putting "rap on trial."[18] In those cases, "prosecutors misrepresent rap music to judges and juries, who rarely understand the genre conventions of gangsta rap or the industry forces that drive aspiring rappers to adopt this style."[19] This chapter adapts this concept to examine the stigmatizing rhetoric used by both prosecutors and judges in HIV-related prosecutions in Michigan and Tennessee—both in actual jury trials and in the far more numerous cases resolved through plea bargaining.

In the courtroom, the words used to represent and describe HIV and HIV-positive defendants are far from toothless talk. Lawyers and judges wield stigmatizing rhetoric as a hammer; ignorant and prejudicial views of HIV serve as justifications for harsh sentences demanded by prosecutors and imposed by judges. At times, the law on the books appears as almost an afterthought, as judges and prosecutors find creative ways to work around or simply ignore sections of the written law that would appear to limit the law's scope. In invoking such misleading and stigmatizing rhetoric, trial courts codify outdated and inaccurate depictions of HIV into case law—thereby opening the door to more cases, more convictions, and more stigmatizing rhetoric. While some readers may think of law enforcement as a straightforward translation of the laws on the books, stigmatizing language is an important moderating variable that shapes the application of HIV law in practice. In this sense, this chapter

TABLE 2   HIV ON TRIAL: BY THE NUMBERS

	Michigan (N = 58)		Tennessee (N = 45)	
How case was decided				
Plea	87.9%	51	87.6%	39
Trial	10.3%	6	6.7%	3
Unknown	1.7%	1	6.7%	3
Type of sentence				
Probation (including suspended)	13.8%	8	24.4%	11
Jail/prison	86.2%	50	68.9%	31
Unknown		–	6.7%	3
Average length of sentence (months)				
Average term of probation		23.3		52.7
Average term of jail/prison		24.6		77.7
Median length of probation sentence		21		36
Median length of jail/prison sentence		20.5		48

echoes the work of other sociolegal scholars who have argued that the language used in the courtroom is more than "just words"; in shaping how HIV is governed under the law, stigmatizing rhetoric is a function of power.[20]

This chapter analyzes fifty-eight convicted cases involving fifty-four defendants under Michigan's 1988 felony HIV disclosure law (95 percent of all convictions in that state through 2010) and forty-five convicted cases involving forty-two defendants under Tennessee's 1994 felony HIV exposure law (see table 2; figure 15 shows the number of HIV cases in those states from 1991 to 2010).[21] The bulk of this analysis focuses on the 6,654 pages of transcripts obtained from courtroom proceedings associated with 194 courtroom proceedings from seventy-eight criminal cases.[22] Notably, these include nine cases that actually went to trial (six in Michigan and three in Tennessee) as well as the far more numerous cases in which the defendant entered a plea of guilty or no contest. While cases that involve plea bargains can be brief, they nonetheless frequently feature debate over the severity of the sentence that should be imposed; thus, although these defendants are not technically on trial, their cases reveal how HIV shapes the application of the criminal law.

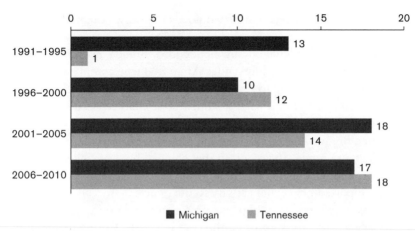

FIGURE 15. HIV on trial: Number of cases in Michigan and Tennessee, by year. Source: Trevor Hoppe.

Laws in Michigan and Tennessee are typical of those enacted nation-wide: Michigan law makes it a crime for HIV-positive people to engage in "sexual penetration" (defined broadly) without first disclosing their HIV status. Tennessee law is even more broadly construed so as to crim-inalize any form of HIV exposure, including not only sexual contact but also nonsexual contact such as spitting, biting, or scratching. Prosecu-tors and judges apply their state's law in ways that reinforce and repro-duce HIV stigma.

"A CARRIER OF DEATH": HIV STIGMA IN EARLY CASE LAW

The investigation into Brenda J. was one of those proceeding "quietly in the wings" as Jeffrey's case unfolded in nearby Lake County, Michigan. Brenda, a thirty-two-year-old White woman living in Muskegon County, was described as having an IQ "above the level considered developmentally disabled."[23] In court, it was revealed that her IQ was 72, which was in fact only two points above the *Diagnostic and Statisti-cal Manual of Mental Disorders* threshold for a diagnosis of disability.[24] After reports surfaced that she was having sex without disclosing her HIV-positive status, local health officials sought to have Brenda quarantined under the provisions of the state's health-threat-to-others statute (discussed in chapter 3), which allows officials to confine an individual deemed to be a threat to public health.[25] The prosecutor reported to media outlets that he would also "review potential criminal sanctions."[26]

Not long after her civil confinement ended, Brenda again found herself in legal jeopardy in July 1994. After frequent complaints to her legal guardian about the foster care home in which she resided, Brenda was allowed to move into what would later be characterized in court as a run-down motel notorious for sex work and drug use.[27] Only two days later, Brenda begged her legal guardian for permission to return to the foster care home. She reported that she had been having sex with a man named John, another tenant in the motel; her legal guardian subsequently reported her sexual activity to the police.

Just as in Jeffrey's case, both the prosecutor and police utilized unusually aggressive tactics to bring the case to court. Approximately two weeks after the alleged sexual encounter, police visited John at his place of employment; courtroom testimony reveals that he initially declined to testify over concerns that, because of her limited intelligence, sexual assault charges could be brought against *him*. When the preliminary examination hearing began in August 1994 (preliminary examinations, like grand juries, determine if there is sufficient evidence to indict a defendant), the prosecution informed the court that it could not locate John.[28] However, soon thereafter, police arrested and jailed John for failing to pay fines associated with six outstanding traffic offenses (including drunk driving). Although it is not known precisely why police chose to arrest John at this particular point in time (as the six tickets were long outstanding), his confinement had the effect of giving prosecutors leverage to secure his testimony. Prosecutors visited John in jail to offer a deal: testify against Brenda, and they would

1. grant him immunity from prosecution for having sex with Brenda;

2. agree to hear all of the six traffic cases against him at the same time; and

3. guarantee that all six sentences associated with those six cases would run concurrently, minimizing any time he might be ordered to spend behind bars.[29]

John finally complied and testified against Brenda at the final day of the preliminary exam in December 1994 as well as at trial the following spring.

Brenda's case was tried by jury in March 1995. Although the prosecutor only needed to prove that Brenda had engaged in "sexual penetration" without first disclosing her HIV status, he laid out his case by framing Brenda as a "carrier of death" who needed to be locked up:

> She had been told and discussed with her repeatedly that she should not have sex with another person unless she first told them of her HIV status. It was a condition that was made clear to her that . . . could in fact kill another individual, another human being. The facts will show . . . that she knew that she was literally a carrier of death in this situation. . . . It is the facts of this case, that the disease was a fatal one, that in fact she passed it onto another person.[30]

While these statements prompted a sustained defense objection preventing the prosecutor from making similarly inflammatory comments again, the image of a "carrier of death" had already been planted in jurors' minds, as had the prosecutor's false assertion that she had "passed" the disease on to the complainant (who did not contract HIV).

To make his case, the prosecutor echoed popular tropes of people living with HIV as sexually insatiable and predatory, describing Brenda as acting out of "self- fulfillment, someone that wanted to satisfy her own sexual desires."[31] Switching to the first person and a rough grammatical style, the prosecutor told the jury that Brenda did not tell her partners she was positive "because that means that he won't keep coming back to give me more sex and to satisfy my sexual desires."[32] Instead of basing his case on the potential HIV risk Brenda might pose to others in the community, the prosecutor relied on HIV stigma to make his case, painting her as a selfish "carrier of death." These stigmatizing statements served to create the illusion of harm in the place of evidence that Brenda had infected someone.

The prosecutor's explosive rhetoric mirrors the way many Americans view casual sex: reckless, irresponsible, and ultimately dangerous. HIV stigma serves to compound those social attitudes, creating an opportunity for a prosecutor seeking to paint Brenda as a threat to society. These views are further compounded for women with cognitive disabilities like Brenda, who have historically been portrayed as sexually threatening.[33] Notably, eight of the fifty-eight defendants convicted in Michigan (13.8 percent) and five of the forty-eight defendants convicted in Tennessee (10.4 percent) had or were suspected of having a mental illness or disability.[34]

Brenda never denied having sex with the complainant and maintained that she told him about her HIV status; specifically, she claimed that they had discussed the widespread newspaper coverage of her previous quarantine. Nonetheless, the jury found Brenda guilty. At sentencing, the judge declared that her irresponsibility while "carrying a deadly weapon" warranted taking her "out of circulation":

> She is carrying a deadly weapon with her and . . . she could go around killing people by her lack of concern. . . . I think she has a feeble understanding of how dangerous she can be in a public setting such as that in which she was placed by her so-called guardian. . . . I feel that, for the protection of our community, that I have to take [Brenda] out of circulation.[35]

The judge sentenced her to thirty-two months in prison.

While Brenda was one of thirteen defendants convicted under Michigan's HIV disclosure law before treatment was introduced in 1996, only one defendant faced charges under the 1994 Tennessee law during that time. Tennessee law differs from Michigan in two important ways, First, unlike under Michigan statute, prosecutors in Tennessee are not limited to prosecuting sexual exposures; the law provides for criminal charges in cases in which an HIV-positive defendant does one of three things:

1. *engages in "intimate contact"* with another person (defined as "the exposure of the body of one (l) person to a bodily fluid of another person in any manner that presents a significant risk of HIV transmission");

2. provides, donates, or *transfers "potentially infectious body fluids* . . . in any manner that presents a significant risk of HIV transmission"; or

3. sells or *shares a nonsterile syringe.*[36]

Second, the Tennessee law includes some consideration of risk—at least on paper. Both the first and second scenarios described under the law stipulates that intimate contact or exposure to bodily fluids must be done in a "manner that presents a significant risk of HIV transmission" in order to be criminally sanctioned.

On its face, the wording of Tennessee's statute would seem to rule out prosecuting cases in which the state could not prove that the defendant placed a person in harm's way. In practice, however, this has not been the case. This became apparent in 1995 when the first charges were filed under the newly enacted statute against a thirty-three-year-old White man named Ronald T. The details of Ronald's case were not well described in the court proceedings. However, the thin description that was presented in court speaks volumes about the standing of people living with HIV under Tennessee law. Ronald was arrested in June

1995 after breaking into the home of a woman and, according to court-room testimony, stealing a "ceramic eagle"[37]:

Judge: Tell me what you did?

Defendant: On June 9th I entered [a woman's] house without permission and unlawfully took a ceramic eagle.

Judge: And then what happened?

Defendant: After that I was apprehended by Sumner County police department, and there was a struggle between me and the officers, and that was basically it.

Judge: Did you spit on the officer?

Defendant: I was sprayed with Mace and stuff. I can't say what happened.

Judge: You feel it is in your best interests to enter this plea?

Defendant: Yes, ma'am.

Although he enters a no contest plea, Ronald does not fully corroborate the officer's story. He perfectly parrots the case presented by the prosecutor in some of his answers ("I entered [a woman's] home without permission and unlawfully took a ceramic eagle"), but when he is asked if he actually spat on the officer, he states that he was sprayed with Mace and "can't say what happened"—suggesting that he may not have fully believed the officer's account. Nonetheless, his plea was accepted and he was sentenced to three years in prison for spitting on the officer.

Ronald's case represents the first of five convicted cases between 1995 and 2010 in Tennessee involving an allegation that an HIV-positive defendant spit at, bit, or got blood on a police officer. Despite the fact that the law stipulates that a transfer of a body fluid must be shown to pose a "significant risk" of HIV transmission, the word *risk* is never so much as uttered in court in any of these cases. Although there has never been evidence that spitting is likely to transmit HIV, media coverage of Ronald's case noted that "the officer has so far tested negative for the virus, but must be tested periodically, officials said."[38]

If Tennessee law explicitly stipulates that there must be a "significant risk of transmission," why was risk never mentioned in these proceedings? Perhaps it is because many Americans mistakenly believe that HIV is transmitted through saliva. In 1985, for example, a *New York Times*–CBS poll found that 32 percent of Americans believed that kissing could transmit HIV.[39] In 2001, a Kaiser Family Foundation poll found a remarkably similar proportion—31 percent—of Americans still held this belief.[40] Five years later, the Kaiser Family Foundation found that the number of Americans who believed HIV could be transmitted through kissing had actually *increased* to 37 percent. Although polling data specific to Tennessee is not available, a 2015 survey of residents of a Southern neighbor, Georgia, found that 33 percent of respondents believed kisses can transmit HIV.[41]

Layered on top of this pervasive belief about HIV is the fact that these cases involved HIV-positive defendants engaging in what police characterize as assaultive behavior against law enforcement. In short, prosecutors may not have felt that they needed to prove that spitting, biting, or getting blood on the uniform of an officer posed a significant risk because many Americans would simply presume that having HIV necessarily makes these defendants a threat.

The cases against the defendants discussed in this section reveal an important distinction in how HIV stigma operates in American courtrooms.[42] Prosecutors and judges in Jeffrey's and Brenda's cases invoked *explicit stigma* in their rhetoric about HIV and people living with the disease. They explicitly labeled Brenda as a selfish "carrier of death" and Jeffrey as handing out "death notices." This rhetoric served to create the illusion of harm in the absence of evidence that these defendants endangered their partners. The case against Ronald, on the other hand, exhibits *implicit stigma,* an unspoken, unconscious form of bias. Although the prosecutor did not use the same kind of explosive rhetoric that the prosecutors in Brenda's or Jeffrey's case used, the case against Ronald implicitly relied on the notion that spitting poses a "significant risk" (a notion then disseminated to the public through the media, which reported that the officer in question "must be tested").

As the rest of the chapter will demonstrate, the stigma codified into case law through these early convictions had implications for years to come. Despite the introduction of effective treatment in 1996 that reshaped HIV into a chronic, manageable disease, the stigma of these early years appears to trump science.

"DEATH TO INNOCENT THIRD PARTIES": HIV ON TRIAL IN AN ERA OF EFFECTIVE TREATMENT

In 1999, Oakland County, Michigan, prosecutors charged Franklin C. for not telling a new roommate that he was HIV positive before they engaged in oral and anal sex. According to testimony, the complainant in the case did not ask Franklin, a thirty-four-year-old White gay man, about his HIV status until the following day. When the defendant then revealed his HIV status, the complainant "basically freak[ed]," returned home, found the defendant's HIV medication, and went to a hospital where he was prescribed post-exposure prophylaxis (a course of medicine that can reduce one's risk of contracting HIV after an exposure takes place). Hospital attendants also performed a rape kit and encouraged the complainant to contact the police.[43] Franklin was subsequently charged; he pleaded not guilty and exercised his right to trial by jury.

The police had secured a signed confession from Franklin nine months after the alleged incident, in which he wrote, "I didn't hide it. I didn't say I was. I had took meds and had meds all over my room, et cetera. I had thought he knew."[44] However, Franklin testified that he had, in fact, told him that he was HIV positive. His defense also aimed to counter the prosecution's claim that Franklin had exposed the complainant to "that deadly virus" by arguing that Franklin's viral load (the amount of virus in his blood) was "undetectable" and thus the risk of transmission was low.[45] As discussed in chapter 2, studies now definitively show that treatment renders people living with HIV virtually noninfectious.[46] However, although many had long suspected this to be the case, nearly a decade would pass after Franklin's trial before any major scientific statement on the subject (the "Swiss statement" of 2008).[47] Given the signed confession and a recent Michigan Supreme Court ruling upholding the statute's constitutionality, basing the defendant's defense on viral load may have been the only strategy apparent to his counsel.[48]

The prosecution argued that the defendant was obliged to disclose even if his viral load was undetectable: "It's like saying, 'Well, I'm only a little bit pregnant.' I mean, you're either pregnant or you're not pregnant."[49] In explaining his argument, the prosecutor directly quoted from the recent Michigan Court of Appeals decision in *People v. Jensen (On Remand)* (1998), which had affirmed the HIV disclosure law's constitutionality, in part, by ruling that not disclosing one's HIV status leads to "death to innocent third parties":

> If you know you have AIDS or you know you have HIV and you don't disclose, well, what does that achieve? "Only further dissemination of a lethal, incurable disease, in order to gratify the sexual or other physical pleasure of the already-infected individual." And I am reading off of something here because I don't want to get the words wrong ... "Indeed, the probable results accompanying the nondisclosure are fairly predictable: Death to innocent third parties."[50]

In only four of the fifty-eight Michigan cases (and five of the forty-three Tennessee cases) did the complainant or complainants allege to have contracted HIV from the defendant—less than 10 percent overall. Despite this, prosecutors and judges (and even the Michigan Court of Appeals) frequently invoked analogies to murder and death sentences throughout the study period.

Because jury trials were rare in these cases, the defense and prosecution rarely engaged in arguments over HIV in contesting the defendant's guilt; the vast majority of defendants pleaded guilty or no contest at the outset. In that sense, Franklin's case is quite rare. For example, none of the three defendants found guilty at trial in Tennessee raised any issues related to HIV in their defense; instead, those cases boiled down to whether or not the jury believed the complaining witness's testimony. In general, beyond securing medical records to prove that the defendant had been diagnosed as HIV positive, prosecutors rarely need more than the testimony of the complainant in order to press charges. For these reasons, the fact that Franklin's viral load was even brought up as a potential factor makes his case unique. His sentencing hearing, on the other hand, closely resembles the way that HIV was litigated in Michigan and Tennessee courtrooms.

When a felony defendant in Michigan is sentenced, the judge completes a spreadsheet containing an assortment of variables that assigns points based on the severity of the crime in question. The higher the score, the more time the defendant will spend behind bars or on probation. Although courtroom testimony directly showed that Franklin's partner tested HIV negative after the incident, the prosecutor argued that the offense variable (OV) for "physical injury to a victim" should be scored at 25 points, defined as "life threatening or permanent incapacitating injury occurred to a victim."[51] Despite defense objections, the judge agreed and added 25 points to his offense score: "I cannot think of anything more life-threatening."[52] Scolding Franklin for his "callous disregard for life," the judge ultimately sentenced Franklin to fifty-eight months to fifteen years in prison.[53]

Commonly used HIV tests have a window of up to six months between an exposure and the ability to detect an infection—although the CDC reports that 97 percent of people will develop detectable antibodies within three months after infection.[54] (Called antibody tests, these tests do not test for the virus but for the body's immune response to it.) Yet, in a dozen cases analyzed for this chapter, prosecutors and judges invoked the lingering possibility of infection, even in cases where the window period had clearly lapsed. This rhetoric served to create the illusion of harm in order to justify harsh punishment. For example,

Montcalm County, Michigan, officials sentenced Gerald C., a thirty-two-year-old White man, *eight months* after the last sexual encounter alleged by four women. The prosecutor had argued that "they're not out of the woods yet. They still may come down with this fatal disease."[55] The judge agreed, sentencing Gerald to thirty to forty-eight months in prison: "You have impacted, as [the prosecutor] has indicated, you know, potentially given four others a life sentence and that's something this Court cannot overlook."[56]

In Tennessee courtrooms, some victims made dramatic claims about the possibility of becoming infected years after having sex with the defendant. Tennessee law expressly allows crime victims to testify at sentencing to provide what is known as "impact testimony" about the impact the crime had on their life.[57] The inaccurate testimony of victims who had no medical training or expertise has affected sentencing in some cases. For example, Antonio F. pleaded guilty in 2004 in Davidson County Circuit Court to charges that he failed to disclose to a woman with whom he had an ongoing sexual relationship. Antonio was sentenced eight months after their relationship ended. The woman testified that she had so far tested negative, but added, "I can show up positive anywhere up to ten years."[58] The prosecutor drew on these statements to argue for harsh punishment, saying that the woman has "to go for the next ten years and wonder what is going to happen" with her life.[59] This argument appeared to hold sway over the judge, who ruled that Antonio would serve *ten years'* probation—by far the lengthiest probation term handed down in either state. As part of his sentence, the judge ordered him to pay for the woman to be tested *daily* during that ten-year period: "That means for ten years you are also going to be paying for . . . the amount of money it takes them to test every day. I don't care if they've got TennCare or other insurance. I want you to pay for their testing."[60]

Scott B., a thirty-six-year-old White male, pleaded guilty in 2007 in front of the same Davidson County Circuit Court judge, Judge Cheryl A. Blackburn., who had previously heard Antonio's case. Scott admitted having sex twice with a woman he was dating without disclosing his HIV-positive status. Four months after their sexual contact ended, the woman took the stand at Scott's sentencing hearing to claim that she would *never* know whether or not Scott infected her:

> *Complainant:* I'm still taking tests. I just got done with my three-month test, and I came back negative. But there are a lot more tests, I'm nowhere done. I'm nowhere in the clear. . . . I just got done with my three-month test and I have a six-month test and I have a year test and a two-year

> test. . . . I think I even have a five-year test if the two-year test comes back negative.
>
> *Prosecutor:* Okay. At any point can they say definitively that you do not have it?
>
> *Complainant:* I mean, there's never any time because people have showed up like ten, twelve, fifteen years later with it.[61]

She concluded her testimony by imploring Judge Blackburn to hand down the maximum sentence: "Right now my tests have come back negative, but that's not saying that they're always going to come back negative. And three years is not worth the value of a life."[62] The prosecutor parroted the woman's testimony, arguing that the woman's anxiety should render Scott ineligible for a diversion sentence that would have resulted in his record being expunged after a period of probation.[63] "The best case scenario is a lifetime of uncertainty for her," he argued.[64] "She's got to be worried about this and . . . got to tell everybody that she's going to have a relationship with about it, . . . Three years is not sufficient for that type of thing."[65] Ruling the crime "especially violent, shocking, reprehensible," Judge Blackburn agreed with the prosecutor, denying Scott both diversion and probation, and sentencing him to the maximum—three years in prison—for "destroy[ing] somebody's life."[66]

It is important to note that the lingering possibility of infection did not always sway judges to apply sentence enhancements. In 1998, for example, Chester B., a thirty-one-year-old Black man, pleaded guilty in Hamilton County, Tennessee, to charges that he failed to tell a woman he was having sex with that he was HIV positive. Although she had tested negative six months after the encounter, a representative from Chattanooga CARES, an AIDS service organization, testified that "we do advise people to continue testing for a full year."[67] The judge expressed concern that, although the woman "has been clear up to this point . . . we don't know that she's going to be permanently clear."[68] The judge even went on to compare the crime to murder: "It's, I guess, analogous to putting a couple of bullets in a revolver and spinning the chamber and pointing at somebody's head and pulling the trigger, because it's a very significant death, it does create a risk of death, not just serious bodily injury, but death."[69] Despite these explicitly stigmatizing comments (comparing HIV to a bullet that kills instantly, people living with HIV to weapons, and the risk of transmission to the one in six of Russian roulette), the judge rejected applying the sentence enhancement factor for putting another person at a risk of death. However, he did so because he believed that putting the victim at risk of death is "part of the underlying offense"—thus, applying the aggravating factor would be "double-dipping."[70] Although the judge did not apply that particular sentence enhancement factor, he did deny Chester probation because he believed the HIV exposure law needed "teeth" to work.[71] He sentenced Chester to four years in prison.

In both Michigan and Tennessee courts, one way that prosecutors and judges frequently made sense of the criminal cases before them was to compare HIV to a lethal weapon. In Chester's case, the judge was merely ad-libbing in front the courtroom, presumably in order to shame the defendant and communicate the threat he saw in the defendant—similar to the judge in Brenda's case remarking that she was "carrying a deadly weapon." But in some cases, that metaphor became material during sentencing. Valerie J., a fifty-four-year-old heterosexual White woman, was convicted in both Clare and Isabella Counties, Michigan, in 2010 for not disclosing her status to the same male partner. In one of those counties, the judge and prosecutor debated whether they should score the offense variable marked for "aggravated use of a weapon" at 20 points, defined as "the victim was subjected or exposed to a harmful biological substance, harmful biological device":[72]

> *Judge:* Any comment, [prosecutor], on OV two? That's like the use of a weapon . . . . Do you think it fits?
>
> *Prosecutor:* I looked at that and I think it does. I looked up the definition of the harmful biological device. . . . Yeah, it says it means a bacteria, virus or other micro-organism or toxic substance derived from or produced from an organism that can be used to cause death, injury or disease in humans, animals or plants. So I do think that that fits.[73]

The question echoes a controversial case that played out earlier that same year in which an HIV-positive Michigan man in Macomb County was charged under a law intended to combat bioterrorism after he bit a neighbor.[74] Indeed, Valerie's defense attorney specifically cited the judge's ruling in the Macomb County case, which dismissed the bioterrorism charge on the grounds that being HIV positive in itself does not constitute the unlawful manufacture or possession of a harmful biological substance.[75] The Clare County prosecutor countered, "If we want to talk about aggravated use, the fact that she continued to have sexual relations . . . each time, placing him in risk of loss of his life, I think it's an appropriate scoring."[76] While he noted his respect for his Macomb County colleague's opinion, Clare County judge Thomas Evans agreed with the prosecutor and ruled that "the bodily fluids; specifically, the vaginal fluids of an HIV positive woman do contain a potentially harmful biological substance and, therefore, the Court does find the award of the points is appropriate." The judge in Isabella County agreed. Valerie was sentenced to eleven months in jail in Isabella County and seventeen to forty-eight months in prison in Clare County.

These cases reveal how crime victims and prosecutors can influence the way that judges utilize the various sentencing levers at their disposal. In Antonio's case, the victim's erroneous claim that she must wait ten years to definitively know whether he infected her with HIV appears to have directly influenced the ten-year probation term handed down by the judge. In Scott's and Chester's cases, judges relied on the victims' potential infection—at least in part—as a rationale for denying them probation. In Valerie's case, the prosecutor's argument that HIV should be considered a weapon increased her presumptive sentence. In the end, however, these cases reveal the discretionary power of judges in HIV exposure and nondisclosure cases to interpret technical matters that can directly influence sentencing.

"THAT'S NOT IN THE STATUTE": PUNISHING THE ILLUSION OF HARM

Billy T., a forty-one-year-old Black man, was convicted in Washtenaw County, Michigan, in 2001 of not disclosing his HIV status to a woman with whom he had sex after they had smoked crack together one evening. The complainant initially told the police that she was raped— "the victim of a carjacking, and a kidnaping by two unknown Black men."[77] However, she later admitted that she had fabricated the story and that she had, in fact, gone willingly to the defendant's house seeking drugs and sex. Billy admitted to having sex without telling the woman of his HIV status, but he said that he believed he had abided by the law because he used a condom. Despite serious inconsistencies in the woman's account, Billy pleaded guilty to both criminal sexual conduct charges and a felony HIV nondisclosure charge.

At sentencing, the prosecutor argued for Billy to be sentenced at the top end of the guidelines: twenty-eight months. His defense attorney argued that Billy should be treated with leniency because he took precautions to avoid transmitting the virus. To make this case, he repeatedly tried to distinguish Billy's case from a more egregious, hypothetical case: "He wasn't just some predatory crack-head out there doing whatever it was that he felt and that—to hell with the consequences." Billy not only used a condom, but his viral load was undetectable; he was not "in full-blown AIDS status and going about knowingly infecting people."[78] The prosecutor disagreed, arguing that risk is irrelevant under Michigan law:

> The fact that the argument is being made that [the defendant] thought that he was adequately protecting the Complainant, because he was wearing a condom. Well, that's not in the statute. It doesn't say if you wear a condom it's only a misdemeanor or—or anything like that.[79]

The judge came close to acknowledging that the risk of transmission might matter to the case, but only in order to dismiss defense claims that Billy's use of a condom made him less blameworthy: "While that might make—make some sense, the risk is so overwhelming in any regard. . . . You don't need a statute to tell you that this is behavior which is just absolutely reprehensible."[80] Arguing that Billy "did manipulate and take advantage of the victim," the judge agreed with the prosecutor's recommendation and sentenced Billy to twenty-eight to seventy-two months in prison.[81]

The scientific literature available at the time, however, showed that the risk in Billy's case was far from "overwhelming." One widely cited study published in 1999, for example, estimated condoms to be 87 percent effective at preventing heterosexual HIV transmission.[82] Another widely cited study published in 1998 estimated the per-incidence risk of male-to-female vaginal transmission *without a condom* to be roughly 1 in 1,000.[83] Thus, had the judge consulted the scientific literature available at the time, he would have discovered that contemporary scientists estimated the theoretical risk of male-to-female HIV transmission during condom-protected vaginal intercourse to be 1 in 7,500. Today, more recent studies have demonstrated that Billy's undetectable viral load would have even further reduced the risk of transmission. Even using the conservative estimate that HIV treatment reduces the risk of heterosexual transmission by 96 percent, one could estimate the risk of transmission in Billy's case to be roughly 1 in 190,000—a risk so low as to be negligible. Given even the evidence available to the sentencing judge in 2001, describing a 1 in 7,500 risk of transmission as "overwhelming" appears far-fetched.

While there were many cases in which the level of risk was arguably small to negligible, some might contend that any level of risk is sufficient grounds for prosecution. The most persuasive examples of the *illusion of harm* punished under HIV disclosure and exposure laws would be cases in which the complainant was exposed to no risk at all. Such is the case against Melissa G., a twenty-three-year-old White woman arrested in Cass County, Michigan, in 2009 after police raided the strip club where she was employed. The prosecutor justified the raid by describing the club as a "dangerous common nuisance due to ongoing drug activity, prostitution and repeated acts of lewd behavior."[84] Initially charging Melissa with prostitution and drug-related offenses, the prosecutor tacked on felony HIV disclosure charges after it was discovered that she was HIV positive. In order to minimize time spent in jail, Melissa accepted a plea deal. During an otherwise routine plea hearing, the detective testified as to what allegedly transpired between Melissa and her client, a confidential informant:

> *Prosecutor:* Let me focus you particularly on a situation involving a penetration with his nose or nasal area of his face.
>
> *Detective:* He would pay her twenty dollars a song for a lap dance, and on this occasion she was topless, she began dancing, started grinding on him, trying to arouse his penis. At one point she exposed her vagina area to him and placed it on the tip of his nose and began grinding on his nose with her vagina.
>
> *Prosecutor:* Did the confidential informant indicate that his nose actually went inside or penetrated her vaginal area?
>
> *Detective:* Yes, it did.[85]

There are many conceivable pathways for HIV to be transmitted during intimate contact; nasal-vaginal penetration is not among them. Yet at sentencing, the prosecutor alleged that Melissa's actions "clearly threatened the health and safety of specific individuals as well as the general public. The disease she carried is terminal."[86] Judge Michael E. Dodge sentenced Melissa to five months in jail and she will be labeled a felon for the rest of her life.

In Tennessee, spitting and biting prosecutions continued well into the study period. Although the majority of these cases (five out of seven) involved alleged altercations between defendants and police officers, this was not always the case. In July 2010, David S. attempted suicide. David, a thirty-six-year-old White gay man, was found in a "bathtub full of blood" and taken to a local hospital for treatment and monitoring.[87] His same-sex life partner came to visit him in the hospital, and an argument broke out. A hospital attendant demanded that David's life partner leave, at which point David allegedly became very angry and pushed the attendant into a wall. (Although the court records do not make clear the basis for the argument, there are numerous accounts during this period of hospitals denying same-sex partners access to their lovers' hospital rooms.[88]) When the attendant then grabbed David to defend himself, David bit the attendant on the forearm. Hospital staff called the police, who arrived at the emergency room just after midnight that evening; David was subsequently charged under Tennessee's felony HIV exposure law.[89]

At sentencing, his publicly appointed defense attorney stated that they entered a plea on the charge "because of the proof against my client, and quite frankly, because of his previous criminal history."[90] David's criminal history that included assaulting a police officer and lewd and lascivious conduct—a charge that led to being registered in Tennessee as a sex offender. Despite the fact that Tennessee statute explicitly requires demonstrating a "significant risk of transmission," contesting the charges at trial could have resulted in much more severe penalties being imposed because of his criminal history. In this sense, David is like many defendants in the United States who enter pleas rather than contest their charges, even in cases where they do not believe themselves to be guilty. Poor defendants like David may do so because they cannot afford to post bail, meaning that they must remain in jail for months or even years as they await trial; a guilty plea can offer the prospect of a timelier release (albeit on probation and with a criminal record).[91]

In spite of David's plea, the prosecutor argued that the judge should sentence David to prison, denying him probation because his supposedly impending death would make rehabilitation all but impossible: "There's a lack of potential for rehabilitation due to the fact that this man has the sword of Damocles hanging over his head now."[92] When David took the stand, the prosecutor went so far as to allege that the defendant also exposed the victim to hepatitis and methicillin-resistant *Staphylococcus aureus* (MRSA). However, he seemed to have a shaky understanding of either disease or the defendant's medical record:

Prosecutor: And did you also say that in addition to—you said you did not have the hepatitis, correct? . . . .

Defendant: No, sir, I was tested in 2005 and the test was negative.

Prosecutor: Negative, I'm sorry. . . . Okay. But you did have MRSA, is that correct?

Defendant: MRSA, sir, is an air-born virus almost like anthrax. It's in hospitals, courtrooms, schoolrooms. It only affects people with a weakened immune system and the elderly.

Prosecutor: I understand, but it can be transmuted [sic] by bodily fluid, too, can it not? And that's another risk this man is facing as well, correct?

Defendant: Whenever I was tested at [the hospital] I was treated for it with a drug called—uh . . .

Prosecutor: It's basically a flesh eating staph infection, isn't it?

Defendant: I was treated and successfully. It dissipated at [the hospital].

As David pointed out to the prosecutor, MRSA is a common infection among the elderly and hospital patients. However, a study published in *Annals of Internal Medicine* in 2008 cited a series of cases involving HIV-positive gay men in U.S. urban centers.[93] Gay men's health advocates criticized media outlets who sensationalized the study's findings with headlines declaring that gay men were "spreading" a "flesh-eating super bug." Activists described such reports as stigmatizing because they implicitly blamed gay men for "spreading" the disease, because they overemphasized a rare presentation of the disease (necrotizing fasciitis), and because they failed to clearly communicate that MRSA is generally treatable.[94] Although Tennessee law makes no mention of MRSA, the prosecutor's rhetoric suggests he may have been nonetheless attempting to stain David's case with the stigma of both HIV and MRSA.

Like the vast majority of cases brought under both Michigan and Tennessee law, no medical evidence was presented to link biting to a significant risk of transmitting HIV as seemingly required under the law. Nonetheless, the judge viewed David as potentially homicidal, noting that "an intentional biting, under the circumstances, you know, I think this similar thing sometimes have been brought as attempted murder."[95] He measured the seriousness of the offense, in part, by the anxiety inflicted on the bitten hospital attendant and by the possibility that, despite nearly a year having passed since the incident, he might yet become infected with HIV: "It's an act of exposing someone to a very serious incurable condition, and certainly the fact that the victim . . . has been in a state of anxiety for a year already, and maybe will have to have some issues of anxiety for another several months."[96] Citing these concerns, the judge denied David probation and sentenced him to three years in prison.

Taken together, the convictions of Billy, Melissa, and David reveal the argument that HIV-specific criminal laws protect the public from harm to be false. Although extreme in their tragic absurdity, these cases reveal the contours of HIV criminalization in America: that a woman can be made into a felon for allowing a man's nose to penetrate her, that a suicide patient can be imprisoned for biting a hospital attendant, and that heterosexual sex with a condom can be ruled an "overwhelming" risk. Underneath the illusion of harm lies a naked, uncomfortable truth: the punishable offense in these cases is merely being HIV positive.

PUNISHING HIV

Although prosecutors and judges routinely compared HIV to a death sentence and defendants to murderers, the research for this chapter uncovered only one death associated with a criminal case. William K., a fifty-two-year-old White gay man, was convicted in Allegan County, Michigan, in 2004 after being accused of not disclosing his HIV status to a casual male sex partner before engaging in receptive anal intercourse. At sentencing, William told the court that he was unaware that the law existed and that he thought he was protecting his partner by using a condom. Unsympathetic, the judge suggested that William might have killed his partner.

> *Defendant:* I had no idea that the law even existed, and I know that ignorance is not a justification of it but I did what I thought I was supposed to do. We did it safely and I thought that was the way it was supposed to be done
>
> *Judge:* It never occurred to you that you might kill the man?
>
> *Defendant:* I was recently diagnosed. I mean we practiced safe sex which is basically the only thing you can do.
>
> *Judge:* Well, I guess if you knew what you had when you did this there's always a huge risk that you could infect somebody with a horrible disease.[97]

As in so many of the proceedings brought under Michigan and Tennessee law, the judge introduced no evidence to support the claim that there was a "huge risk" to his partner—ignoring the contemporary research that he might have turned to in order to estimate the odds of transmission from a receptive to insertive anal sex partner while using a condom (roughly 1 in 12,820, using estimates published in 1999).[98] Nonetheless, in August 2004, the judge sentenced him to twenty-four months' probation.

Nearly a year later, William was charged with two counts of violating his probation. His alleged violation: "The first would be Count 1, violation of Term #3 in that the defendant failed to provide a truthful report to [his probation officer], specifically by lying about his attendance at treatment. Count 2, violation of Term 3.3 in that the defendant failed to attend his specified treatment as directed."[99] In short, William was arrested for not seeing his therapist and for telling his probation officer that he had. While such a minor infraction might appear petty to those unfamiliar with the criminal justice system, technical violations such as

William's can result in a judge revoking the defendant's probation and ordering incarceration.[100] On August 5, 2005, William was arraigned on probation violation charges; he was nonresponsive when the judge asked him a question, and then later complained that he did not feel well and asked to sit throughout the proceedings.[101] The prosecutor successfully argued for a "significant bond" (set at $10,000) to keep William behind bars while he awaited a contested hearing on the charges.[102]

At the contested hearing, William represented himself (what's known as pro se representation) and appeared ready to plead guilty to the second count, but he explained that he had trouble getting in touch with his provider—complicated by the fact that his preferred provider was moving away: "It was hard for me to get a hold of him. And so would call and leave him messages and then not get returned phone calls back. . . . I didn't even know he was leaving. Now I have to find somebody else who is really good at what they do." The judge appeared frustrated with William's hedging on pleading guilty—telling him repeatedly that "I don't care." William, for his part, appeared confused as to what was happening and what his legal options were at the hearing:

> *Judge:* Well, let's put it this way [William]. Either you missed treatments that you were supposed to go to or you didn't. You can either plead guilty or not guilty, *I don't care* which way you go. I just need to have a definitive statement. . . .
>
> *Defendant:* Why didn't they check with him?
>
> *Judge:* Look, I can't answer you. I don't know anything about it, period. I don't know whether you went, whether you didn't go, all I can either take your plea and you admit that you didn't go or we have a hearing and I'll decide if they have evidence that says you didn't go. You've got your choice. What do you want to do?
>
> *Defendant:* Can I change the hearing later or not?
>
> *Judge:* No. If you have a hearing—you're here today for a hearing. We're either going to have a hearing or you're going to enter a plea, one of the other. *I don't care* which.
>
> *Defendant:* Can I plea bargain something?
>
> *Judge:* Talk to the prosecutor. Go ahead, talk to him. *I don't care.* (italics added)[103]

After a repeated back and forth with the prosecutor, they failed to come to an agreement and William declared that he wished to contest the charges. Although he could have ordered a continuance to give William time to sort out his legal issues, the judge immediately opened the hearing and called William's probation officer to the stand. After the prosecutor briefly questioned the officer, the judge then turned to William to present his defense.

> *Judge:* [William], it's your opportunity to present testimony or evidence. Do you have any testimony you want to present?
>
> *Defendant:* I guess I'm just a little confused.
>
> *Judge:* Well, you said you wanted a hearing, you weren't going to plead, we're having the hearing. You have testimony against you. The prosecutor has put his case in.
>
> *Defendant:* The other—I'm sorry. The other gentleman told me that we would have a trial and do all that kind of stuff.
>
> *Judge:* We are having a trial right now. This is the day set for your contested hearing.
>
> *Defendant:* Well, he told me we would have it next month.
>
> *Judge: I don't care* what he told you. We're not having it next month, we're having it today. (italics added)

William continued by explaining that, while he did miss some sessions, he was sick and it was difficult to get a hold of his counselor. The judge promptly found William guilty of violating his probation: "Now I don't know that you did so because you're a mean, evil person, you probably were sick but it doesn't matter, you violated the terms and conditions of your probation order so you're guilty as charged."[104]

Bond was continued at $10,000, leaving William incarcerated as he awaited his September 16, 2005, sentencing. William would not appear again in court, however; he died eleven days later, on August 29, just days before he was to be sentenced for not seeing his therapist.[105] He was pronounced dead upon arrival at a regional hospital; the official causes of death listed on his death certificate are cryptococcal meningitis (a fungal infection associated with untreated HIV) and "advanced AIDS/HIV."[106] Although a medical doctor might say that William died of AIDS-related complications, sociologically speaking, the legal proceedings against him seem at the very least to be a complicating factor. Although the judge accused William of potentially killing his partner, it was William who would ultimately not survive the allegations.

. . .

William's tragic case reflects many of the critical problems faced by the poor when interacting with the American criminal justice system—particularly how technical probation violations can create a vicious cycle of supervision and punishment. Unable to afford to hire a lawyer to represent him, William appeared to stumble through the probation violation hearings, unaware of how they would unfold. But while William's case resembles many non-HIV related cases, his death reveals how HIV can compound these factors for people living with HIV. If the goal of probation was to rehabilitate William and promote his well-being, the system clearly failed.

More broadly speaking, William's case reveals the bluntness of the law as a tool for managing social problems. William was ordered to see a health care provider—and for failing to do so, he faced being locked up. As studies on addiction have demonstrated, punishment is not an effective way to handle medical problems.[107] Health care providers are encouraged to demonstrate compassion, not scorn.[108] The courtroom is a place for punishment, the hospital a place for recuperation. The tools for one job appear not well-suited to accomplish the goals of another.

As this chapter demonstrates, in order to put HIV on trial in American courtrooms, judges and prosecutors translate HIV from the language of medicine (risk, treatment) to the language of the law (harm, punishment). Judges and prosecutors conduct this translation through the language they use to discuss and interpret the cases. HIV is not a virus or a chronic disease, but a "deadly weapon." Defendants are not merely people living with HIV; they are potential killers. These analogies assign blame and establish victimhood in a system that deals in prisons and handcuffs rather than hospitals and pills.

The language used in court by victims, prosecutors, and judges is not just meaningless banter: their implicitly and explicitly stigmatizing rhetoric creates the illusion of harm in these cases, a veil under which prosecution and conviction seem the logical response to the defendant's actions. The words used to describe and represent HIV ("a death sentence"), the risk of transmitting HIV ("Russian roulette"), and HIV-positive defendants ("carrier of death") matter. That such highly stigmatizing and woefully ignorant views can shape the court's decisions is inextricably tied to broader political and power struggles in American society. For example, that so many Americans are so ignorant of HIV is at least partially a result of impoverished sexual education standards in many states. It is also the product of a media landscape in which HIV is represented as a disease impacting the "4-H club"—thus mitigating the need for many Americans to better understand it. If all the people in the courtroom were required to discuss HIV in medically accurate terms, it would be far more difficult to build a criminal case against many of the defendants.

The translation achieved through this stigmatizing discourse from "sickness" to "badness" is what sociologists would describe as a "moral passage."[109] It is not unique to HIV; other conditions, such as excessive drinking, have been relabeled as disease and in some contexts as crime (when pregnant, for example).[110] This transformation from disease to crime explains why medical evidence was largely irrelevant in trial courts. Indeed, in only one criminal case did a prosecutor or judge describe HIV in medically accurate terms as a manageable or chronic disease.[111] This reflects the fundamentally different ways that prosecutors and doctors make sense of the social world: whereas the prosecutors assign blame, promote justice, and impose due punishment, doctors are supposed to remain neutral, promote health, and offer treatment. What might seem like compelling evidence to a doctor (viral load, condom use, and so on) may seem entirely irrelevant to a prosecutor—and vice versa.

To better explain the implications of this moral passage, the next chapter explores which communities are being prosecuted and convicted under HIV-specific criminal laws. Although activists charge that the enforcement of these laws follows discriminatory patterns based on race and sexuality, the data tell a more complicated story.

CHAPTER 6

Victim Impact

*HIV Threat and the Disparate Impact of
HIV Criminalization*

During the summer of 2014, an explosive arrest was splashed across
Midwestern newspapers: Michael J., then twenty-two years old, stood
accused of exposing six male partners to HIV without telling them he
was HIV positive; two allegedly contracted the disease. A young Black
man in a conservative county in Missouri, Michael and the accusations
against him quickly became a flashpoint for racial and sexual politics.
The fact that Michael went by the highly racialized name "Tiger Mandingo" on gay dating social networking applications made the case
immediate fodder for virulently racist White supremacy websites that
bashed both Michael and his partners for engaging in "bestiality."[1]
News media frequently referred to that name while featuring sexually
charged pictures of Michael downloaded from social media. A critic of
such coverage lamented, "Arrested and charged in an overwhelmingly
white community where anti-gay beliefs are widespread, the gay, black
'Tiger' never stood a chance."[2]

Activists charged that Michael's case demonstrated how HIV exposure
and disclosure laws disproportionately impacted gay Black men. Eighty-
nine Black gay men—including writers, activists, and academics—penned
an open letter to Michael to express their solidarity with him in the days
before his trial was set to begin in May 2015. In the letter, the authors
pointed out that "legally requiring disclosure privileges the lives of White
people not living with HIV over Black people who are living with HIV.
These laws feed into stereotypes that assume Black gay men are irrespon-

sible and hypersexual."[3] The fact that Michael was set to be tried just ten miles away from a town that had come to symbolize racial injustice in America, Ferguson, only exacerbated the sense among activists that Michael was the target of a racist and homophobic witch hunt.[4]

Critics noted that of the fifty-one potential jurors, "about half" raised their hand when asked whether they believed being gay was a choice.[5] Moreover, court transcripts reveal that seventeen potential jurors stated in court that they believed being gay was a sin.[6] Although only one of those seventeen was ultimately selected, the prevalence of homophobic attitudes confirmed the belief of some critics that the case was stacked against the defendant—especially because all but one of the selected jury panel was White.

At trial, charges of racism ratcheted up as the prosecutor built a case that seemed to reinforce racist, predatory images of Black male sexuality.[7] For example, despite the fact that Missouri's law is extremely broadly written so as to punish a wide range of HIV exposures regardless of risk, the prosecutor repeatedly raised allegations that the defendant refused to use condoms because his penis was too large. In his opening statements, the prosecutor stated: "He had asked the defendant to wear a condom. . . . The defendant refused, claiming, falsely, that they don't make condoms in his size and so they had unprotected intercourse."[8] Regarding another count involving a different complaining witness, the prosecutor recounted a similar story: "He provided [Michael] a condom and said here, put this on. The defendant complained it was too tight and then claimed it broke and took it off."[9] He went on to describe especially lurid details about the encounters, including some that bore no relationship to HIV or its transmission risk, such as "dipping that HIV mixed semen in [the complainant's] face."[10]

In some ways, Michael's case resembles those reviewed in the previous chapter. For example, complainants reported testing an extraordinary, unnecessary number of times to confirm their HIV-negative status, while HIV was a framed as a "deadly" disease (although the defense countered this characterization). What is exceptional about Michael's case, however, is not the role that HIV figured in his prosecution but the way that race loomed over his trial. Race provided a lens through which observers interpreted the case's particularities, leading many to conclude his conviction was a foregone conclusion under a legal system that overtly discriminated against Black gay men.

Michael's case, of course, was not the first HIV-related prosecution to be clouded by accusations of racism. Perhaps the most widely reported such case involved a nineteen-year-old New York defendant, Nushawn W., accused in 1996 of infecting nearly a dozen young women—many of them White and some of them underage (described in chapter 2). As New York does not have an HIV-specific criminal law, Nushawn was tried and convicted under criminal sexual conduct laws. A book examining the media spectacle surrounding his case, *Notorious H.I.V.*, reveals how the politics of race, class, and sexuality fomented the public outcry.[11]

Years later, as Nushawn was approaching his expected release from prison in 2008, New York correctional officials used a state law enacted in 2007, the Sex Offender Management and Treatment Act, to justify keeping Nushawn behind bars *indefinitely* under a program known as "civil confinement" (briefly described in chapter 1). Although keeping criminals behind bars long after their sentences have ended would seem in conflict with constitutional protections against double jeopardy, the Supreme Court ruled in *Kansas v. Hendricks* (1997) that indefinitely detaining sex offenders was not punishment at all; rather, "civil confinement" amounted to a kind of "treatment" and thus was constitutionally sound.[12] Nushawn was still behind bars at time of publication, after a New York State Court of Appeals decision in 2016 rejected his bid for freedom.[13]

Nushawn's ongoing legal battle and Michael's sentence to thirty years in prison would appear to reinforce critics' arguments that states aggressively fight to keep young HIV-positive Black men behind bars for the majority of their lives. This chapter attempts to bring science to bear on these claims of racial injustice by evaluating evidence of discrimination under state HIV exposure and disclosure laws. Specifically, this chapter analyzes an original dataset of convictions under six state HIV-specific laws to address several questions. First, are Black men—gay or straight—disproportionately convicted under HIV exposure and disclosure laws?[14] What factors might be driving such a disparity, if it exists? Second, when Black men are convicted under these laws, are the sentences handed down by judges more severe than the sentences imposed on White men? What can social science tell us about which factors might shape any observed sentencing disparities?

This chapter wrestles with these questions in order to offer a specific diagnosis for how race, gender, and sexuality shape the application of HIV-specific criminal laws. With a more precise account of how the law is enforced against different communities, policy experts might be better positioned to evaluate different reform proposals—and activists might better lobby for them. The chapter begins with an analysis of the demographic characteristics of defendants convicted under HIV disclosure and exposure laws. Then, the chapter turns to sentencing data to examine whether there are disparities in how particular groups are punished under the law.

EVIDENCE OF DISCRIMINATION? UNDERSTANDING FORM, BASIS, AND CONTEXT

Over the past decade, stark, depressing statistics from social research have galvanized some Americans to consider the devastating impact of mass incarceration on communities of color. One 2004 paper, for example, found that nearly 60 percent of Black men who were born between 1965 and 1969 and who dropped out of high school went to prison by 1999—compared to just 11 percent of their White male peers.[15] Advocates for change have harnessed these figures to argue that mass incarceration operates as a new form of Jim Crow, maintaining racial inequality through imprisonment.[16] In response, social scientists have sought to identify discriminatory policies and practices that might be to blame for these dramatic differences between Blacks and Whites in America. This section introduces three key ways to categorize discrimination that can help sharpen our understanding: the *form* of discrimination, the *basis* for discrimination, and the *context* for discrimination.

Form: To help researchers and policy makers make sense of discrimination under the law, scholars sometimes distinguish between disparate-treatment and disparate-impact discrimination.[17] Though this distinction is mostly invoked in civil law proceedings (since discrimination is generally a matter for civil rather than criminal courts in the United States), there are parallels under the criminal law. Disparate treatment is what most Americans probably think of when they hear the term *discrimination;* it refers to practices that explicitly treat groups differently. A recent example of disparate-treatment discrimination under the criminal law is New York City's controversial stop-and-frisk program under which police stopped Black and Latino youth more frequently than White youth (studies show that African Americans were stopped 23 percent more often than Whites under the program).[18]

Disparate-impact discrimination, on the other hand, is due to practices that are not explicitly related to race, gender, or some other legally protected identity but nonetheless result in a disparate outcome. Perhaps among the most notorious disparate-impact criminal policies were the

1986 federal sentencing guidelines for crack cocaine versus powdered cocaine, resulting in a 100:1 sentencing disparity.[19] The sentencing guidelines made no mention of the race of the person arrested for possessing either drug, nor were judges accused of treating Black defendants differently under those guidelines. Instead, the discrimination resulted from racially patterned drug use: because African Americans are more likely to be arrested and convicted for possessing crack cocaine than its more expensive, powdered cousin, the more extreme penalties for crack cocaine were more frequently imposed against Black men—a disparate impact.

Basis: In their quest to track down evidence of discrimination under the law, scholars have paid close attention to the demographic characteristics of defendants—particularly when it comes to sentencing. For example, scholars have examined whether older or younger defendants are sentenced more harshly (the evidence suggests no difference) as well as whether their gender might play a role (the evidence suggests women are sentenced more leniently than men).[20] Studies have also put these two variables together with race to analyze whether there might be what social scientists call an "interaction" between them; although age alone is not associated with harsher sentencing, the evidence suggests that young Black and Latino men are sentenced more harshly than young White men.[21]

Although much less common, some studies have also examined whether the characteristics of crime victims—rather than just defendants—might be associated with disparate criminal justice outcomes. The most convincing evidence to suggest that victim characteristics might play a role in shaping the application of law comes from studies that examine death penalty cases. One famous study found that Black defendants accused of killing White victims were more likely to receive the death penalty than were Black defendants accused of killing Black victims.[22] These findings reveal that who the crime victim is might play just as important a role as who the defendant is in determining how courts punish criminal defendants.

Context: Finally, scholars have also examined the context for discrimination—specifically, the various points along the path from arrest to conviction to sentencing and beyond at which a defendant might experience discrimination involving distinct authorities. These studies recognize that the law is not a machine that processes people through the criminal justice system objectively; rather, the law in practice is the sum of a range of human decisions that can be highly subjective. To understand how various human decisions impact how the law is enforced, social scientists look at patterns in police arrests, prosecutorial decisions in charging defendants, jury decisions in convicting, and judicial decisions in sentencing. For clarity's sake, here are examples of four scholarly findings of discrimination from each of these categories:

1. One study found that *police* policies result in more African Americans being *arrested* for drug use in Seattle.[23]

2. One study found that *prosecutors* choose to upgrade *charges* against Black homicide defendants more often than other defendants, especially in cases involving White crime victims.[24]

3. One study found that mock *jurors* were more likely to *convict* hypothetical Black defendants of rape in cases where their victim was White.[25]

4. One study found that *judges* more frequently depart from the guidelines to impose harsher *sentences* on Blacks, males, and offenders with low levels of education.[26]

These studies represent the tip of the iceberg of the social science research into discrimination. Their presentation here highlights how social scientists have thought about what evidence of discrimination looks like under the law.

A precise diagnosis of the form, basis, and context of discrimination is necessary in order to offer the most effective prescription for reform. The title of the chapter, "Victim Impact," reveals the focus of this analysis: how and why the victim characteristics in HIV exposure and nondisclosure cases shape the application of the law. However, the analysis that follows also considers other variables. In order to make sense of these data, however, it is important to look at how HIV exposure and nondisclosure cases come to court in the first place.

NAMING, BLAMING, COMPLAINING:
UNDERSTANDING THE ORIGINS OF HIV
EXPOSURE AND DISCLOSURE CASES

Prosecutor: And what did you do in your room?

Complainant: I went around the room looking, you know, for any evidence of medications.

Prosecutor: Did you find any?

Complainant: Yes.

Prosecutor: Do you remember what the medications were or whose name was on the medications?

Complainant: Yes.

Prosecutor: Whose medications were they?

Complainant: Franklin [C.'s].[27]

When Franklin told the complainant, his roommate, that he was HIV positive the day after they had consensual sex, his roommate wondered if it was some kind of "sick joke."[28] So when Franklin left for work later that morning, the complainant searched the house looking for medications for HIV in their shared residence. He testified that he found several prescription bottles, wrote down the names of the drugs, and went to the closest pharmacy to confirm their purpose. Upon confirming their purpose, he testified that he felt "really nauseous . . . like I was just going to like die."[29]

He immediately walked to a friend's house nearby and asked her to drive him to the hospital, where he was admitted to the emergency room. At the ER, he testified that the health care providers "started to take like a sample of—you know, like of my hair, looked at my rectum, and blood work."[30] Although the sex was consensual, ER doctors performed a rape kit exam on the defendant; they also started him on a prescription of post-exposure prophylaxis, a treatment regimen that can reduce the risk of contracting the disease if begun within seventy-two hours after an exposure. Two social workers from a local rape crisis center quickly arrived, who ultimately brought the complainant to the rape crisis center, where he would stay for several weeks. He went to the police station the next morning to file a complaint.

Franklin's case is unusual in some respects. For example, as discussed in chapter 5, his defense team (unsuccessfully) argued that his undetectable viral load should be considered as a mitigating factor. However, his case is illustrative in a chapter on discrimination because it reveals the complicated set of factors that can influence someone to decide to file a criminal complaint with police. As the witness's testimony reveals, medical providers responded to his case as if it were sexual assault, doctors performed a rape kit exam, and representatives from a local rape crisis center showed up to support him. These interventions may well have helped to mold the complainant's perspective of the events that transpired.

Sociolegal scholars refer to this transformative process from an unrealized injury to the decision to make a formal legal claim as "naming, blaming, and claiming."[31] While sociolegal scholars theorized this transformation in relation to tort law disputes, this process is nonetheless relevant to criminal HIV exposure and disclosure cases because of the unusual characteristic of the offense: potential complainants do not generally realize a crime has been committed until long after the sexual encounter is finished. Complainants in HIV exposure cases must first view themselves as victims of an injurious offense ("naming"); they then must place explicit blame for that offense on their sexual partner ("blaming"). Finally, they must decide to report their partners to law enforcement by filing a criminal complaint. Although sociolegal scholars studying civil law disputes refer to this step as "claiming," this chapter calls it "complaining" under the criminal law to refer to the formal transformation of the individual filing the complaint into a criminal *complainant.*

It is not always possible to know all the factors that shaped every step in this transformation into complainant. However, because of the nature of these cases, a potential complainant's discovery that a prior sexual partner is HIV positive typically prompts the naming step. Franklin's case reveals how prescription drug medications can play an important role in this step. Although Franklin disclosed his status earlier that morning, the prescription drug bottle played the role of cold, hard evidence that set in motion a process that ultimately led to his partner filing criminal charges.

There are exceptions to this description of naming, most notably in cases involving sexual assault and prostitution; in them, the state generally files charges unrelated to HIV and later tacks on HIV-related charges when it is discovered that the defendant is HIV positive. However, most cases are like Franklin's in that the complainant initiated the investigation into the defendant. In the 103 convictions analyzed in chapter 5 (representing the majority of convictions under Michigan's HIV disclosure law and Tennessee's HIV exposure law between 1992 and 2010), the catalyst that prompted the prosecutor to file charges was evident in fifty-eight cases:

1. in thirty cases, an individual discovered that a prior sexual partner was HIV positive and then filed a complaint with law enforcement;

2. in twenty-two cases, police discovered that a defendant accused of a different crime or already arrested was HIV positive (thirteen involved sexual assault; six involved a defendant who spit at or bit a police officer; three involved prostitution-related charges[32]);

3. in four cases, police had initiated investigation into the defendant;

4. in one case, a hospital attendant who had been bitten by an HIV-positive patient filed a complaint with law enforcement;

5. in one case, the health department had asked the prosecutor's office to investigate a defendant;

Thus, state authorities filed the original criminal complaint in twenty-seven cases. Conversely, in thirty-one of the cases analyzed (the thirty involving prior sexual partners and the one case involving a hospital staff member), the complainant's decision to report the defendant to law enforcement sparked the investigation that ultimately led to the prosecutor filing criminal charges.

Although it is not clear from court records or newspaper reports whether the state or the complainant initially pursued charges in the remaining forty-four cases, it is highly likely that complainants initiated the vast majority of these proceedings. Cases related to prostitution and sexual assault (which constitute the majority of state-initiated cases) can always be identified because of the additional charges filed alongside HIV exposure and disclosure charges—cases that nearly invariably begin with a police investigation into other, non-HIV-related charges. Consequently, state-initiated cases are usually easy to identify. By comparison, in complainant-initiated cases, court records may not mention the case's origins.

In the thirty cases in which a complainant reported a prior sexual partner to law enforcement after discovering that the partner was HIV positive, complainants learned of the defendant's status from six types of sources:

1. in twelve cases, *a third party* informed the complainant of the defendant's HIV-positive status;

2. in five cases, the complainant found *medication* for treating HIV belonging to the defendant or other medical records;

3. in five cases, *the defendant* told the complainant after sexual intercourse had taken place;

4. in four cases, the complainant learned of the defendant's HIV status from a *television or news report;*

5. in two cases, *the health department* informed the complainant of the defendant's HIV status;

6. in two cases, *the complainant* deduced the defendant's HIV status after testing positive for HIV.

As this analysis reveals, complainants most commonly find out that the defendant is HIV positive through a third party—such as an ex-girlfriend, a neighbor, or a friend. (It is worth noting that revealing another person's HIV status is a criminal offense in Michigan.[33] Nonetheless, records did not suggest that charges were ever filed against the third parties in these cases).

This section has detailed the importance of *context* when considering discrimination under the law. These findings suggest that the "complaining" moment when a potential complainant decides whether to call the police plays a critical role in shaping the application of HIV exposure and disclosure laws. As the analysis in the following sections reveals, the evidence suggests that complainants in HIV exposure and disclosure cases influence the law's application in surprising ways.

TRENDS IN CONVICTION UNDER STATE HIV EXPOSURE AND DISCLOSURE LAWS, 1992–2015

This chapter analyzes an original dataset of 431 convictions in six states: Arkansas, Florida, Louisiana, Michigan, Missouri, and Tennessee between 1992 and 2015.[34] Because each state law was enacted at different points in time and data were not available throughout the entire period studied for every state, the data represent 122 state-years. Figure 16 illustrates both the actual number and the moving three-year average of convictions in the six states combined. Excepting Michigan, the trend is consistent: the number of convictions rises over time.

This upward trend is consistent with concurrent rise in HIV prevalence in the United States during the same period. In mid-1996, for example, the Centers for Disease Control (CDC) estimated that there were over 200,000 people living with HIV in the United States.[35] Because of new treatments introduced that year, people living with HIV began living much longer lives; consequently, the number of people living with HIV climbed year over year as new individuals were diagnosed with the disease. At the end of 2013 (the latest year such figures were available at time of publication), the CDC estimated that over 1.2 million Americans were living with HIV.[36] Although the number of convictions continued to climb over time in most states, the sixfold increase in people living with HIV outpaced that growth; the annual number of convictions roughly tripled during the same period.

Table 3 depicts the demographic characteristics of convicted defendants in two groups. In the second column, the table presents descriptive statistics of the entire six-state population. Because partner gender data were not available for cases in Arkansas, Florida, and Louisiana, the table presents the data for only those three states in the third column.

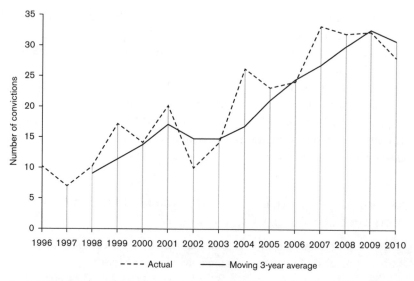

FIGURE 16. Total number and moving average of HIV convictions in six states (AR, FL, LA, MI, MO, TN), by year. Source: Trevor Hoppe.

These data reveal a surprising trend: while many assume that most defendants in HIV exposure and disclosure cases would be gay men, courts convict heterosexual men in far greater numbers. Overall, the vast majority of convicted defendants in all six states are men (76 percent); the majority of those convicted men are Black (62 percent of male defendants and 48 percent of defendants overall); and, in the three states in column 3, the majority of the Black male defendants were accused of not disclosing by female complainants (72 percent of Black male defendants). Heterosexual Black male defendants constitute over one-third of the 206 convictions involving an allegation of nondisclosure before sex (41 percent)—more than straight and gay White men combined. Including straight White male defendants (17 percent) and other heterosexual defendants (1 percent), heterosexual male defendants make up more than 50 percent of convicted defendants—more than twice the number of gay male defendants.

These raw figures are suggestive of several possible trends. For example, it would appear that heterosexuals are most frequently convicted under HIV exposure and disclosure laws. But of course, most Americans are heterosexual; does that difference actually represent a disparity? To evaluate this possibility, it is necessary to compare these figures

	Six states		Three states *Partner gender available*	
States:	Arkansas, Florida, Louisiana, Michigan, Missouri, Tennessee		Michigan, Missouri, Tennessee	
Total number of convictions:	431		231 (206)[a]	
Defendant gender	*Frequency*	*Percent*	*Frequency*	*Percent*
Male	328	76%	196	85%
Female	103	24%	35	15%
Defendant race				
White	170	40%	96	42%
Black	245	58%	130	56%
Other	10	2%	5	2%
Complainant gender (men)				
MSW	–	–	121	72%
MSM	–	–	47	28%
Race, gender				
White men	112	26%	74	32%
White women	58	14%	22	10%
Black men	202	48%	118	51%
Black women	43	10%	12	5%
Other men	9	2%	4	2%
Other women	1	0%	1	0%
Race, complainant gender (men)				
White MSW	–	–	34	20%
White MSM	–	–	25	15%
Black MSW	–	–	85	51%
Black MSM	–	–	21	13%
Other MSW	–	–	2	1%
Other MSM	–	–	1	1%

NOTE: Numbers presented are rounded to the nearest whole number for ease of review.

[a] The analyses including partner gender data are based on 206 convictions in three states. That number does not equal the total number of convictions in those states because it includes only convictions involving sexual contact and convictions for which partner gender data was available.

against the HIV-positive population at large. For example, more than half of women incarcerated in the United States are White, and roughly 30 percent are Black.[37] One could read these data and conclude that White women are more likely to be incarcerated in the United States. However, this would ignore the fact that there are far more White women in the United States than Black women. When accounting for population size, studies reveal that Black women are incarcerated at rates three times greater than White women.[38] Taking into account the population size is critical to evaluating whether discrimination might exist under the law. In the next section, the raw figures presented here are compared to the demographic characteristics of individuals diagnosed as HIV positive during the same time period.

RATES OF CONVICTION UNDER STATE HIV EXPOSURE AND DISCLOSURE LAWS, 1992–2015

To estimate and compare the rate of conviction by race, gender, and sexuality, this section compares the demographic characteristics of convicted defendants against new HIV diagnoses reported by each state health department during the same period. Health department data were not available for Arkansas, so it is excluded from this analysis. As previously mentioned, partner gender data were not available for cases in Florida and Louisiana, so they are excluded from the analyses that rely on those data. Consequently, this section analyzes data from 387 convictions reported in Florida, Louisiana, Michigan, Missouri, and Tennessee between 1992 and 2015.

In the previous section, raw figures reveal that heterosexual men, especially heterosexual Black men, are the most common defendants in HIV exposure and nondisclosure criminal cases. Does this trend reveal a disparity, or is it merely a reflection of the number of heterosexual men who are HIV positive? As it turns out, while most men in the United States are heterosexual, most HIV-positive men are gay men and other men who have sex with men (MSM). Of the men diagnosed as HIV positive during the study period in the three states for which partner gender was available, public health records reveal that just 24 percent were heterosexual. Thus, if criminal charges were filed randomly against HIV-positive defendants, we would expect to find that 24 percent of male defendants would be heterosexual. In fact, nearly the opposite is true: straight men make up the vast majority (72 percent) of male convictions.

This complete reversal of epidemiological trends is reflected in the rates per 10,000 HIV diagnoses presented in table 4. In the three states for which complainant gender data were available, heterosexual men are convicted at far greater rates than their gay counterparts. Overall, HIV-positive heterosexual men were convicted at rates *seven times greater* than gay men. In the state with the fewest number of HIV infections, Missouri, the difference between straight and gay male defendants is enormous: straight male defendants are convicted at a rate of 1,353 per 10,000 HIV diagnoses—compared to just 23 per 10,000 diagnoses for gay men. In Missouri, this study estimates that HIV-positive heterosexual men are nearly *59 times* more likely to be convicted under that state's HIV exposure law than gay men are.

As table 4 demonstrates, Missouri is in its own class. The state has by far the fewest HIV diagnoses during the study period (estimated at 10,680); yet, it has the largest number of convictions and the highest overall rate of conviction (98 per 10,000 HIV diagnoses—more than Florida, Louisiana, Michigan, and Tennessee combined). These findings reveal that nearly all HIV-positive people—straight, gay, Black, or White—are at far greater risk of conviction if they live in Missouri than if they live in any of the other three states analyzed in this section. In nearly every demographic category, the estimated rates of conviction observed are greatest in Missouri (with the exception of White women and White gay men).

The previous section reported that heterosexual Black men were the most common defendant in HIV exposure and disclosure cases, representing more than a third of all cases. Does this mean that they, too, were convicted at greater rates? If we take a cross-section by race alone and compare Black and White defendants, some differences emerge, but they are inconsistent across states and thus not conclusive. If we add gender to the analysis, some differences between Black men and White men appear, but they again vary across states. When sexuality is added as a third dimension for Michigan, Missouri, and Tennessee, the evidence does not suggest that Black straight men are at a higher risk of conviction than White straight men are.

How could this be, if Black straight men constitute nearly a third of all defendants? The answer lies in the public health figures on HIV diagnoses: although heterosexual men overall constitute only a quarter of HIV diagnoses, Black heterosexual men make up nearly 70 percent of all straight male cases. Consequently, accounting for these population sizes suggests that, in fact, White straight men are at a higher risk of

TABLE 4 ESTIMATED RATES OF CONVICTION PER 10,000 HIV-POSITIVE DIAGNOSES IN FIVE STATES

	Florida	Louisiana	Michigan	Missouri[a]	Tennessee	TOTAL
Time period	1996–2015	1992–2013	1992–2010	1996–2015	1995–2013	1992–2015
Number of convictions	98	58	58	105	68	387 (206)[d]
Number of HIV diagnoses	162,590[b]	27,627	17,441	10,680[c]	18,818	237,156
Convictions per 10,000 diagnoses	6	21	33	98	36	13
Defendant gender						
Male	4	22	34	109	40	16
Female	13	20	32	49	26	18
Defendant race						
White	13	30	58	96	35	28
Black	8	18	20	115	40	20
Other	1	–	43	–	–	3
Complainant gender (men)						
MSW	–	–	44	1,353[b]	213	146[e]
MSM	–	–	17	23[b]	15	20[e]
Race, gender						
White men	7	18	44	93	33	24
White women	43	94	152	118	47	22
Black men	7	24	26	142	49	25
Black women	10	7	3	24	22	11
Other men	2	–	45	–	–	–
Other women	–	–	35	–	–	–

Race, complainant gender (men)

White MSW	–	57	1,284[b]	211	108[e]
White MSM	–	29	21[b]	15	9[e]
Black MSW	–	40	1,449[b]	234	47[e]
Black MSM	–	7	28[b]	16	8[e]
Other MSW	–	43	–	–	–
Other MSM	–	19	–	–	–

NOTE: Numbers are rounded to the nearest whole number for ease of review.

[a] Risk category for male cases with "no risk reported" in Missouri was imputed. See appendix 1 for details.

[b] Diagnosis data for Florida were available for the years 1996–2014. 2015 values are estimated using 2014 figures by demographic category.

[c] Diagnosis data for Missouri were available for the years 2006–2014. 1996–2005 values are imputed using an average of 2006–2015 figures by demographic category. 2015 values are estimated using 2014 figures by demographic category. See methodological appendix for additional details on imputation methods.

[d] The analyses including partner gender data are based on 206 convictions in three states. That number does not equal the sum of the total number of convictions in those states because it includes only convictions involving sexual contact and convictions for which partner gender data was available.

conviction than Black straight men—with rates of conviction observed of more than twice that of Black straight men.

This chapter began with a highly racially charged case involving a Black gay male defendant. Some activists charge that these laws target gay Black men. But does the evidence bear this out? Black gay men make up 50 percent of HIV diagnoses among gay men and other MSM and account for a similar proportion of convictions among gay men (45 percent). This study estimates that White and Black gay men are convicted at similarly low rates: about 9 convictions per 10,000 diagnoses for White gay men and 8 for Black gay men. This trend is roughly the same in all three states studied, with the exception of Michigan, where White gay men are observed to experience higher rates of conviction.

The figures presented in table 4 are equally surprising for women. As mentioned previously, studies have shown that Black women are incarcerated in the United States at rates more than three times that of White women. This would suggest that similar disparities might exist in conviction under HIV exposure and disclosure laws. However, as the previous section already demonstrated, Black women account for just 12 percent of all convicted defendants and White women make up 16 percent. There might still be a disparity in rates of conviction if White women were to account for an overwhelming majority of HIV diagnoses. Yet, the opposite is true: Black women account for over 60 percent of HIV diagnoses among women. In every state analyzed, White women are convicted at rates far greater than those observed for Black women. In Michigan, for example, HIV-positive White women are convicted at rates *fifty times* that of Black women. Overall, this study estimates that HIV-positive White women are convicted at a rate of 22 per 10,000 diagnoses as compared to 11 per 10,000 diagnoses for Black women.

VICTIM IMPACT: THE CASE FOR DISPARITY-GENERATING CRIME REPORTING

When counselors brought Franklin's partner from the hospital to the rape crisis center, he had to decide whether to call the police. Although it is not possible to know what went through his mind, partners who discover that a lover, a fling, or a one-night stand is HIV positive but did not tell them likely grapple with several questions: Was what happened a crime? If it was, should I report it? They may not realize that what happened was a prosecutable offense. Even if they are aware of HIV-specific criminal laws in their state, they may not wish to pick up the phone and call police to report their partner. They could hesitate for several reasons. They may not wish to discuss their sex lives with the police. They may not trust the police to treat them with dignity and respect. Alternatively, they may not believe that their partner deserves criminal sanction.

There is good reason to believe that there are different patterns of crime reporting between groups. For example, studies show that gay and lesbian crime victims are less likely to report crimes to the police than heterosexuals are; other studies show that crime is less likely to be reported to the police when the offender is White or when the victim is male or White.[39] Could the trends in conviction outcomes observed in this analysis be due to reporting?

This study shows that HIV-positive, White heterosexual men and White women were both convicted at greater rates than their Black counterparts. This would make some sense from a reporting perspective. Although it is not possible to know the race of the complainant in most cases, studies show that Americans tend to couple with partners of the same race. Although rates of interracial marriage are on the rise, a recent study reveals that only 15 percent of marriages in 2010 were between spouses who identified as a different race (compared to 6.7 percent in 1980). This trend is especially true for heterosexual Black women: only 9 percent of Black female newlyweds marry a man of a different race (compared to 24 percent of Black men).[40] Thus, while there is certainly some variation, it is reasonable to assume that most defendants were accused by complainants of the same racial background.

Heterosexual Black men and Black women may be less likely to be convicted than heterosexual White men and White women because their Black partner is not as likely to report them to the police—either because they do not trust the police or because they do not believe it is a legal matter. Similarly, a reporting-based theory posits that gay men are convicted at lower rates because they do not trust police or they do not believe that police should get involved.

A second, related explanation for these disparate reporting practices may be the coinciding differences in HIV prevalence in the communities studied. As shown in table 5, gay men have the highest HIV prevalence, by far, of any community in the United States; one recent study estimated that 8 percent of all gay men and 21 percent of Black gay men are living with HIV.[41] In such a high prevalence context, many gay men would not be shocked to discover that someone they had sex with is living with HIV. As this table illustrates, using crudely estimated HIV prevalence

TABLE 5   ESTIMATED HIV PREVALENCE COMPARED TO ESTIMATED CONVICTION
RATES

Group	Estimated HIV prevalence	Conviction rate
White MSW[a]	0.01%	108
White women[a]	0.05%	22
Black MSW[a]	0.32%	47
Black women[a]	0.82%	11
White MSM[b]	5.52%	9
Black MSM[b]	21.02%	8

[a] Estimated prevalence rates for White MSW, White women, Black MSW, and Black women are crudely estimated using 2013 Census population estimates of adults 16 years or older and CDC estimates of the population of Americans living with HIV at year-end 2013.

[b] Estimated prevalence rates for White MSM and Black MSM are taken from David W. Purcell, Christopher H. Johnson, Amy Lansky, Joseph Prejean, Renee Stein, Paul Denning, Zaneta Gau, Hillard Weinstock, John Su, and Nicole Crepaz, "Estimating the Population Size of Men Who Have Sex with Men in the United States to Obtain HIV and Syphilis Rates," *Open AIDS Journal* 6 (September 7, 2012): 98-107.

rates for heterosexual men and women, there appears to be a nearly perfect inverse relationship between HIV prevalence and rates of conviction under HIV-specific criminal laws. If HIV prevalence is high in particular demographic group, this study suggests that the corresponding prevalence of convictions under HIV specific criminal laws will be low.

These findings suggest perceived *HIV threat* may in part explain differences in reporting: if you have sex with a person from a low-prevalence demographic group, it may be particularly shocking and alarming to discover he or she was living with the disease. This argument is related to but different from racial threat hypotheses of crime control, which posit that greater proportions of people of color will result in White authorities enacting more strident and punitive policies to control them.[42] In this case, however, greater proportions of people living with HIV are theorized to be associated with fewer HIV exposure and disclosure cases being reported to law enforcement, thereby lessening the burden of the criminal law in a particular population. Straight White men and women make up less than 4 percent of people living with HIV in the United States, yet they constitute 27 percent of convictions analyzed in this study; conversely, gay men constitute more than half of all people living with HIV in the United States, but they represent just 23 percent of convictions.[43] While there are likely multiple factors driving these disparities, the reaction of a potential complainant to the news that a prior sexual partner is HIV positive likely plays a key role.

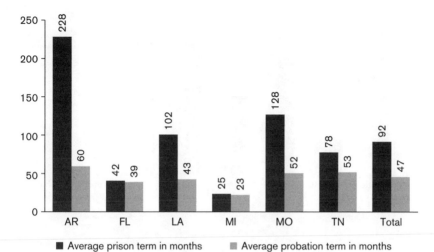

FIGURE 17. Average prison and probation sentences in six states (AR, FL, LA, MI, MO, TN), by number of months, 1992–2015, Source: Trevor Hoppe.

PUNISHING HIV: ANALYZING TRENDS IN SENTENCING, 1992–2015

The findings of the previous sections would seem at odds with an argument that HIV exposure and disclosure laws are applied in discriminatory ways. However, conviction outcomes are not the only possible way to evaluate whether discrimination exists under the law. As outlined earlier in the chapter, there are multiple contexts for discrimination under the criminal law. One frequently analyzed context is sentencing. Although Black men and women may be less likely to be convicted under the law, are they punished more harshly than White men and women when they are convicted? The first analyses on overall trends and demographic trends by race and gender are based on 393 convictions in Arkansas, Florida, Louisiana, Michigan, Missouri, and Tennessee. The subsequent analyses on sexuality are limited to those three states for which partner gender and sentencing data were available, representing 190 convictions in Michigan, Missouri, and Tennessee.

Figure 17 illustrates the average prison and probation sentences handed out by each of the six states. Notably, sentences at the low end of the spectrum in Michigan include 2 years in prison or 2 years on probation. At the long end of the spectrum in Arkansas, defendants sentenced to prison (rather than probation) are ordered to serve an average of 228 months, or 19 years. The average sentence in all six

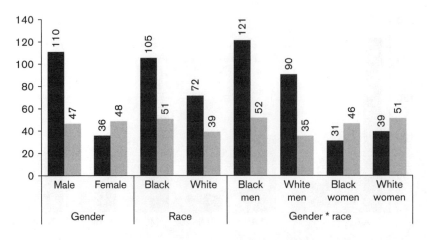

FIGURE 18. Average prison and probation sentences in six states (AR, FL, LA, MI, MO, TN), by gender, race, and gender by race. Source: Trevor Hoppe.

states was 92 months in prison (nearly 8 years) or 47 months on probation (four years). Average sentences waxed and waned slightly over the study period, with an average prison term of 63 months observed between 1995 and 1998; 115 months between 1999 and 2002; 79 months between 2003 and 2006; and 93 months between 2007 and 2010. The proportion of cases receiving prison sentences declined about 3 percent every four years, from an average of 88 percent in 1995–1998 to an average of 77 percent between 2007 and 2010.

Sentences under HIV exposure and disclosure laws varied along a number of demographic lines. Figure 18 illustrates the average prison and probation sentences by gender, race, and gender by race. At first glance, there appear to be several important differences. Men were sentenced to prison sentences that were three times longer on average than their female counterparts (110 versus 36 months)—a trend that was consistent in five states. Second, it appears that Black defendants were sentenced more harshly than White defendants, ordered to serve an additional 33 months in prison—a trend consistent across three states. Finally, Black male defendants were sentenced to serve nearly three more years in prison than White men—a trend consistent across four states (Arkansas, Louisiana, Michigan, and Tennessee).

However, some of these observed differences are primarily driven by large differences between defendants who accept a plea bargain versus

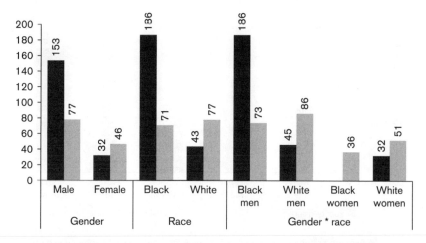

FIGURE 19. Average prison sentences by trial and plea in three states (MI, MO, TN), by gender, race, and gender by race. Source: Trevor Hoppe.

those who take their case to trial. As it was possible to conduct this analysis on the data from only Missouri, Michigan, and Tennessee, figure 19 illustrates the same demographic variations shown in figure 18 for the 27 defendants who took their case to trial and for the 139 defendants who pleaded guilty or no contest. There are extreme differences between sentences handed out at trial to Black men and to White men (186 months versus 45 months). However, there are no similar differences between sentences handed out by plea bargain. These differences varied by state, however. In Michigan, Black men were sentenced more harshly than White men at both trial and by plea bargain; in Missouri and Tennessee, Black men were sentenced much more harshly than White men at trial but not by plea bargain (223 versus 51 months in Missouri at trial; 182 months versus 36 months in Tennessee).

Overall, Black women were slightly less likely to be sentenced to prison or jail than White women: 85 percent of White women defendants were incarcerated versus 77 percent of Black women defendants. On average, White women received longer prison and probation sentences than Black women did (no Black women took their cases to trial in the three states examined in figure 19). However, because of the small number of Black women convicted overall, what appears to be a systematic trend is really driven only by a small number of cases in Tennessee. No Black women were sentenced to prison in Arkansas, Louisiana,

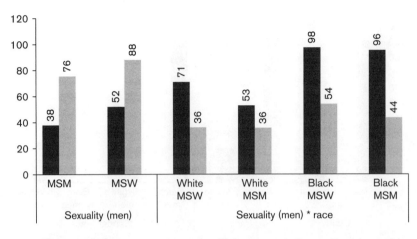

FIGURE 20. Average prison sentences in three states (MI, MO, TN), by sexuality (men) and sexuality by race (men). Source: Trevor Hoppe.

Michigan, or Missouri, for example. Sentences were comparable in Florida (26 months for Black women and 25 months for White women). In Tennessee, however, they were quite different but involved a very small number of defendants: three White women were sentenced to an average prison term of 130 months, while four Black women were sentenced to an average of 36 months. Therefore, sentencing data for female defendants across race are difficult to interpret.

Figure 20 illustrates sexuality for male defendants and sexuality crossed by race for the three states (Michigan, Missouri, and Tennessee) in which partner gender data was available. This analysis is limited to men because women are accused by only male complainants in HIV disclosure and exposure cases.[44] Overall, heterosexual men or MSW were sentenced to prison terms roughly a year longer than their gay or MSM counterparts. Overall, Black heterosexual men were sentenced to similar prison terms as Black gay men, and Black heterosexual men were slightly less likely to receive a prison or jail sentence than Black gay men were—an unexpected trend that was consistent in all three states. White gay men were sentenced to an average of 18 fewer months in prison than White straight men were. As shown in figure 21, however, several of these differences are driven by large differences in trial sentencing. Among just the cases settled by plea bargain, Black and White straight men were sentenced equivalently whereas

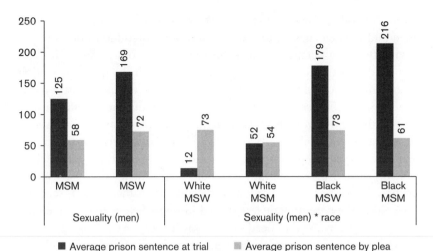

FIGURE 21. Average prison sentences by trial and plea in three states (MI, MO, TN), by sexuality (men) and sexuality by race (men). Source: Trevor Hoppe.

Black and White gay men were sentenced less harshly than their straight counterparts.

There was some variation in prison and jail dispositions for straight and gay defendants. Seventy percent of gay or MSM defendants were sentenced to jail or prison, compared to 83 percent of straight or MSW defendants. This trend was consistent across all three states. White straight men were far more likely to receive a prison or jail sentence than White MSM were: 94 percent versus 60 percent, respectively. This trend was consistent in all three states, with the greatest difference observed in Missouri, where just 38 percent of White gay male defendants were incarcerated compared to 89 percent of White straight male defendants. Heterosexual Black defendants were less likely to be incarcerated than their White straight male counterparts (79 percent versus 94 percent). The trend is reversed for gay and other MSM defendants: Black gay male defendants were more likely to be incarcerated than their White gay male counterparts (85 percent versus 60 percent). Both trends were consistent across all three states.

LENIENCY FOR GAY MEN OR BENEVOLENT SEXISM?

Do the findings presented in the previous section reveal a "gay bonus" or a "straight penalty" when it comes to sentencing under state HIV exposure and disclosure laws? In fact, the sentencing patterns between men and women suggest that it may not have anything to do with the sexuality of the defendant; instead, it may have something to do with the gender of the complainant. Data presented in the previous section consistently showed that men were sentenced to lengthier prison terms than women. This echoes other findings throughout the criminal justice system that show women are treated more leniently than men. This suggests that women defendants are viewed as less of a threat and, perhaps, with greater empathy by prosecutors and judges—a form of what scholars of gender-based prejudice would call "benevolent sexism."[45] Although the bias benefits women defendants in these cases, scholars argue that they are nonetheless rooted in sexist beliefs that women are weak, vulnerable, and in need of male protection.

The trend between straight and gay defendants, on the one hand, and male and female defendants, on the other, may in fact *both* be products of benevolent sexism. If judges and prosecutors view women defendants with greater empathy, it would be reasonable to assume that their biases would also extend to their view of crime victims. This would echo analyses of death penalty cases that show that Black defendants are more likely to receive the death penalty when their victim was White. In this case, both Black and White defendants accused of not disclosing their status to female complainants who plead guilty are treated more harshly than defendants accused of not disclosing to male complainants.

There is less evidence to support the alternative hypothesis that defendants who are gay are treated more leniently. Most theories of discrimination based on sexual orientation would predict that heterosexual judges and prosecutors would typically view gay male defendants as more threatening. For example, studies have shown that gay men convicted of child molestation are more likely to receive prison sentences than heterosexual male defendants are.[46] Although gay men are treated more leniently, in effect, in HIV exposure and disclosure cases, the evidence suggests that has less to do with their sexual orientation and more to do with the gender of their partners.

CONCLUSION: VICTIM IMPACT

Over the past four decades, victims have come to play an increasingly significant role in shaping the application of the criminal law in America. The victim rights movement persuaded many state legislatures to enact laws that guaranteed crime victims certain rights as law enforcement authorities investigate, prosecute, and sentence criminal defendants. The title of this chapter refers to the statements that victims are allowed to present at criminal sentencing hearings. These "victim-impact statements"—some of which are analyzed in chapter 5—serve as an outlet for victims to communicate the harm inflicted upon them by the defendant; they can also directly influence how prosecutors and judges adjudicate a particular case, as the analysis in chapter 5 demonstrated.[47] This chapter harnesses this concept to consider how crime victims shape the application of HIV exposure and disclosure laws in the United States—both within and outside American courtrooms.

The first section of this chapter argued that complainant characteristics drive the application of HIV exposure and disclosure laws. Far from showing a disparate impact on racial and/or sexual minorities, the findings presented in this chapter evidence a seemingly perplexing trend: heterosexual White men and women bear the brunt of the application of HIV exposure and disclosure laws. How could this be? The argument presented in this chapter is that not all potential complainants are equally likely to report criminal cases or "complain" to the police. Two theories are offered to explain why this would be the case.

First, given that gay men and Black women are infrequently prosecuted, it appears that their partners—typically other gay men and straight Black men, respectively—are the least likely to file complaints. As it turns out, these partners belong to the same groups that one would expect might be hesitant to call the police. After all, gay sex was illegal in many states until relatively recently, when the Supreme Court decided *Lawrence v. Texas* (2003). In a 2005 report on police brutality against LGBT Americans, Amnesty International concluded that "LGBT people continue to be targeted for human rights abuses by the police based on their real or perceived sexual orientation or gender identity."[48] Empirical studies back up these claims, suggesting, for example, that many police officers hold antigay attitudes;[49] that many LGBT victims of hate crimes do not report their crimes to police because they fear police mistreatment;[50] and that reports of police misconduct and inaction in cases involving LGBT crime victims are persistent over time.[51] Therefore, even if gay male potential complainants "name" their experience as a criminal offense and "blame" their partners, gay male potential complainants ultimately may decide not to file a formal "complaint" with law enforcement.

As for why Black men may not choose to report cases of HIV nondisclosure to the police, evidence of mistreatment of African Americans in the criminal justice system demonstrates a pervasive pattern of abuse and discrimination that has created a hostile and adversarial relationship between law enforcement and Black communities.[52] Legal scholars argue that these trends extend beyond police and front-line law enforcement personnel to prosecutors who wield considerable discretionary power in deciding who to charge and for what offense.[53] This combative legal context may understandably discourage many Black men from inviting the state into their private lives.

While some potential complainants may hesitate to make a "complaint" to police, there is also reason to believe others still may not "name" or "blame" their partners. As shown in table 5, the evidence suggests a nearly perfect inverse relationship between the prevalence of HIV in a particular demographic category and the risk of conviction for members of that community. Perceived HIV threat may be shaping the law's applications. For example, because straight White men and women have prevalence rates of less than 1 percent, many heterosexual White Americans have likely never even entertained the *possibility* of sex with an HIV-positive person—much less the reality. Thus, finding out that a partner was HIV positive is likely to be met with a much more violent and upset reaction—and a sense that a grave injustice was committed. In such cases, potential complainants may be more likely to "name" the failure to disclose as criminal and "blame" their partners for not telling them. By contrast, with estimated prevalence rates of more than 20 percent among Black MSM, the odds of having sex with another HIV-positive person are quite high for members of that community; in such a context, "naming" and "blaming" may be less likely.

Notably, these arguments do not mean that race and sexuality never figure in the prosecution of Black defendants. This chapter opened with a discussion of a particularly inflammatory case against a young gay Black man in Missouri, Michael J. To say that gay Black men are not more likely to be convicted than other groups does not negate the fact that Michael was demonized in court specifically because of his race and sexuality. Indeed, the sentencing data presented in this chapter suggest that—if charged—Black gay male defendants who take their case to trial like Michael face stiff penalties under the law at sentencing. When Black men are convicted at trial, this chapter reveals that they are punished more harshly than their White counterparts; this trend is consistent for both heterosexual Black men and Black MSM like Michael. Therefore, his sentence of thirty years in prison reflects larger patterns.

As this chapter also revealed, both Black and White gay men who plead guilty or no contest are sentenced less harshly than their heterosexual counterparts. Black and White women are treated far more leniently than their male counterparts. These trends are explained as the product of benevolent sexism: judges and prosecutors view women as vulnerable and less threatening, leading to reduced sentences for female defendants *and* for increased sentences imposed against male defendants accused of not disclosing to their female partners and who accept plea deals.

This chapter began with a discussion of how social scientists theorize discrimination under the law by categorizing its form, basis, and context. What does this chapter reveal about the application of HIV exposure and disclosure laws in the United States? First, what form does it take? The first section of the chapter argues that patterns in the law's enforcement suggests a disparate impact. Disparate-impact discrimination is driven by policies that are neutral on their face but in practice disproportionately impact certain communities. Although many people would suspect that HIV exposure and disclosure laws would disproportionately impact racial and sexual minorities, the observed disparate impact does not align along conventional expectations; rather than gay men and racial minorities being impacted disproportionately, heterosexual White men and women shoulder the burden of the law. This chapter argues that victim characteristics serve as the basis for the law's disparate impact. This chapter explains the disparate impact by arguing that the likelihood of a potential complainant reporting a partner's failure to disclose varies along demographic lines—with gay men and Black men the least likely to report their partners. This chapter further argues that the context for this disparate impact is at the stage of reporting.

The second section of the chapter analyzes sentencing outcomes. Rather than a disparate impact, these findings suggest that different defendants are treated differently at sentencing in certain contexts. The demographic characteristics of both the defendant *and* the complainant appear to form the basis of this disparate treatment. Black men are punished more harshly than White men at trial and men are punished more harshly than women. In addition, men accused of not disclosing to women complainants are treated more harshly than men accused of not disclosing to male complainants in cases where a defendant pleads guilty or no contest. The context for these findings is the sentencing stage of law enforcement.

If these theories are correct, then what would such a diagnosis offer anticriminalization advocates who wish to reform the law's application? First, the evidence suggests that reporting drives disparities in the law's application. The remedy for this disparate impact is not automatically clear, however. Equality could result from either prosecutors charging gay men more frequently or prosecuting straight people less frequently. Presuming most advocates would believe the latter proposal to be more appealing, then the only potential strategy would seem to be reach out to heterosexual communities with the goal of making HIV less threatening. Most straight Americans (not to mention gay Americans) likely have no idea that treatment all but eliminates the possibility of sexual HIV transmission. If the theory of HIV threat is true, then normalizing HIV would ultimately translate into fewer prosecutions.

Second, these findings—as well as those presented in chapter 5— reveal the importance of focusing on sentencing as a potential context for discrimination under the law. Chapter 5 reveals that ignorant statements about HIV and its transmission can directly influence the punishment handed out in criminal courts. The findings presented in this chapter reveal that different kinds of defendants and complainants are associated with different sentencing outcomes. This again raises the question, what is the remedy? Equality could mean punishing women and gay men more harshly or punishing straight men more leniently. Presuming that less-harsh sentencing is the goal, there are several recourses available to advocates. First, judges and prosecutors typically rely on sentencing guidelines issued by the state that are specific to a particular law; these administrative guidelines are often the most critical factor in shaping how judges and prosecutors approach sentencing in a particular case. Advocating for their reform might prove one potential recourse. In addition, educating judges and prosecutors about HIV and its transmission might reduce the frequency with which ignorance seems to directly inform sentencing in HIV-related prosecutions.

These proposals are but a few of many that likely could affect the application of HIV exposure and nondisclosure laws. They are presented as a tool for generating ideas that respond to the specific diagnosis offered in this chapter. Targeting the factors that most clearly shape the law's application will maximize the impact of any efforts toward reform. For example, this chapter did not raise issues relating to whether a defendant is found guilty or not (the context of juries, for example). This was purposeful. Only a tiny fraction of cases is decided by a judge or jury. To this point, a 2015 study from the Williams Institute at UCLA revealed a startling statistic: when prosecutors charged a defendant under one of California's HIV-specific laws, they secured a conviction in 389 cases out of 390 (99.8 percent).[54] During the course of research for this book, only a small handful of cases were ever identified in which the defendant was acquitted or the charges dismissed. Once charges are brought, conviction is nearly inevitable. Focusing on the areas of the law's application that reveal its uneven application may prove a useful strategy in a society that places great value on equal justice under the law.

Punishing Disease

On March 13, 2016, Corey Rangel was pulled over in southwest Michigan for having a loud muffler.[1] A police officer cited Rangel for driving without corrective lenses and without an operating license; however, the more serious issue was that Rangel was driving after his curfew. Rangel was nine months into his probation for felony drug charges. His case was diverted to Cass County's Adult Drug Treatment Program. According to Rangel, his probation officer initially brushed off the altercation with police, indicating to him that he did not want to violate him for such a minor incident. This might have been the end of it—except that Rangel was different from other individuals under probation: he was HIV positive. Hours later, he received an ominous phone call from probation officials: Report to jail immediately. And bring your cell phone.

When Rangel reported to jail, he brought his cell phone as requested. Officials demanded that he hand over his phone and provide them with the password to access information in it. Over the next several days, what began with a traffic stop for a loud muffler spiraled into a serious investigation that threatened to put Rangel behind bars for years. Rangel told reporters that a few days after arriving in jail, a local police officer showed up to ask him a few questions: "He asked me whether or not I was disclosing to my sex partners. . . . I told him I was. And he said he was going to contact them and ask them—to see if our stories matched up."[2]

Police admit to going through Rangel's phone and finding digital photographs of Rangel engaged in sex with other men. They admit to then calling several of his phone contacts hoping to discover whether they knew that Rangel was HIV positive. According to one of the men who received one of these calls, Nico, police made it clear what information they were after without ever actually using the term *HIV*. Nico told reporters that they asked "basically just, you know, about him, like making me come out and say, 'You mean his status?,' you know. So, 'About that,' and I'm like, 'Yeah, I know about it. He told me already.'"[3]

In effect, police were investigating Rangel for not disclosing his HIV status on the basis of nothing more than the fact that he was HIV positive. That investigation failed to yield any legally actionable information. A police representative told a reporter, "It could have been a crime. We have investigated, and we found nothing criminal happened. The criminal case has been closed." But even though the investigation into his HIV-disclosure practices may have been closed, the saga had just begun for Rangel. Over the next several months, authorities moved to dismiss Rangel from the drug treatment court. At the hearing to consider his dismissal, the drug court coordinator, Dr. Barbara Howes, testified about what led her to conclude that Rangel was a danger to society. Although she denied being made aware of the sexual photos police found on Rangel's phone, she said that she was aware of his HIV status. The prosecutor inquired, "Would you consider that to be a potential danger to the public?" "Yes," she responded. The prosecutor then asked whether she believed his traffic violation—the reason the case came to court in the first place—made him a danger to the public. "Possibly," she said. "If he was consuming drugs or alcohol."[4]

Corey Rangel was ultimately dismissed from the drug treatment court, which had the effect of violating the terms of his probation on felony drug charges. He entered a plea of guilty to probation violation charges in front of the very same judge who in 2009 had sentenced Melissa G. to five months in jail for allowing a client's nose to penetrate her vagina, Judge Michael E. Dodge (discussed in chapter 5). Judge Dodge sentenced Rangel to 36–240 months in prison.[5]

While this book focuses on the cases brought under HIV exposure and disclosure laws, cases like Corey Rangel's demonstrate that these laws can have effects that extend far beyond the cases brought directly under them—in Rangel's case, by prompting law enforcement to view him with suspicion. Would an HIV-negative person on probation cited for a traffic violation have his phone seized and sexual partners contacted? Clearly, Rangel was treated differently because of his HIV status and viewed as a threat to public safety, as Dr. Howes herself said.

Although she did not cite Michigan's felony disclosure law, nonetheless a pall of criminality associated with being HIV-positive loomed over Rangel's case.

When gay and lesbian rights organizations fought for four decades to get states to repeal their anti-sodomy laws, they did so in part because those laws symbolically validated what so many Americans believed: that gay sex was a crime. Similarly, HIV exposure and disclosure laws reinforce the view that sex for HIV-positive people is a potentially criminal affair, leading law enforcement to view people living with the disease with suspicion. In Corey Rangel's case, that suspicion led police to seize his phone and investigate his sex life. Law enforcement did not wait for a person to come to them to report Rangel; he was presumed guilty from the start by virtue of his HIV status.

These views are reflected in stories told in chapter 3 by Michigan health officials tasked with monitoring and controlling HIV-positive people in their counties. While the state's felony HIV disclosure law makes clear that the only legal obligation required of people living with HIV is to disclose their status to sexual partners, the civil health-threat law granting health authorities the authority to surveil and control the behavior of people living with HIV was more open to interpretation. When asked to describe the surveillance practices employed to identify potential heath-threat cases, some health officials conflated failing to disclose with failure to use a condom. For example, in some counties, testing positive for a sexually transmitted infection was reported to be a sufficient rationale for labeling someone a health threat—despite the fact that a positive test result for gonorrhea does not indicate whether a person disclosed his or her HIV status. Underlying these surveillance practices is the assumption that sex for HIV-positive people is necessarily dangerous.

At the heart of these assumptions are distinctions between "risky" and "safe" behaviors that are not particularly nuanced. For example, as chapter 5 described, as many as one in three Americans continue to believe that HIV can be transmitted by kissing. But can we blame them? In 1997, the Centers for Disease Control (CDC) published a report of a woman who acquired HIV from "deep kissing" with an HIV-positive man.[6] The *New York Times* proclaimed that the case was the "first linked to kiss" but went on to reveal that both individuals had gum disease and that she had recently had oral surgery (a root canal). The report notes that the CDC "has long recommended against deeply kissing an infected individual and said that individuals who did should be tested."[7] Was it really *kissing* that was the risk factor in this case—or the improbable scenario of both partners having gum disease and one recently having undergone a root canal? The obsession in public health practice to distinguish between "risky" and "safe" has made it a challenge to effectively communicate about HIV risk to the American public. In the face of rare cases or theoretical possibilities, some doctors and public health experts feel ethically obligated to emphasize risk rather than safety.

This dichotomous view of risk is often coupled with a special focus on individual behaviors stripped of any contextual factors. That HIV has been labeled a sexually transmitted infection has exacerbated this issue: Health authorities carve up the sexual act into an array of who-put-what-into-wheres, which are often distinguished in black and white terms as either safe or not. This is more likely for diseases we consider to be sexually transmitted and to HIV in particular. Would the CDC put out a news release if a new Zika or flu infection was "linked" to grocery shopping or going to the gym? Although both individuals in the CDC release cited above had gum disease, the link promoted was not the relatively rare probability of two people kissing who both have gum disease but instead the altogether commonplace behavior of kissing. Intentional or not, the effect is to absurdly exaggerate the risk of commonplace behaviors in the minds of many readers. Context, in fact, matters.

Even a handful of the Michigan health officials who formed the backbone of their counties' HIV/AIDS programs struggled to accurately evaluate the risk of transmission in particular scenarios. In a survey completed by officials interviewed for chapter 3, each official was asked to assign a risk probability to various scenarios along a scale of factors of 10—from less than 1 in 100,000 to 1 in 1. In sixteen of the twenty scenarios given, health officials on average overestimated the risk of transmission—sometimes by more than a factor of 10. For example, they were asked to evaluate the average risk of transmission for an HIV-negative woman who has vaginal sex *without a condom* once with an HIV-positive man. CDC estimates this risk to be less than 1 in 1,000 on average—not taking into account the HIV-positive partner's viral load. Seventeen of twenty-five (68 percent) health officials rated the risk at least a factor of 10 greater: two rated it at 100 percent; six rated it at 1 in 10; and nine rated it at 1 in 100. On average, health officials also evaluated identical behaviors (for example, oral sex) as posing a greater risk in scenarios involving gay men than in those involving heterosexual couples. If trained professionals consistently overestimate the risk of transmission, it is no wonder that lay Americans and legal professionals do the same. For most Americans, where there is sex, so too must there be its accompanying risk—and where there is risk, there is the potential for harm. This slippery syllogism facilitates efforts to punish disease.

Yet, despite the fact that risk is ubiquitous for all Americans, the label of "risky" is selectively applied to certain social contexts—most frequently those involving marginalized groups, stigmatized behaviors, or undesirable social locations. Those social contexts then become the battleground for disease control. As chapter 1 made clear, the most intrusive and coercive measures aimed at controlling risk have at times been historically reserved for marginalized populations. From Seattle's Firland tuberculosis clinic-turned-detention center for poor alcoholics to the prison camps built in World War II to house sex workers suspected of spreading venereal disease, disease control efforts have turned punitive when they are driven by social bias.

This process of labeling and stigmatizing echoes the way America has historically dealt with other socially undesirable groups. For example, during the first few months of his presidency in 2017, President Donald J. Trump signed an executive order banning nationals from seven majority-Muslim countries from entering the United States for ninety days.[8] While the president argued that the policy was necessary in the face of a growing threat of terrorism, CNN anchor Chris Cuomo rebuffed those claims on the air, arguing instead that the policy was driven by "phobias, not facts."[9] Cuomo's argument echoes much of the evidence presented in this book; while authorities in both cases frequently invoke discourses of risk as a veneer to justify harsh and coercive measures, a closer inspection of the evidence reveals the fear, ignorance, and stigma lurking beneath the surface.

Although punitive disease control is not new, HIV stigma facilitated the rise of an unprecedented criminal justice response to infectious disease. To be sure, there have been attempts historically to criminalize diseases, primarily sexually transmitted infections like syphilis. However, never in American history have states been so systematically aggressive in using the criminal law to punish individuals because of their illness—and in many cases, the real offense does appear to be HIV-positive status. Although HIV disclosure and exposure laws are, at least in theory, premised on punishing behavior, these laws are often written so broadly that they can transform even a garden-variety lap dance at a strip club into a felony.

The criminalization fever has arrived, and recent developments suggest it may be contagious. In 2014, Iowa reconsidered its HIV-specific criminal law after a widely reported case involving an HIV-positive gay man accused of having sex while wearing a condom yielded a twenty-five-year prison term and lifetime sex offender registration.[10] After a statewide advocacy campaign, the Iowa legislature moved to reduce the penalties for cases involving low risk—a success that was widely heralded by advocates as a sign of "modernization." Less discussed was the simultaneous move to add a bevy of other infectious diseases to the criminal law, including tuberculosis, hepatitis, and meningococcal disease. Indeed, left-leaning advocacy groups even celebrated this shift as a triumph over AIDS stigma. The state's LGBT rights organization, One Iowa, noted in a press release, "Rather than single out HIV, the law now includes other infectious diseases."[11] Iowa's legislative reform came on the heels of a similar expansion in Tennessee, where the legislature voted to extend the state's HIV-specific criminal statute to individuals infected with hepatitis B or C.[12] These developments suggest that the logic of criminalizing diseases is spreading and becoming more deeply entrenched in American society.

THE CRIMINALIZATION OF SICKNESS: A CONCEPTUAL MAP

Chapter by chapter, this book has implicitly been informed by a conceptual model of the social contexts and social forces that ultimately led to the criminalization of HIV. In what follows, this model is made explicit by explaining how the pieces of the puzzle fit together at three levels: the cultural level, the criminal justice and policy level, and the event level.[13] As depicted in box 1, cultural attitudes and biases that provide the backdrop for efforts to regulate HIV include three social phenomena—stigma, responsibility politics, and ignorance and fear. These three factors are mostly outside the control of any individual person or organization but nonetheless have played a pivotal role in facilitating criminalization efforts at the criminalization and policy level. They act as resources for the institutions, authorities, and stakeholders that make up the second level to draw on in their efforts to promote or enact criminalization. For example, politicians have drawn on stigmatizing views of homosexuality and played on public fears of HIV to drum up support for new HIV-specific criminal laws. Finally, the third level consists of triggering events—sensationally reported arrests and ambitious politicians—that ignite efforts to criminalize HIV. While imperfect, this conceptual map illustrates the relationships between the different kinds

---

Box 1. Conceptual Map of Criminalization

1. Cultural Level
   a. Stigma
   b. Responsibility politics
   c. Ignorance and fear
2. Criminal Justice and Policy Level
   a. Crime policy
   b. Complainants, law enforcement, and public health
   c. State governments
3. Event Level
   a. Moral entrepreneurs
   b. Sensationally reported crimes
   c. Interest group lobbying

---

of social phenomena identified as driving criminalization throughout this book.[14]

1. The Cultural Level

a. Stigma. Throughout the book, stigma—against not just HIV but also gay men and sex workers—has repeatedly reared its hoary head to drive efforts to criminalize HIV. As chapter 4 illustrated, early efforts to criminalize HIV were fueled by antigay and antiprostitution biases; there was considerable anxiety that HIV could bleed over from "high-risk groups" into the "general population"—a rhetorical othering that is characteristic of stigmatizing campaigns. In the case of prostitution, stigma against sex workers prompted police in states across the country to pressure lawmakers to enact a rapid succession of felony, HIV-specific prostitution laws. That HIV was steeped in homophobia and social anxieties around sex from the start made it prime fodder for lawmakers looking for new problems to punish.

b. Responsibility politics. This book has argued that the way we conceptualize disease has implications for how it is socially regulated. From the outset, conservative Americans blamed HIV-positive people for contracting the disease. But as chapter 2 revealed, in popular discourse HIV-positive people were nonetheless often discussed as "AIDS victims." This changed over time, especially when treatment was introduced in the mid-1990s. Suddenly, people were *living* with HIV and thus deemed responsible for taking care of themselves. Public health responded by shifting resources away from campaigns telling HIV-negative people to use a condom and toward telling HIV-positive people not to infect their partners—a trend that has reinforced the idea that people living with HIV carry the greater share of the responsibility for managing the epidemic. The responsibility has often been conceptualized as belonging to the individual person living with the disease (for example, "HIV stops with me") rather than something shared between people. As chapter 2 argued, characterizing HIV-positive people as individually responsible for preventing HIV transmission complements criminalization by implicitly assigning blame and victimhood—a characteristic feature of the criminal justice system.

Notably, pre-exposure prophylaxis (PrEP) threatens to reorganize these politics. (As discussed in chapter 2, PrEP is a strategy for preventing HIV in which an HIV-negative person takes medication to protect against HIV.) The first indications of PrEP's impact on responsibility politics were visible in the wake of a highly publicized prosecution in San Diego, California, involving a gay male defendant accused of infecting a male partner with HIV. The complainant in the case gave a media interview in which he expressed regret for not being more educated about HIV, telling a reporter that "I didn't know about PrEP. . . . I was not as educated as I needed to be and I think a lot of people aren't."[15] His comments are suggestive that the burden of responsibility may be ever so slightly shifting in the shadow of PrEP. Yet, the uptake of the drug has so far been slow among the communities hardest hit by HIV— with 12 percent of prescriptions being issued to Latino patients and 10 percent to Black patients (by contrast, the CDC estimates that 45 percent and 24 percent of new HIV diagnoses in 2015 were among Black and Latino people respectively).[16] Moreover, as most efforts to promote PrEP (and most of its subsequent uptake) remain limited to gay men, PrEP as it presently is being rolled out has done little to reshape the responsibility politics in the population identified in this book as hardest hit by criminalization: heterosexuals.[17]

c. Ignorance and irrational fear. As described throughout the book, many Americans (including the prosecutors, judges, and health officials tasked with enforcing the law) have a simplistic understanding of HIV. Lacking a nuanced or even a medically sound understanding of HIV and its transmission facilitates the generic conclusion that sex = risk =

harm. This pervasive ignorance acts as a moderator, clearing the path for criminalization to push ahead in the face of mountains of contrary scientific evidence. If HIV was a more normalized part of social life, criminalization would likely be less pervasive. Indeed, as shown in chapter 6, there appears to be a nearly perfect inverse relationship between communities most impacted by HIV and communities most impacted by criminalization—suggesting that criminalization flourishes in those communities that are least familiar with the disease.

2. The Criminal Justice and Policy Level

a. Crime policy. As described in chapter 4, laws enacted in twenty-eight states provide the infrastructure or foundation upon which criminalization is built. Although there were attempts to use laws already on the books (such as assault with a deadly weapon or attempted murder), a series of prosecutorial failures led many lawmakers and prosecutors to believe that the general law—with its problematic requirement to prove malicious intent—was not well suited for criminalizing unintentional HIV exposures; in twenty-eight states, lawmakers constructed a new system of legal infrastructure built to specification. This strategy differs from that of criminal justice authorities in Canada, who rely on existing sexual assault law to punish people living with HIV who do not disclose their status to partners.[18] But the criminal code in Canada is federalized, while the United States has a decentralized criminal justice system in which criminal codes vary by state. This makes it possible for different states to enact widely different policy approaches. The particularities of each state law shape the cases that flow from it. For example, chapter 5 analyzed the cases brought under Michigan law (which criminalizes a failure to disclose before engaging in "sexual penetration") and Tennessee law (which criminalizes "exposing" another to HIV). Because sex is built into Michigan law, spitting and biting cases that are relatively common in Tennessee are largely unknown to Michigan courts.

b. Complainants, law enforcement, and public health. Complainants, health officials, prosecutors, and judges are steering the ship. Their collective decisions, which were analyzed in chapters 3, 5, and 6—to call the police, to report a client, to press charges, to sentence harshly—ultimately determine how the laws in twenty-eight states described above are enforced. Their individual decisions are important, but they also are in many cases interdependent. For example, if a complainant decides not to report a client to police, the prosecutor cannot push forward; alternatively, if a prosecutor drops charges or a judge tosses a case out, the complainant cannot prosecute on his or her own. Although their hands are all on the ship's wheel, as it were, their influence is somewhat constrained by the laws in their respective states.

c. State governments. Lawmakers and the legislative branch of government ultimately hold the authority to decide the scope of criminalization efforts. As analyzed in chapter 4, this is a story that plays out mostly at the state level; federal agencies, such as President Reagan's Presidential Commission on the HIV Epidemic, play an institutionalizing role. Ultimately, state lawmakers determine the wording of the law and what criminal penalties get attached to it. While judges and prosecutors do not determine what the law says, as chapter 4 revealed, along with the general public they nonetheless attempt to exert their influence on state lawmakers. Police unions have often successfully lobbied state lawmakers to enact HIV-specific criminal laws, but, in the end, it is the lawmakers whose votes decide the fate of a particular bill.

3. The Event Level

Chapter 4 revealed how individual events and actors can trigger enormous change. Given enough sensational media coverage, a single arrest of an HIV-positive prostitute triggered entire campaigns to enact new HIV-specific criminal laws in many states. Chapter 4 also showed how individual actors (so-called moral entrepreneurs), such as Illinois representative Pullen, have been able to mobilize an array of resources at the federal and state levels to help catapult a model law to legislatures across the United States. In the right institutional and cultural contexts, these seemingly minor events and people can play an outsize role in shaping criminalization efforts.

Taken together, these levels offer a conceptual map for HIV criminalization. It is not intended to be a perfect or exhaustive list of every single factor that can play a role; rather, it provides an overview of the most critical puzzle pieces. Although it will not provide a perfect template for other diseases, efforts to criminalize sickness in the future will almost certainly share many of the same elements. Stigma, pervasive ignorance, and a belief that people with a particular disease are to blame for their infection are likely hallmarks of efforts to criminalize sickness. But they alone are not enough.

WHY NOT PUNISH DISEASE?

Some readers may wonder what is so bad about criminalization? Criminalization magnifies many of the problems that plague coercive strategies for managing public health problems analyzed in chapter 1. Because the risk of criminalization spreading to other areas of American life appears high, it is especially important to address this question head-on. This section will discuss five of the most distressing problems posed by criminalizing sickness.

1. *It often gets it wrong.* As chapter 1 revealed, coercion is nothing new in public health history. Although there are successful examples of coercive practices historically, there is also evidence that the state often implements coercive practices in ways that do little to control the spread of disease. For example, cordons sanitaires were a common tool to control the plague in medieval times, yet these blockades did little to stop the disease vector, rats, from traveling and spreading infected fleas to people in other neighborhoods. In the case of HIV criminalization, the tool promoted by the state for controlling disease is HIV-status disclosure rather than blockades. But there are good reasons to believe that disclosure is just as shoddy a tool for managing the spread of HIV.

First, many people who are HIV positive do not know that they are infected and believe themselves to be HIV negative. The CDC recently estimated that approximately 15 percent of people living with HIV in the United States are not aware of being infected.[19] People who do not know they are infected with HIV obviously cannot disclose their status to partners. This is a much bigger problem that it may seem: evidence shows that individuals who are HIV positive but do not know it also tend to be the most infectious. This is because people with HIV who are undiagnosed and thus not yet on a treatment regimen can have up to a *million* copies of the virus in every milliliter of their bodily fluids, making it far more likely that a sexual partner will contract the disease; after diagnosis, however, doctors prescribe antiretroviral treatment that clamps down on the virus's ability to replicate—often to the point that the virus becomes undetectable. To this point, one study estimated that 54–70 percent of all new sexually transmitted HIV infections were attributable to sexual contact with someone unaware of their HIV-positive status.[20]

In addition, as chapter 2 described, there is a growing consensus among public health experts that people living with HIV who are on treatment and whose viral load is undetectable cannot infect their partners. By contrast, because the most commonly used HIV antibody tests do not always detect infection until up to six months after transmission, the results of a nonreactive HIV-antibody test from *yesterday* may not reliably indicate someone's actual HIV status. Taken together, these findings suggest that the best way to contract HIV is to have condomless sex with someone who thinks he or she is HIV negative. Mandating disclosure implicitly promotes this risk by making it appear as though sex with HIV-negative partners is safe; in many cases, however, choosing to have sex only with HIV-negative people may result in a greater risk of infection. In short, if preventing HIV is the goal, then promoting disclosure is the wrong strategy.

2. *It is subject to abuse.* Chapter 1 revealed how coercive strategies have often been mired by the ignorance and/or prejudice of the officials in charge of implementing them. Seattle's tuberculosis sanitorium became a de facto prison for homeless alcoholics, while turn-of-the-century efforts to control an outbreak of the plague in San Francisco led to racist policies that selectively quarantined Chinatown. As chapters 4 and 5 revealed, HIV exposure and disclosure laws were borne out of stigmatizing views of HIV that continue to guide the hands of law enforcement as they punish people living with HIV today. Blatantly ignorant views of HIV are codified into case law by judges who have no expertise in infectious disease but nonetheless accept a prosecutor's claims that a victim may wind up testing positive decades after a sexual encounter.

3. *The stakes are high.* While quarantine programs generally end relatively quickly, incarceration can last for years—and under new state sexual predator laws, perhaps even for life. After inmates are released from prison, they go back to a life marred by the label of a felon, facing not just the loss of rights like voting and social benefits like food stamps, but also patterned unemployment and a high risk of poverty.[21] Defendants convicted in Louisiana and Tennessee also face having to publicly register as a sex offender. In Louisiana, that means having the phrase SEX OFFENDER printed in red capital letters underneath one's driver's license photo. In short, criminalization can have devastating effects on convicted defendants that can be both immediate and long-lasting.

4. *It is hard to change.* Even in cases where lawmakers agree that the criminal justice system is broken and in need of change, actually

enacting that change is an uphill battle. Once a criminal law is on the books, it is exceedingly difficult to get it removed. This problem did not recently arrive alongside the gridlock in American governance in recent years; it has a long history driven by American lawmakers and political parties locked in a race to be seen as ever tougher on crime.[22] In a context in which repealing a criminal law can make a lawmaker vulnerable to losing the next election, criminal laws tend to accumulate ad infinitum. This tendency has led some legal philosophers to argue that criminalization ought to be a last resort.[23]

In contrast to the criminal justice system, epidemiology and medical science can change overnight, as new treatments, vaccines, and prevention measures are developed. These advancements radically change the context for people living with a particular disease. When most state legislatures decided to criminalize HIV, the virus was largely untreatable and, for many, terminal. Today, one recent study estimates that a twenty-year-old gay man diagnosed with HIV who starts treatment immediately will live to be 89.3 years old (as mentioned in chapter 2, this is several years longer than life expectancy estimates for twenty-year-old men in the general population).[24] HIV is not the same disease it was in 1985 (or 2015, for that matter), yet the laws regulating it have scarcely been touched since they were enacted.

Even if a cure for HIV is developed, these laws will not automatically disappear. Recent developments for hepatitis C raise ominous signs for how an HIV cure might play out in a legal context. While the hepatitis C drugs cure the disease in most patients, the pharmaceutical companies making them charge upward of $100,000 for a course of treatment—making these life-saving medications out of reach for many people living with the disease.[25] If a $100,000 cure for HIV comes to market, will the poor continue to face legal sanction for not disclosing their status? Because the move to criminalize hepatitis C in Iowa came one year *after* the FDA approval of one of these revolutionary hepatitis C therapies, all signs point to an emphatic yes.

5. *It does not accomplish what we want it to do.* Why do we punish? Experts on criminal justice have long held that there are several schools of thinking when it comes to answering this question. Four are worth describing here as they each represent one yardstick by which we might measure the "success" of criminalization efforts. In each case, the evidence suggests that these laws are either not effective or are vastly disproportionate to the offense in question.

Retributive theories of punishment argue that we punish because people who break the law deserve social sanction. Of the four schools of thought presented in this section, retribution is by far the predominant narrative in HIV disclosure and exposure cases. In particular, in many of the victims' narratives described in chapter 5, they explicitly plead with the court to impose harsh punishment because of the harm the defendant inflicted. But as chapter 5 illustrated, the harm may often be illusory and in many cases largely based on ignorant views of HIV. Indeed, the laws are worded in such a way that the crime is failure to speak, a crime of omission; the state is not required to prove that defendants actually inflicted physical harm (or even the risk of harm) on their partners. Psychological duress—rooted in many cases in an irrational fear of HIV—seems in many cases to be the only measurable harmful outcome. If psychological duress is the primary harm punished under HIV exposure and disclosure laws, then an average prison sentence of nearly nine years seems out of step with most just deserts theories of punishment.

Rehabilitative theories of punishment argue that we punish to improve criminals so that they can be reintegrated back into society. Rehabilitation narratives were few in HIV disclosure and exposure cases. Although most cases received prison sentences, the minority of cases sentenced to probation often included terms that required the defendant to seek treatment or counseling, requirements that seem to exhibit a rehabilitative spirit. Although this study did not systematically evaluate whether these terms were effective, the case of William K. (discussed in chapter 5) reveals that, at least in his case, the system utterly failed. When William missed several appointments with a counselor, the court violated his probation and threatened to put him behind bars, ignoring his complaints that he felt unwell. William died of cryptococcal meningitis days before he was to be sentenced for violating his probation for missing appointments with a counselor. While his case is but one, it reveals the hollow, empty vision of rehabilitation practiced in some criminal justice contexts; beneath the thin veil of rehabilitation lies a system built for retribution. Rehabilitation might be an effective approach in these cases, but its spirit is largely unknown in the application of HIV-specific criminal laws today.

Incapacitation theories argue that we punish in order to separate dangerous individuals from society in the interest of public safety. For example, when Brenda J. was sentenced to prison in 1995 in the Michigan case described in chapter 5, the judge explicitly argued that he was sentencing her to prison in order to protect the public. Although some defendants may pose a threat to society, the law does not require that the state prove that anyone was put in danger by the defendant; instead, it presumes that the failure to disclose is itself dangerous. This presumption may have been arguably more sustainable when HIV was untreatable and largely terminal, but in a contemporary context the argument loses steam. Today, both defendants and complainants have at their fingertips tools that can stop sexual transmission dead in its tracks: condoms, pre-exposure prophylaxis (PrEP), and effective treatment. These technologies make it harder to categorically describe all cases of nondisclosure as inherently dangerous. Consequently, incapacitation seems an increasingly untenable justification for most state HIV exposure and disclosure laws.

Finally, *deterrence* theories argue that we punish so that other people will think twice before engaging in the same criminal behavior. Some people might argue that having HIV exposure and disclosure laws on the books is important because they deter nondisclosure. Studies have actually attempted to evaluate whether HIV-specific criminal laws have an effect on people's sexual practices. For example, a study published in 2007 found that individuals living in a state with an HIV-specific criminal law (Illinois) did not differ in their self-reported HIV risk behaviors from individuals living in a state without such a law (New York).[26] Similarly, a study published in 2010 found that the reported rates of condomless sex among MSM living with HIV did not vary between states with and without an HIV-specific criminal law.[27] A separate study of 384 people living with HIV in Michigan published in 2012 found that awareness of their state's HIV disclosure law was not associated with increased likelihood of disclosing their HIV-status to all potential sexual partners.[28] Finally, a 2017 study found no association between state-level HIV diagnoses rates and criminal HIV-exposure laws.[29] Taken together, these findings suggest that HIV-specific criminal laws are not an effective strategy for changing the behaviors of people living with HIV.

CONCLUSION: BEYOND BLAME

As this book makes clear, no one lawmaker, defendant, or interest group could reasonably be said to be solely responsible for criminalizing HIV. In chapter 4, Representative Pullen is described as Lawmaker Zero with tongue planted firmly in cheek. Rather than an attempt to blame a particular person for bringing HIV criminalization to pass, the notion of a Lawmaker Zero and this book more generally are attempts to turn the classic public health model of studying the HIV epidemic on its head. Scholarship on HIV tends to focus on the practices of people living with the disease or those at risk of contracting it. We know far less about the lawmakers, prosecutors, and health officials who manage the epidemic. However, as this book shows, their practices, beliefs, and institutional contexts play a significant role in shaping our response to the epidemic—and thus the epidemic itself.

Some readers may have found the Lawmaker Zero concept a bit silly precisely because popular discourse on communicable disease control is not filled with images of prosecutors or elected officials. The notorious figures in infectious disease history such as Patient Zero and Typhoid Mary are fictions created to stigmatize individuals living with infectious diseases. And yet, the stigmatizing efforts of conservative leaders have contributed far more to inflaming HIV stigma and thus the epidemic than any one French Canadian flight attendant could have ever done. In the popular imagination, the responsibility for HIV has not been equally shared by people living with the disease and the authorities who manage our response to it. In that sense, *Punishing Disease* is a plea to turn our critical gaze to the political leaders, institutional forces, prosecutors, and judges that also play a critical role in the social life of HIV.

There are signs that states are responding to critics such as UNAIDS that charge that these laws are overly broad.[30] Notably, in 2012, Illinois amended its felony HIV-specific criminal law to require proof of intent; to prevent prosecution for oral sex, kissing, spitting, or biting; and to provide an affirmative defense for condom use.[31] As already mentioned, Iowa lawmakers amended their state law to reduce the penalties for the least egregious types of cases. A Tennessee appeals court ruled in 2012 that courts must have a medical professional testify that a defendant's actions actually posed a "significant risk" to their partner or victim as seemingly required under the law (although the impact of this ruling remains unclear, as prosecutors continue to file HIV exposure charges related to spitting and/or biting incidents).[32] Whether other states will follow their leads remains to be seen.

Even as state lawmakers and appeals courts winnow their laws in ways that would seem to limit their scope, the basic notion that punishment is an appropriate tool for controlling disease remains unchallenged. Ultimately, if we are to resist the impulse to punish disease, we

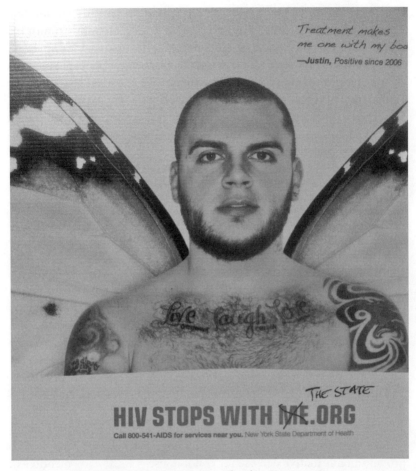

FIGURE 22. HIV Stops with the State. Source: Theodore Kerr.

must find a way to move beyond blame.[33] The following three strategies might help communities do that.

1. *Promote collective responsibility.* Although it makes for a great slogan, HIV does not truly ever stop with "me." The responsibility for managing, containing, and preventing the spread of HIV rests on the shoulders of not just individuals but also communities, organizations, institutions, state governments, and international agreements. In 2016, an unknown AIDS activist defaced an HIV Stops with Me campaign poster in Brooklyn, New York, to make a similar point, crossing out "Me" and writing in black marker "THE STATE" (see figure 22).

As this book has shown, promoting a model of individual responsibility facilitates the transformation of HIV as a medical problem to HIV as a criminal problem. Recontextualizing people living with HIV within their broader communities and institutional environments would make it more challenging to frame HIV as a criminal problem.

What might that look like in practice? Many of the testing campaigns targeting HIV-negative individuals reviewed in chapter 2 provide some clues. Those campaigns placed the decision to get tested for HIV-negative individuals in the context of their intimate relationships, families, and friends. But more than just making an appeal based on interpersonal relationships, public health might seek to highlight the ways that institutions such as health care, public health, housing, and the economy shape the ways in which people navigate HIV. This could entail putting doctors, health officials, hiring managers, and landlords at the center of a public health campaign. Instead of focusing on promoting an ethic of individual responsibility among people living with HIV, this hypothetical HIV Stops with *Us* campaign might instead promote the ways that authority figures in our lives can help to normalize HIV and make disclosure a nonevent.

2. *Promote alternatives to responsibility.* Responsibility—shared or individual—is not the only social good worth promoting in the name of public health. As previously mentioned, recent debates over pre-exposure prophylaxis (PrEP) are often framed in terms of whether its users might interpret the drug as giving license to individuals to behave "irresponsibly." But there are other frameworks other than individual responsibility for understanding PrEP's public health significance. In January 2017, the Los Angeles LGBT Center launched a public health campaign that promoted PrEP without emphasizing responsibility. Its campaign slogan, "F*ck without fear," instead highlighted the liberatory aspects of PrEP to free its users from the fear of contracting HIV.[34]

Although the LGBT Center did not say so explicitly, the F*ck without Fear campaign was likely a tacit response to efforts by the nation's largest AIDS-service organization, the AIDS Healthcare Foundation (AHF, also based in Los Angeles). The organization's executive director, Michael Weinstein, has been an outspoken critic of PrEP; he has previously derided the HIV prevention tool as a "party drug" and even taken out full-page advertisements in LGBT news outlets criticizing PrEP[35] AHF has instead aggressively promoted condom use, sometimes by using nationalist and punitive tactics. In 2012, the foundation launched a Condom Nation campaign (complete with an Americana motif and a slogan that intentionally rhymes with "condemnation") and later fought to put an initiative on the California ballot in 2016 that would have required adult film actors to wear condoms or face punitive fines (the initiative was defeated at the ballot box).[36]

Whatever position on PrEP's utility that one takes, the LGBT Center's campaign reveals that promoting responsibility (and/or blame) need not be the sole strategy for HIV prevention practitioners. Given the resonance that responsibility rhetoric can have with efforts to punish people living with HIV, public health organizations wishing to resist efforts to criminalize sickness may strive to imagine alternative approaches when designing interventions.

3. *Combat stigma and ignorance.* Let's face it: People living with HIV are often afraid to disclose their HIV status because many Americans hold extremely prejudiced and ignorant views of the disease. Although some readers may presume that most Americans are well informed about HIV, surveys suggest otherwise. As previously noted, upward of one-third of Americans report believing that HIV can be transmitted through casual contact such as kissing—a figure that hasn't changed much since the 1990s. Data such as these suggest that many Americans grossly overestimate the risk of transmitting HIV through sexual contact—not to mention ignoring how HIV treatment and undetectable viral loads can mitigate risk. Consequently, fighting for comprehensive sex education that includes scientifically accurate information about HIV could be one key strategy in a movement to combat HIV stigma. This is especially needed for low-HIV-prevalence communities that are disproportionately affected by criminalization (as chapter 6 revealed).

Finding ways to normalize HIV and people living with HIV is key to reducing stigma. Beyond primary schools, this could include featuring HIV-positive characters in popular media. For example, in 2015, the popular ABC drama *How to Get Away with Murder* included a story line featuring a gay couple in which one person tests HIV positive and the other begins taking pre-exposure prophylaxis (PrEP).[37] To write the story line, writers worked with CDC staff to accurately portray PrEP and HIV.[38] That coverage undoubtedly provided countless American households with their first exposure to the idea that HIV transmission could be prevented by taking a daily pill. According to Nielsen data, episodes of *Murder* during that season reached an average of 13 million households—far more than any billboard or bus poster campaign could ever hope to reach.[39]

The success of *Murder* and its PrEP story line reveals how cooperation between Hollywood and public health can produce effective results.

However, because the story line depicts a gay couple negotiating HIV risk, it is conceivable that heterosexual audiences will not view it as especially relevant to their own lives. Yet, as chapter 6 revealed, it is these heterosexual audience members who are disproportionately affected by the criminal law. In the minds of many TV viewers, HIV infection remains a thing that happens to other people. Precisely because of its infrequency, destigmatizing HIV in low-prevalence communities will be an especially challenging task.

4. *Promote alternatives to prosecution.* In cases where legal reform is unlikely or not possible in the short term, it may be possible at the local level to institute alternative programs aimed at reducing the number of felony cases filed. As incarceration rates have exploded over the past three decades, advocates have increasingly called for authorities to devise and implement restorative justice and alternatives to criminal prosecution. Instead of spending years in prison, a defendant might instead be called on to volunteer or engage in community service, to make financial amends to the crime victim, or to meet with the crime victim directly for mediation or arbitration.[40] Given that the harm in the vast majority of HIV exposure and disclosure cases is limited to psychological duress, this seems to be a proportionate and particularly suitable strategy for keeping HIV-related cases from proceeding to prosecution.

5. *Speak the same language (or at least try to translate).* This book has argued that lawmakers and prosecutors translate HIV from the language of medicine to the language of criminality. For legal authorities, the impetus to criminalize HIV does not depend on medical evidence; it is instead a matter of morality and ethics. Those are the grounds of debate. Many critics of criminalization begin their critique on the basis of public health evidence; as this book shows, these arguments were uniformly unsuccessful in courts of law. They are also unlikely to sway lawmakers who view the problem in moral terms.

Trying to persuade lawmakers and prosecutors to move beyond blame will require either speaking the language of the law or translating between law and medicine. To the first point, critics might seek ethical and moral grounds upon which to defend individuals accused of not disclosing their HIV-positive status to sexual partners. To do so, they might frame their arguments in the language of privacy rights or other constitutionally guaranteed protections. This is, admittedly, likely to be an uncomfortable proposition for many HIV advocates, who are far more fluent in the language of science and public health. For those unable or unwilling to mount a moral or ethical defense of nondisclosure, it may be possible to instead translate between the language of the law and the language of public health. That translation necessarily begins with an acknowledgment of both perspectives in an effort to find a common understanding. This will require grappling with complicated and difficult questions such as what is the difference between "risk" (a public health concept) and "harm" (a legal concept).

These strategies are not exhaustive, by any means. Instead, they are presented to begin a conversation about how we can control infectious disease while also avoiding shaming, blaming, and punishing. Those tactics are counterproductive and do not end epidemics. If this book has demonstrated anything, it is that the causes and effects of criminalizing sickness are themselves social ills. Stigma begets stigma. Ignorance begets ignorance. To break the link between disease and punishment, we need new tools.

Methods

On Analyzing the Anatomy of a Social Problem

There is a standard approach to studying HIV. Although there is a wide array of methodologies in the social and behavioral science universe, a dominant model towers over others: (1) identify a "high risk" group; (2) identify "high risk" behaviors among members of said risk group; (3) demonstrate associations between "high risk" behaviors and other negative indicators (typically psychological measures such as self-esteem); (4) develop interventions designed around this evidence; (5) repeat. This conventional approach has formed the basis of countless careers in public health and the behavioral sciences, and it is certainly not unique to HIV. Yet, while it has utility for helping to understand one aspect of the epidemic, its predominance has the effect of keeping the critical gaze of most researchers fixated on ordinary people and their "risky" behaviors.

Sociologists have helped broaden the picture.[1] Scholarship from ethnographers like Claire Decoteau, Sanyu Mojola, and Robert Wyrod have helped us to understand how and why social context—including gender, inequality, and social policy—so deeply matters for understanding the epidemic.[2] Cultural sociologists such as Marian Burchardt, Iddo Tavory, and Ann Swidler have employed qualitative research methods (including interviews but also nonstandard approaches such as diaries) to reveal how cultural perceptions directly shape how people respond to HIV.[3] Sociologists working under the umbrella of science and technology studies, such as Steven Epstein, have employed policy and content analysis research methods to analyze how AIDS activists and expert discourses shaped the American response to AIDS.[4]

Punishing Disease draws on many of these methodological approaches to studying HIV but also employs the complementary tools offered by demography, criminology, and sociolegal studies. For example, criminal justice scholars have analyzed the disparate impact of mass incarceration on different communities using population-level demographic data. Studies in this tradition have shown how devastatingly the high level of mass incarceration for African Americans is deepening racial inequality in America.[5] Criminologists have also long employed quantitative-based methods for analyzing associations between demographic characteristics and disparate criminal justice outcomes. Scholars working in this tradition have shown, for example, that Black men who murder White men are more likely to receive the death penalty than those who murder Black men.[6] Finally, sociolegal scholars have employed a range of mostly qualitative methods to analyze how people's perceptions shape how the law is applied in action. Scholars working in this tradition have employed, for example, the tools of discourse analysis to show how gendered perceptions haunt how rape is litigated in trial courts when the victim is a man.[7]

Punishing Disease draws on this range of methods in order to analyze what can best be described as the anatomy of a social problem. *Punishing Disease* dissolves traditional boundaries of crime, medicine, public health, and law. This is a work of medical sociology and of criminology. It is a project steeped in sociolegal studies. It is certainly a critical examination of the sociology of punishment. And yet it is much more than any one of these. Even recently proposed frameworks for thinking about the overlap between the law and medicine, such as the "medico-legal borderland," while useful, do not adequately capture the intellectual, methodological, and ultimately, epistemological promiscuity present in this project.[8]

Each chapter takes a different view on the punitive regulation of disease and HIV in particular. Thus, addressing the questions raised particular domains (who gets punished? what role do health officials play?) necessarily requires different methodological approaches. In the following pages, I describe how the data for each chapter were collected and analyzed.

CHAPTER 1: CONTROLLING TYPHOID MARY

Chapter 1 employs the methods of comparative historical research to analyze the rise, fall, and return of coercion in public health practice. This chapter is based on a systematic review of secondary historical literatures in public health, history, and the history of medicine. It is particularly indebted to public health law scholars such as Lawrence O. Gostin, who have contributed significantly toward our understanding of the history of coercion in public health practice, particularly as it pertains to the HIV epidemic. Sources reviewed include those that analyzed the history of

1. a particular disease control policy, such as quarantine;
2. a notable figure in the history of disease control, such as Mary Mallon;
3. a particular epidemic, such as the plague.

An analysis of these secondary sources is presented in chronological order, in order to illustrate how the use of coercion has changed over time.

CHAPTER 2: "HIV STOPS WITH ME"

Chapter 2 analyzes broad shifts in HIV prevention policy since the emergence of the HIV epidemic. Using the tools of discourse analysis, this chapter analyzes what Steven Epstein has called the "politics of knowledge" as it pertains to how responsibility for HIV has been framed in public health practice. It draws on primary sources, such as Centers for Disease Control policy announcements, as well as a critical review of medical and public health literatures on the transmission of HIV, on people living with HIV, and on the effectiveness of particular prevention technologies such as condoms and treatment. It also uses Google's Ngram tool, which measures how often a particular phrase or word is found in the corpus of English-language texts digitally scanned by Google. This tool helps track the rise and fall of specific ways of talking about HIV.[9]

CHAPTER 3: THE PUBLIC HEALTH POLICE

This chapter primarily draws on qualitative interviews with Michigan health officials. Michigan is divided into forty-five local health jurisdictions, sixteen of which are classified by the Michigan Department of Community Health (MDCH) as high-morbidity jurisdictions for HIV infection. Each of these sixteen jurisdictions has its own program for handling HIV/AIDS, which includes staff responsible for managing and responding to health-threat-to-others (HTTO) cases. The remaining twenty-nine jurisdictions, classified as low-morbidity jurisdictions, share one overarching, centralized HIV/AIDS program. Thus, there are seventeen proper cases (defined as local public health agencies charged with investigating HIV HTTO cases) suitable for analysis in this project: sixteen high-morbidity jurisdictions and one omnibus low-morbidity jurisdiction.

With assistance from MDCH staff, I identified two actors whose organizational roles and institutional responsibilities are most closely tied to responding to and managing HTTO cases: the HIV/AIDS services coordinator and the disease intervention specialist (DIS). The coordinator is responsible for overseeing the jurisdiction's programs and services that are related to HIV/AIDS, and the DIS is charged with making site visits and organizing and implementing interventions developed to deal with HTTO cases. Notably, these roles are not distributed evenly: in smaller counties, they were sometimes united in the same person, while larger counties had multiple DIS positions. In cases where there were multiple DIS positions, I interviewed only staff who had direct experience with HIV HTTO cases.

In coordination with MDCH, I visited fourteen of the seventeen local health jurisdictions, where I interviewed twenty-five staff members. Two jurisdictions declined to participate because of recent staff turnover, and one never responded to requests to participate. Each in-depth, 45- to 90-minute, semistructured interview was audio recorded. I asked each participant to choose a pseudonym, which are the names used in this book. I conducted all the interviews myself and coded transcripts using NVIVO software. In particular, I coded interviews for general techniques of surveillance (such as using partner services or testing data), participants' awareness and opinion of the HIV disclosure law, and direct experience with regulating HIV-positive clients. I obtained approval to do research with human subjects from both the University of Michigan's Health Sciences and Behavioral Sciences Institutional Review Board and MDCH's Institutional Review Board.

CHAPTER 4: MAKING HIV A CRIME

This chapter draws on an original archive of primary sources related to HIV exposure and nondisclosure criminal bills introduced in the United States. I began by requesting legislative histories of bills known to have passed in the United States; from there, I reached out to state libraries and archivists in all fifty states to identify bills that did not pass, that were vetoed, or that were repealed. In sum, 162 bills from forty-five states were identified. Once identified, all relevant historical documents were requested. For states with robust archiving policies, such as California, this entailed thousands of pages of records—including committee hearing records, bill analyses, and statements of support or opposition. In most states, however, the most that was typically available for review was the bill itself and the House and Senate journals describing its progression through the legislative process. The range of data available in these forty-five states can be categorized in this way:

1. *Bill only* (26): Alabama, Arizona, Arkansas, Connecticut, Delaware, Georgia, Hawaii, Idaho, Indiana, Iowa, Kansas, Kentucky, Louisiana, Maryland, Minnesota, Mississippi, Nebraska, New Hampshire, New Jersey, New York, North Carolina, Pennsylvania, Rhode Island, South Dakota, West Virginia, and Wyoming.

2. *Bill plus transcripts or audio of hearings* (3): Alaska, Colorado, and Illinois.

3. *Bill plus committee records* (9): California, Missouri, Montana, Nevada, North Dakota, Ohio, Oklahoma, South Carolina, and Wisconsin.

4. *Bill plus transcripts or audio and committee records* (7): Florida, Michigan, Tennessee, Texas, Utah, Virginia, and Washington.

Collectively, this archive includes 547 files, or 14,257 pages of documents. (Notably, in keeping with the spirit of the state's colloquial motto regarding size, 6,435 pages are associated with bills in Texas alone.)

In addition to these primary sources, I also conducted a systematic analysis of newspaper reports using Newsbank for references to "AIDS" and "crime" or "felony." As a result, 596 newspaper articles were archived for analysis.

CHAPTER 5: HIV ON TRIAL

To analyze how trial courts litigated HIV exposure and nondisclosure cases in Michigan and Tennessee, I obtained public records of convictions from the Michigan State Police Information Center and the Tennessee Administrative Office of the Courts. These de-identified data described the county and dates in which defendants were convicted under their state's respective law. I attempted to identify the defendant in each case by reviewing local newspaper archives, searching for any mention of a case within two weeks of the sentencing date indicated in the police data (this was easier in Michigan, where the de-identified data included specific sentencing dates; Tennessee data included only the year).

In Michigan, I successfully identified the defendant in twenty-nine cases using newspaper reports and in another twenty-nine cases using county clerk records and Internet searches. In these ways, I identified the defendant in 95 percent of the known sixty-one convictions between 1992 and 2010 in Michigan.

It is not possible to know precisely how many defendants were convicted under Tennessee's law given the information provided, which reported only counts rather than individual cases (defendants in Tennessee were often charged with multiple HIV exposure counts—up to twenty-eight in one case). However, it was possible to rely on the state's sex offender registry as a source of data, since defendants convicted under that state's HIV exposure law are required to publicly register as a violent sex offender for life.[10] In total, forty-three defendants convicted under Tennessee's HIV exposure law between 1995 and 2010 were identified.

In the 103 cases in which the defendant was identified, I ordered courtroom transcripts from the county circuit court. I obtained 194 court transcripts totaling 6,654 pages associated with 78 cases. In the 12 cases for which no transcripts were available, I requested copies of other documents in the court file that detailed the basic facts of the case and relevant legal matters. For the purposes of this analysis, I also drew on 125 local newspaper reports located through archival research, Internet searches, and electronic newspaper database queries. This research design was reviewed by a University of Michigan ethics board and determined to be exempt from review.

Upon receipt, I digitized records using a scanner and a computer outfitted with ABBY FineReader text recognition software. Once they had been digitized, I read and coded the court transcripts using ATLAS.ti qualitative analysis software. For the purposes of this analysis, I coded for framing devices employed by legal actors to justify punishing defendants. This includes public health framings (such as "they're a risk to public health" or "exposed another to a risk of contracting HIV") and moral framings that depart from medical science (such as "they're a reckless killer" and "they sentenced another to death"). I also coded for references to medical science, such as undetectable viral loads, transmission probabilities, and HIV virology.

CHAPTER 6: VICTIM IMPACT

This analysis is based on an original dataset of convictions in Arkansas, Florida, Louisiana, Michigan, Missouri, and Tennessee. The methods used to obtain the Michigan and Tennessee case information have already been described. The methods for the remaining states were similar. The primary agency or source of data for each of the remaining states were the following:

1. the Arkansas Department of Corrections;

2. Florida's Office of the State Courts Administrator;

3. Louisiana's state sex offender registry, which requires that defendants convicted under the HIV exposure register for fifteen years;[11] and

4. Missouri's Office of the State Courts Administrator.

De-identified case reports were identified using news reports and sex offender registry reports. In Florida, data was de-identified but included cases numbers that could be entered as a search term in most county circuit court clerk websites. In total, the defendant was identified in 431 convicted cases. This research design was reviewed by the University of Michigan Health Science and Behavioral Sciences Institutional Review Board and determined to be exempt from review.

Defendant demographic characteristics were obtained from a variety of sources, including mugshot websites, news reports, department of corrections databases, and sex offender registry reports. In cases for which this information could not be garnered from electronic sources, data was requested directly from the county circuit court clerk. The most labor-intensive datapoint, by far, was partner gender, which is not generally recorded in a systematic way. Partner gender was systematically collected from case files in Michigan, Missouri, and Tennessee. Because of costs (costs associated with obtaining court files for this project approached $20,000), it was not possible to collect partner gender data in additional states.

In order to examine differences between the demographic characteristics of convicted defendants and HIV-positive residents generally, I requested data from the state departments of health describing the population of people newly diagnosed with HIV over the same periods as the court data obtained. Notably, in cases in which the health department data indicated "{{lt}}5" HIV diagnoses instead of specifying a definite number of individuals for a particular risk group, I substituted either an indirectly determined precise figure or an average estimator. For example, if the data indicated that seven HIV-positive women were diagnosed between 1992 and 2010 in a particular county and that five of those HIV-positive women were White and zero were "Other," then necessarily two were Black, because these categories were mutually exclusive. In other instances where it was not possible to deduce the precise figure, an average of the possible values was substituted. For example, if the data indicated that eight HIV-positive women were diagnosed in a particular county and that four of them were White, {{lt}}5 were Black, and {{lt}}5 were "Other," I used the average of the minimum and maximum possible values as an estimator. In this example, since the sum of the possible values could not exceed four, the estimate substituted would be the average of 1 and 3, or 2.0. In Michigan, for example, of the 352 data points for the twenty-two jurisdictions analyzed, it was necessary to substitute twenty-five such estimates. Because the estimators were necessary only in cases with very small numbers, this strategy has a negligible effect on the validity of the overall estimates for HIV-positive diagnoses in these jurisdictions.

Because of the large number of "no risk reported" (NRR) cases, Missouri reports imputed estimated total HIV diagnoses by risk category (in addition to actual reported HIV diagnoses) on an annual basis. However, these figures are not differentiated by race. For example, in 2007, Missouri reports 240 known MSM-associated HIV diagnoses but, after including estimated NRR cases, estimates 451 MSM diagnoses. These imputed estimates are not reported based on race, however. To estimate imputed total diagnoses by race, Missouri diagnoses data are imputed based on the annual proportional composition for each demographic category (for example, 46 percent of actual reported MSM cases in 2007 were among Black MSM; therefore, the imputed estimate for Black MSM for 2007 is $0.46 * 451 = 208.59$).

The analyses conducted in this book treat both defendant data and health department data analytically as populations because they represent the vast majority of all possible cases during the study period (95 percent in Michigan, for example). Because both sets of data include nearly the entire population, statistical significance tests are unnecessary because the probability that the differences observed between the two data sets were the result of random error (or "chance") due to sampling is negligible. Statistical significance figures for the analyses conducted in this paper would estimate the probability that the differences observed between groups were the result of random error due to sampling rather than actual differences in the population. Because these two sets of data represent entire populations (or in the case of the conviction data, 95 percent of the entire population), statistical significance tests are inappropriate. Consequently, statistical significant tests are not presented. This assumption is consistent with a previously published, peer-reviewed analysis of the Michigan data.[12]

State HIV Bills

TABLE A.I STATE HIV EXPOSURE AND DISCLOSURE BILLS, SORTED BY YEAR AND
THEN BY STATE

STATE	Bill Number	Year Introduced	Penalty	Final Action
New Jersey	Assembly Bill No. 3577	1985	Not applicable	Not passed
Pennsylvania	House Bill No. 1787	1985	Felony	Not passed
Colorado	House Bill No. 1144	1986	Felony	Not passed
Florida	House Bill No. 1313	1986	Misdemeanor	Enacted
Florida	House Bill No. 1055	1986	Misdemeanor	Not passed
Florida	Senate Bill No. 787	1986	Misdemeanor	Not passed
Florida	House Bill No. 1245	1986	Misdemeanor	Not passed
Hawai'i	House Bill No. 2289	1986	Felony	Not passed
Idaho	House Bill No. 662	1986	Felony	Not passed
Idaho	House Bill No. 653	1986	Not specified	Not passed
Maryland	House Bill No. 1282	1986	Unknown	Not passed
New Jersey	Assembly Bill No. 1443	1986	Not applicable	Not passed
Oklahoma	House Bill No. 1698	1986	Felony	Not passed
South Dakota	Senate Bill No. 193	1986	Misdemeanor	Not passed
West Virginia	House Bill No. 1393	1986	Unknown	Not passed
Alabama	House Bill No. 338	1987	Misdemeanor	Enacted
Illinois	Senate Bill No. 651	1987	Misdemeanor	Amended out before passage
Louisiana	House Bill No. 1728	1987	Felony	Enacted
Louisiana	House Bill No. 1634	1987	Felony	Not passed
New Jersey	Assembly Bill No. 4069	1987	Felony	Not passed

Pennsylvania	House Bill No. 2009	1987	Felony	Not passed
Pennsylvania	House Bill No. 2274	1987	Felony	Not passed
Rhode Island	Senate Bill No. 449	1987	Felony	Not passed
South Carolina	Senate Bill No. 508	1987	Not specified	Enacted
Georgia	House Bill No. 1281	1988	Felony	Enacted
Idaho	House Bill No. 433	1988	Felony	Enacted
Illinois	Senate Bill No. 110	1988	Misdemeanor	Not passed
Iowa	House Bill No. 2344	1988	Felony	Not passed
Michigan	House Bill No. 5026	1988	Felony	Enacted
Missouri	House Bill Nos. 1151 & 1044	1988	Felony	Enacted
New Jersey	Assembly Bill No. 966	1988	Not applicable	Not passed
Oklahoma	House Bill No. 1798	1988	Felony	Enacted
Rhode Island	House Bill No. 8444	1988	Infraction	Not passed
Rhode Island	Senate Bill No. 2595	1988	Civil	Not passed
Rhode Island	Senate Bill No. 2638	1988	Felony	Not passed
Rhode Island	Senate Bill No. 2673	1988	Felony	Not passed
South Carolina	House Bill No. 2807	1988	Felony	Enacted
Virginia	House Bill No. 469	1988	Felony	Not passed
Washington	Senate Bill No. 6221	1988	Felony	Enacted
Arkansas	House Bill No. 1496	1989	Felony	Enacted
Illinois	House Bill No. 1871	1989	Felony	Enacted
Illinois	Senate Bill No. 1180	1989	Felony	Vetoed
Maryland	Senate Bill No. 719	1989	Misdemeanor	Enacted
Montana	House Bill No. 661	1989	Misdemeanor	Enacted
Nevada	Senate Bill No. 73	1989	Misdemeanor	Enacted
North Carolina No. 10A NCAC 41A .0202	Administrative Code	1989	Misdemeanor	Not applicable
North Carolina	House Bill No. 191	1989	Civil	Not passed
North Dakota	Senate Bill No. 2049	1989	Infraction	Enacted
North Dakota	Senate Bill No. 2052	1989	Felony	Enacted
Ohio	Senate Bill No. 2	1989	Misdemeanor	Enacted
Pennsylvania	House Bill No. 824	1989	Felony	Not passed
Pennsylvania	House Bill No. 600	1989	Felony	Not passed
Texas	Senate Bill No. 163	1989	Felony	Not passed
Texas	Senate Bill No. 649	1989	Not specified	Not passed
Texas	House Bill No. 1901	1989	Felony	Not passed
Texas	Senate Bill No. 959	1989	Felony	Repealed
Virginia	House Bill No. 1343	1989	Felony	Not passed
Kentucky	House Bill No. 125	1990	Felony	Amended out before passage
Oklahoma	House Bill No. 1012	1991	Felony	Enacted
Tennessee	House Bill No. 52	1991	Felony	Amended out before passage

(continued)

STATE	Bill Number	Year Introduced	Penalty	Final Action
Utah	House Bill No. 435	1991	Not specified	Drafted out before passage
California	Senate Bill No. 982	1992	Felony	Not passed
Connecticut	House Bill No. 5887	1992	Felony	Not passed
Kansas	House Bill No. 2841	1992	Misdemeanor	Enacted
New York	Senate Bill No. 7339	1992	Felony	Not passed
Pennsylvania	House Bill No. 2815	1992	Felony	Not passed
Tennessee	House Bill No. 1673	1992	Felony	Not passed
Tennessee	Senate Bill No. 1676	1992	Felony	Not passed
Wyoming	House Bill No. 8	1992	Felony	Not passed
Connecticut	House Bill No. 5305	1993	Felony	Not passed
Florida	House Bill No. 153	1993	Felony	Enacted
Indiana	Senate Bill No. 24	1993	Not specified	Enacted
Indiana	House Bill No. 1015	1993	Felony	Not passed
Nevada	Senate Bill No. 514	1993	Felony	Enacted
North Carolina	House Bill No. 973	1993	Felony	Not passed
Pennsylvania	House Bill No. 743	1993	Felony	Not passed
Tennessee	Senate Bill No. 398	1993	Felony	Amended out before passage
Tennessee	House Bill No. 585	1993	Felony	Not passed
Texas	Senate Bill No. 1067	1993	Repeal	Enacted
Colorado	House Bill No. 1255	1994	Felony	Not passed
Indiana	House Bill No. 1366	1994	Felony	Not passed
New York	Senate Bill No. 744	1994	Felony	Not passed
Tennessee	House Bill No. 1686	1994	Felony	Enacted
Alaska	Senate Bill No. 91	1995	Felony	Not passed
Alaska	House Bill No. 199	1995	Felony	Not passed
Minnesota	House Bill No. 1700	1995	Felony	Enacted
North Carolina	House Bill No. 801	1995	Felony	Not passed
Utah	House Bill No. 331	1995	Felony	Not passed
California	Assembly Bill No. 380	1996	Sentence enhancement	Not passed
California	Assembly Bill No. 2147	1996	Felony	Not passed
New York	Senate Bill No. 280	1996	Felony	Not passed
Alaska	Senate Bill No. 17	1997	Felony	Vetoed
Connecticut	House Bill No. 5133	1997	Felony	Not passed
Mississippi	Senate Bill No. 2542	1997	Felony	Not passed
Mississippi	Senate Bill No. 2124	1997	Felony	Not passed
Missouri	Senate Bill No. 347	1997	Felony	Enacted
New Jersey	Senate Bill No. 1297	1997	Not applicable	Enacted
New Jersey	Assembly Bill No. 2084	1997	Not applicable	Not passed

Virginia	House Bill No. 1912	1997	Tiered	Not passed
Arizona	House Bill No. 2396	1998	Felony	Not passed
California	Senate Bill No. 705	1998	Felony	Enacted
California	Assembly Bill No. 2287	1998	Felony	Not passed
Indiana	Senate Bill No. 355	1998	Tiered	Enacted
Indiana	House Bill No. 1126	1998	Felony	Not passed
Indiana	House Bill No. 1012	1998	Felony	Not passed
Indiana	House Bill No. 1029	1998	Felony	Not passed
Iowa	House Bill No. 2369	1998	Felony	Enacted
Iowa	House Bill No. 2108	1998	Felony	Not passed
Mississippi	Senate Bill No. 2545	1998	Felony	Not passed
Mississippi	Senate Bill No. 2657	1998	Felony	Not passed
New York	Assembly Bill No. 8861	1998	Felony	Not passed
New York	Senate Bill No. 1592	1998	Felony	Not passed
New York	Senate Bill No. 3017	1998	Felony	Not passed
Pennsylvania	Senate Bill No. 1263	1998	Felony	Not passed
Virginia	House Bill No. 73	1998	Tiered	Not passed
Virginia	House Bill No. 296	1998	Felony	Not passed
Connecticut	House Bill No. 5434	1999	Felony	Not passed
Hawai'i	House Bill No. 819	1999	Felony	Not passed
Indiana	Senate Bill No. 373	1999	Tiered	Not passed
Mississippi	Senate Bill No. 2450	1999	Felony	Not passed
Mississippi	Senate Bill No. 2006	1999	Felony	Not passed
Ohio	Senate Bill No. 100	1999	Felony	Enacted
Pennsylvania	Senate Bill No. 847	1999	Felony	Not passed
Virginia	House Bill No. 296	1999	Tiered	Not passed
Virginia	House Bill No. 1604	1999	Felony	Not passed
Wisconsin	Assembly Bill No. 550	1999	Felony	Not passed
Hawai'i	Senate Bill No. 2602	2000	Felony	Not passed
Indiana	Senate Bill No. 277	2000	Tiered	Not passed
Indiana	House Bill No. 1392	2000	Tiered	Not passed
Mississippi	Senate Bill No. 2249	2000	Felony	Not passed
Mississippi	Senate Bill No. 2044	2000	Felony	Not passed
New York	Assembly Bill No. 1908	2000	Felony	Not passed
New York	Senate Bill No. 464	2000	Felony	Not passed
South Dakota	Senate Bill No. 48	2000	Felony	Enacted
Virginia	House Bill No. 141	2000	Felony	Enacted
Mississippi	Senate Bill No. 2065	2001	Felony	Not passed
Mississippi	Senate Bill No. 2080	2001	Felony	Not passed
Pennsylvania	Senate Bill No. 221	2001	Felony	Not passed
Hawai'i	House Bill No. 2688	2002	Felony	Not passed
Mississippi	Senate Bill No. 2010	2002	Felony	Not passed
Missouri	House Bill No. 1756	2002	Felony	Enacted
New York	Assembly Bill No. 827	2002	Felony	Not Passed
New York	Senate Bill No. 3521	2002	Felony	Not passed
Mississippi	Senate Bill No. 2082	2003	Felony	Not passed

(continued)

STATE	Bill Number	Year Introduced	Penalty	Final Action
Pennsylvania	Senate Bill No. 314	2003	Felony	Not passed
Virginia	House Bill No. 2082	2003	Chemical castration	Not passed
Mississippi	House Bill No. 1298	2004	Felony	Enacted
Mississippi	Senate Bill No. 2810	2004	Felony	Not passed
Nebraska	Bill No. 872	2004	Felony	Not passed
New York	Assembly Bill No. 5278	2004	Felony	Not passed
Virginia	House Bill No. 871	2004	Tiered	Enacted
Virginia	House Bill No. 657	2004	Felony	Not passed
Colorado	Senate Bill No. 17	2005	Misdemeanor	Not passed
Nebraska	Bill No. 377	2005	Tiered	Not passed
New Hampshire	House Bill No. 673-FN	2005	Felony	Not passed
Pennsylvania	Senate Bill No. 505	2005	Felony	Not passed
Wisconsin	Assembly Bill No. 652	2005	Felony	Not passed
Delaware	House Bill No. 417	2006	Felony	Not passed
New York	Assembly Bill No. 9359	2010	Felony	Not passed
West Virginia	Senate Bill No. 599	2010	Felony	Not passed
New York	Assembly Bill No. 2991	2012	Felony	Not passed
New York	Assembly Bill No. 4006	2013	Felony	Not passed

Notes

INTRODUCTION

1. Jimmy Swaggart, "Column: Jimmy Swaggart," *Advocate* (Baton Rouge), July 20, 1985, 5-B. Swaggart is an American televangelist and was at the time a columnist for the Baton Rouge *Advocate* (not to be confused with the LGBT magazine *The Advocate*).

2. UPI Newstrack, "A Conservative Political Action Committee Called Traditional Values Demands . . . ," October 5, 1985, Newsbank. Louis Sheldon founded the Traditional Values Coalition in 1984 and continues to serve as the group's chairman. Designated a hate group by the Southern Poverty Law Center, the group has long championed antigay campaigns nationwide.

3. Don Boys, "Don't Protect Victims at Society's Expense," *USA Today,* June 24, 1988, 8A. Boys is an evangelist, a former member of the Indiana House of Representatives, and the author of *AIDS: A Silent Killer* (Ringgold, GA: Freedom Publications, 1987), which promoted the idea that AIDS was contagious via coughing and sneezing.

4. Joan Parrish, "On the Right Track," *Tulsa World,* February 28, 1989, 7A. Parrish's editorial reflects a populist sentiment at the time: that crime was rampant and authorities were doing little to clamp down on it.

5. George Gallup Jr. and Jim Castelli, "Poll Catalogs Views on AIDS by Religion," *Dallas Morning News,* September 27, 1987, 45A.

6. Lyndon LaRouche is best known for his ballot initiative efforts in California to restrict the rights of people living with HIV. William F. Buckley Jr. founded the conservative magazine *National Review* and famously promoted the idea that newly diagnosed AIDS patients should be tattooed. See, for example, David L. Kirp, "LaRouche Turns to AIDS Politics," *New York Times,* September 11, 1986, http://www.nytimes.com/1986/09/11/opinion/larouche-turns-to-aids-politics .html; William F. Buckley, "Crucial Steps in Combating the AIDS Epidemic;

Identify All the Carriers," *New York Times*, March 18, 1986, https://www.nytimes.com/books/00/07/16/specials/buckley-aids.html.

7. Several AIDS activists have recently penned memoirs that shed light on these debates. See, for example, Sean Strub, *Body Counts: A Memoir of Politics, Sex, AIDS, and Survival* (New York: Scribner, 2014).

8. "There Ought to Be a Law," *Daily News of Los Angeles*, December 4, 1987, N24.

9. For a concise overview of the war on drugs, see "A Brief History of the Drug War," Drug Policy Alliance, accessed January 5, 2017, http://www.drugpolicy.org/facts/new-solutions-drug-policy/brief-history-drug-war-0.

10. "Death for Dealers? Bush Might Buy It," *Miami Herald*, September 2, 1986, 13A.

11. Ronald J. Ostrow, "Casual Drug Users Should Be Shot, Gates Says," *Los Angeles Times*, September 6, 1990, A1.

12. See Doris Provine, *Unequal under Law: Race in the War on Drugs* (Chicago: University of Chicago Press, 2007).

13. See Michelle Alexander, "The Color of Justice," chap. 3 in *The New Jim Crow: Mass Incarceration in the Age of Colorblindness* (New York: New Press, 2010).

14. Justice Policy Institute, *The Punishing Decade: Prison and Jail Estimates at the Millennium*, May 2000, http://www.justicepolicy.org/images/upload/00-05_rep_punishingdecade_ac.pdf; and United States Department of Justice, *Correctional Populations in the United States, 1990* (Washington, DC: Bureau of Justice Statistics, 1992). By contrast, the prison and jail population had increased by about one-third between 1970 and 1980.

15. For a discussion, see David Garland, "Social Change and Social Order in Late Modernity," chap. 4 in *The Culture of Control: Crime and Social Order in Contemporary Society* (Chicago: University of Chicago Press, 2001).

16. Bruce Western, *Punishment and Inequality in America* (New York: Russell Sage Foundation, 2006), 192.

17. Garland, "Social Change."

18. Jonathan Simon, "Project Exile: Race, the War on Crime, and Mass Imprisonment," in *Governing through Crime: How the War on Crime Transformed American Democracy and Created a Culture of Fear* (New York: Oxford University Press, 2007), chap. 5.

19. Roy Walmsley, *World Prison Population List*, 10th ed. (London: International Centre for Prison Studies, 2013).

20. Bureau of Justice Statistics, *Correctional Populations in the United States, 2013* (Washington, DC: Department of Justice, 2014), 13, appendix table 5.

21. Alfred Blumstein and Allen J. Beck, "Reentry as a Transient State between Liberty and Commitment," in *Prisoner Reentry and Crime in America*, ed. Jeremy Travis and Christy Visher (New York: Cambridge University Press, 2005), 50–79.

22. Alexander, *New Jim Crow*.

23. Chris Uggen, Jeff Manza, and Melissa Thompson, "Citizenship, Democracy, and the Civic Reintegration of Criminal Offenders," *ANNALS of the American Academy of Political and Social Science* 605 (2006): 281–310.

24. For a review, see Sara Wakefield and Chris Uggen, "Incarceration and Stratification," *Annual Review of Sociology* 36 (2012): 387–406.

25. David Garland, ed., *Mass Imprisonment: Social Causes and Consequences* (New York: SAGE Publications, 2001).

26. The recent collection of essays *The War on Sex* makes this point. In the book's introduction, David Halperin explains that the war on sex is "a war against sex itself—in many cases, against sex that does no harm but that arouses disapproval on moral, aesthetic, political, or religious grounds. Those grounds provide an acceptable and politically palatable cover for a war on the kinds of sex that are disreputable or that many people already happen to dislike." David Halperin, "Introduction: The War on Sex," in *The War on Sex,* ed. David Halperin and Trevor Hoppe, (Durham, NC: Duke University Press, 2017), 3–4.

27. Trevor Hoppe, "Punishing Sex: Sex Offenders and the Missing Punitive Turn in Sexuality Studies," *Law and Social Inquiry* 41, no. 3 (Summer 2016): 573–94.

28. Ibid.

29. Thomas McKeown famously argued that the biggest declines in mortality from infectious disease were due to better nutrition and sanitation—and that vaccines and antibiotics played a diminished role in squashing infectious disease. Thomas McKeown, R. G. Record, and R. G. Turner, "An Interpretation of the Decline of Mortality in England and Wales during the Twentieth Century," *Population Studies* 29, no. 3 (1975): 391–422. For a discussion of McKeown's legacy, see James Colgrove, "The McKeown Thesis: A Historical Controversy and Its Enduring Influence," *AJPH* 92, no. 5 (May 2002): 725–29.

30. In 1968, psychologists added "hyperkinetic reaction to childhood" as a disorder category in the second edition of the *Diagnostic and Statistical Manual.* Sociologist Peter Conrad quickly picked up on the potential problems posed by this category in his now-famous article "The Discovery of Hyperkinesis." Peter Conrad, "The Discovery of Hyperkinesis: Notes on the Medicalization of Deviant Behavior," *Social Problems* 23, no. 1 (1975): 12–21.

31. Recently, Peter Conrad has followed up on his work to note the development of adult ADHD as an emerging category. Peter Conrad and Deborah Potter, "From Hyperactive Children to ADHD Adults: Observations on the Expansion of Medical Categories," *Social Problems* 47, no. 4 (2000): 559–82.

32. For a lengthy discussion of this process and its many examples, see Joseph Schneider and Peter Conrad, *Deviance and Medicalization: From Badness to Sickness* (Philadelphia: Temple University Press, 1980).

33. Robert C. Gallo, "A Reflection on HIV/AIDS Research after 25 Years," *Retrovirology* 3, no. 72 (2006): 1–7.

34. Even some gay activists were concerned that the use of nitrite inhalants, typically called "poppers," were the actual culprit behind AIDS. When the HIV virus was discovered, some advocates continued to argue that a single-cause theory of AIDS was wrong and instead argued for a multifactorial approach. See, for example, John Lauritsen and Hank Wilson, *Death Rush: Poppers & AIDS* (New York: Pagan Press, 1986).

35. For a discussion of the lasting impact of such associations, see Cindy Patton, "What Science Knows: Formations of AIDS Knowledges," in *AIDS:*

Individual, Cultural, and Policy Dimensions, ed. Peter Aggleton (New York: Routledge, 1990), 1–18.

36. The notion of labeling is often credited to sociologist Howard Becker, whose 1963 book *Outsiders* examined how society responded to marijuana users and dance musicians. Howard Becker, *Outsiders: Studies in the Sociology of Deviance* (New York: Free Press, 1963).

37. This gap has long been of interest to sociologists, often traced back to sociologists working in the late nineteenth and early twentieth centuries, including Émile Durkheim, Leon Petrazycki, and Eugen Ehrlich. For a discussion of the field's intellectual history, see Mathieu Deflem, *Sociology of Law: Visions of a Scholarly Tradition* (Cambridge, UK: Cambridge University Press, 2008).

38. This model is adapted from McGarrell and Castellano's integrative conflict model of crime legislative policy. Edmund McGarrell and Thomas Castellano, "An Integrative Conflict Model of the Criminal Law Formation Process," *Journal of Research on Crime & Delinquency* 28, no. 2 (1991): 174–96.

39. John M. Conley and William O'Barr, *Just Words: Law, Language, and Power,* rev. 2nd ed. (Chicago: University of Chicago Press, 2005).

CHAPTER 1. CONTROLLING TYPHOID MARY

1. Anthony Lanzilote, "Can You Get Ebola from a Bowling Ball?," *New York Times,* October 23, 2014, https://well.blogs.nytimes.com/2014/10/23/can-you-get-ebola-from-a-bowling-ball/.

2. Brad Gerick, "New Yorkers, Twitter Users Wonder Why Dr. Craig Spencer Went Bowling," *New York Daily News,* October 23, 2014, http://www.nydailynews.com/new-york/new-yorkers-dr-craig-spencer-bowling-article-1.1985427.

3. Ibid.

4. Mark Berman and DaNeel N. Brown, "Thomas Duncan, the Texas Ebola Patient, Has Died," *Washington Post,* October 8, 2014, https://www.washingtonpost.com/news/post-nation/wp/2014/10/08/texas-ebola-patient-has-died-from-ebola/.

5. Ibid.

6. Manny Fernandez and Kevin Sack, "Ebola Patient Sent Home despite Fever, Records Show," *New York Times,* October 10, 2014, https://www.nytimes.com/2014/10/11/us/thomas-duncan-had-a-fever-of-103-er-records-show.html.

7. Bate Felix, "Liberia Says May Prosecute Man Who Flew to U.S. with Ebola," Reuters, October 2, 2014, http://www.reuters.com/article/us-health-ebola-liberia-idUSKCN0HR25U20141002.

8. Alex Johnson, "Kaci Hickox, Maine Nurse Quarantined in Ebola Scare, Sues New Jersey Gov. Chris Christie," *NBC News,* October 22, 2015, http://www.nbcnews.com/storyline/ebola-virus-outbreak/kaci-hickox-maine-nurse-quarantined-ebola-scare-sues-new-jersey-n449491.

9. *Daily Mail,* "'I Don't Care If I Have Ebola, I'm Riding My Damn Bike!': *Saturday Night Live* Mocks New Jersey Quarantine Fiasco Ending in Fist-Fight between Governor Chris Christie and Nurse," November 2, 2014, http://www.dailymail.co.uk/news/article-2817468/I-don-t-care-Ebola-m-riding-damn-

bike-Saturday-Night-Live-mocks-New-Jersey-quarantine-fiasco-ending-fist-fight-Governor-Chris-Christie-nurse.html.

10. Laura Wagner, "New Jersey Governor Facing Lawsuit from Nurse Quarantined during Ebola Scare," *NPR News,* October 22, 2014, http://www.npr.org/sections/thetwo-way/2015/10/22/450908372/new-jersey-governor-facing-lawsuit-from-quarantined-nurse.

11. Associated Press, "Judge Tosses Civil Rights Claims of Kaci Hickox, the Ebola-Quarantined Nurse," *Portland Press Herald,* September 8, 2016, http://www.pressherald.com/2016/09/08/judge-tosses-the-civil-rights-claims-of-kaci-hickox-the-ebola-quarantined-nurse/.

12. This chapter uses the term *public health* broadly—referring to a wide range of health promotion practices spearheaded by governmental officials, professionals, and/or advocates who may have very different perspectives. For example, the public health response to Ebola in the United States includes both New Jersey's twenty-one-day quarantine policy as well as the Centers for Disease Control director's criticism of that policy. Nonetheless, some strategies have dominated others in certain historical moments.

13. Many thanks to Scott Burris for his assistance in distinguishing these forms of social control.

14. For a discussion of coercion in public health practice, see Lawrence O. Gostin, "A Theory and Definition of Public Health Law," *Journal of Health Care Law and Policy* 10 (2007): 3–4.

15. Kansas v. Hendricks, 521 U.S. 346 (1997), 362.

16. Ronald Bayer, "Ethics and Infectious Disease Control: STDs, HIV, TB," in *Ethics and Public Health: Model Curriculum,* ed. Bruce Jennings, Jeffery Kahn, Anna Mastroianni, and Lisa S. Parker (Washington, DC: Health Resources and Services Administration, 2003), 133–46.

17. There are other cases in which punitive actions taken by the state are not legally determined to qualify as "punishment" under the Constitution. For example, J. Wallace Borchert examines how consensual sex between same-sex partners is punished within American jails and prisons. The various kinds of internal sanctions meted out against gay and lesbian prisoners include reduced freedom of movement, including administrative segregation, or a lengthier prison term. However, criminal justice authorities do not view these responses to same-sex behavior (or, for that matter, any of the administrative penalties doled out against people incarcerated) as punishment. J. Wallace Borchert, "A New Iron Closet: Failing to Extend the Spirit of Lawrence v. Texas to Prisons and Prisoners," in *The War on Sex,* ed. David Halperin and Trevor Hoppe (Durham, NC: Duke University Press, 2017), 191–210. For a discussion of civil commitment programs, see Laura Mansnerus, "For What They Might Do: A Sex Offender Exception to the Constitution," in Halperin and Hoppe, *The War on Sex,* 268–90.

18. Philosophers term this tendency to blame people for their illness "punishment theory of disease." For a discussion, see Loretta Kopelman, "If HIV/AIDS is Punishment, Who is Bad?," *Journal of Medicine and Philosophy* 27, no. 2 (August 9, 2010): 231–43.

19. Janet Brooks, "The Sad and Tragic Life of Typhoid Mary," *Canadian Medical Association Journal* 154, no. 6 (1996): 915–16.

20. Howard Markel, *Quarantine! East European Jewish Immigrants and the New York City Epidemics* (Baltimore, MD: Johns Hopkins University Press, 1999), 55–56.

21. William H. Park, "Typhoid Bacilli Carriers," *JAMA* 51 (1908): 981.

22. Paul S. Sehdev, "The Origin of Quarantine," *Clinical Infectious Disease* 35, no. 9 (2002): 1071–72.

23. For a discussion, see Robert S. Gottfried, *The Black Death: Natural and Human Disaster in Medieval Europe* (New York: Free Press, 1985), 124.

24. Eugenia Tognotti, "Lessons from the History of Quarantine, from Plague to Influenza A," *Emerging Infectious Diseases* 19, no. 2 (2013): 254–59; and Wendy Parmet, "Legal Power and Legal Rights—Isolation and Quarantine in the Case of Drug-Resistant Tuberculosis," *New England Journal of Medicine* 357 (2007): 433–35.

25. For a history of quarantine, see Parmet, "Legal Power and Legal Rights"; and Tognotti, "Lessons from the History of Quarantine."

26. Tognotti, "Lessons from the History of Quarantine," 257.

27. For a useful brief overview of quarantine, see Peter Tyson, "A Short History of Quarantine," *NOVA*, October 12, 2004, http://www.pbs.org/wgbh/nova/body/short-history-of-quarantine.html.

28. For a thorough history, see Francesco Aimone, "The 1918 Influenza Epidemic in New York City: A Review of the Public Health Response," *Public Health Reports* 125, suppl. 3 (2010): 71–79.

29. Susan Dominus, "In 1918 Flu Outbreak, a Cool Head Prevailed," *New York Times*, April 30, 2009, A19.

30. Alfred Crosby, *America's Forgotten Pandemic: The Influenza of 1918*, 2nd ed. (Cambridge, UK: Cambridge University Press, 2003). Crosby estimates that New York had a death rate of about 6 per 1,000, lower than Boston (7 per 1,000) or Philadelphia (7.5 per 1000).

31. Lawrence O. Gostin, Scott Burris, and Zita Lazzarini, "The Law and the Public's Health: A Study of Infectious Disease Law in the United States," *Columbia Law Review* 99 (1999): 59–128.

32. Barron Lerner, "Temporarily Detained: Tuberculous Alcoholics in Seattle, 1949 through 1960," *American Journal of Public Health* 86, no. 2 (1996): 259.

33. Ibid., 262.

34. See Gostin, Burris, and Lazzarini, "Law and the Public's Health"; Parmet, "Legal Power and Legal Rights."

35. Allen Brandt, *No Magic Bullet: A Social History of Venereal Disease in the United States* (New York: Oxford University Press, 1985), 85.

36. Ibid.

37. See Tyson, "Short History of Quarantine."

38. Troy Thompson, "'A Black Spot': Florida's Crusade against Venereal Disease, Prostitution, and Female Sexuality during World War II," *Florida Public Health Review* 2 (2005): 115.

39. Brandt, *No Magic Bullet*, 167.

40. Judith W. Leavitt, *Typhoid Mary: Captive to the Public's Health* (Boston: Beacon Press, 1996), 122.

41. James Colgrove and Ronald Bayer, "Manifold Restraints: Liberty, Public Health, and the Legacy of *Jacobson v. Massachusetts*," *American Journal of Public Health* 95 (2005): 571–76.

42. Ronald Bayer, "Ethics and Infectious Disease Control," 141.

43. In such cases as *Lessard v. Smith* (1972), the courts established that patients had the right to be treated in the least restrictive setting that met their needs. In 1980, in *Greene v. Edwards,* the West Virginia court of appeals ruled that these protections also applied to tuberculosis patients facing involuntary isolation. *Lessard v. Smith* (1972) also affirmed the doctrine of the least restrictive alternative, under which patients should be offered outpatient treatment before institutional care, which has been extended to tuberculosis patients. See Bayer, "Ethics and Infectious Disease Control"; Ronald Bayer and Laurence Dupuis, "Tuberculosis, Public Health, and Civil Liberties," *Annual Review of Public Health* 16 (1995): 307–26.

44. Centers for Disease Control and Prevention (CDC), "Leading Causes of Death, 1900–1998," accessed January 25, 2017, https://www.cdc.gov/nchs/data/dvs/lead1900_98.pdf.

45. Thomas McKeown famously argued that the biggest declines in mortality from infectious disease were due to better nutrition and sanitation—and that vaccines and antibiotics played a more diminished role in squashing infectious disease. Thomas McKeown, R. G. Record, and R. G. Turner, "An Interpretation of the Decline of Mortality in England and Wales during the Twentieth Century," Population Studies 29, no. 3 (1975): 391–422. For a discussion of McKeown's legacy, see James Colgrove, "The McKeown Thesis: A Historical Controversy and Its Enduring Influence," *American Journal of Public Health* 92, no. 5 (May 2002): 725–29. For the leading causes of death, see CDC, "Leading Causes of Death, 1900–1998."

46. U.S. Public Health Service, "Smoking and Health. Report of the Advisory Committee to the Surgeon General," *DHEW Publication (PHS),* no. 1103 (1964).

47. Centers for Disease Control and Prevention (CDC), "Trends in Cigarette Smoking around High School Students and Adults, United States, 1965–2014," last updated March 30, 2016, https://www.cdc.gov/tobacco/data_statistics/tables/trends/cig_smoking/.

48. Federal Cigarette Labeling and Advertising Act of 1965, U.S.C. 15 (1965) § 1331 et seq.

49. Peter D. Jacobson, Jeffrey Wasserman, and John R. Anderson, "Historical Overview of Tobacco Legislation and Regulation," *Journal of Social Issues* 53, no. 1 (1997): 75–95; and Jonathan Gruber, "Tobacco at the Crossroads: The Past and Future of Smoking Regulation in the United States," *Journal of Economic Perspectives* 15, no. 2 (Spring 2001): 193–212.

50. Jacobson, Wasserman, and Anderson, "Historical Overview of Tobacco Legislation."

51. For an empirical analysis of the impact of California's taxation policies and antismoking media campaigns, see Teh-wei Hu, Hai-Yen Sung, and Theodore Keeler, "Reducing Cigarette Consumption in California: Tobacco Taxes vs.

an Anti-Smoking Media Campaign," *American Journal of Public Health* 85, no. 9 (September 1995): 1218–22.

52. CDC, "Trends in Cigarette Smoking, 1965–2014."

53. See Colgrove and Bayer, "Manifold Restraints"; and Ronald Bayer, "The Continuing Tensions between Individual Rights and Public Health," *Journal of European Molecular Biology* 8 (2007): 1099–103.

54. New York City's efforts to curtail the sale of sugary drinks have been particularly controversial, as the science behind these efforts is not entirely clear. In 2013, a judge blocked the limits, calling the policies "arbitrary and capricious." Michael M. Grynbaum, "Judge Blocks New York City's Limits on Big Sugary Drinks," *New York Times,* March 11, 2013, A1.

55. Alan Petersen and Deborah Lupton, *The New Public Health: Health and Self in the Age of Risk* (Newbury Park, CA: Sage, 1997).

56. Michel Foucault, *Discipline and Punish: The Birth of the Prison* (London: Tavistock, 1977).

57. For a discussion, see Petersen and Lupton, *The New Public Health.*

58. Deborah Lupton, *Risk,* 2nd ed. (New York: Routledge, 2013), 489.

59. National Institutes of Allergy and Infectious Disease, "Finding the Cause of Lyme Disease," last modified June 9, 2008, https://www.niaid.nih.gov /diseases-conditions/finding-lyme-disease-cause.

60. Lawrence Altman, "In Philadelphia 30 Years Ago, an Eruption of Illness and Fear," *New York Times,* August 1, 2006, F1.

61. For a discussion of these issues, see Gostin, Burris, and Lazzarini, "Law and the Public's Health."

62. For an discussion of neoliberalism and its impact on public health policy and practice, see Nike Ayo, "Understanding Health Promotion in a Neoliberal Climate and the Making of Health Conscious Citizens," *Critical Public Health* 22, no. 1 (March 30, 2011): 99–105.

63. Albert R. Zink, Cristophe Sola, Udo Reischl, Waltraud Grabner, Nalin Rastogi, Hans Wolf, and Andreas Nerlich, "Characterization of *Mycobacterium tuberculosis* Complex DNAs from Egyptian Mummies by Spoligotyping," *Journal of Clinical Microbiology* 41, no. 1 (2003): 359–67.

64. Samuel W. Dooley, William R. Jarvis, William J. Marione, and Dixie E. Snider, "Multidrug-resistant Tuberculosis," *Annals of Internal Medicine* 117, no. 3 (August 1, 1992): 257–59.

65. For a review of the disease and global efforts to fight it, see Stephen D. Lawn and Alimuddin I. Zumla, "Tuberculosis," *Lancet* 378, no. 9785 (July 2011): 57–72.

66. New York City Department of Health and Mental Hygiene, "New York City Is Stopping TB," 2009, https://www1.nyc.gov/assets/doh/downloads/pdf /tb/tb_annualsummary08.pdf .

67. See Bayer, "Ethics and Infectious Disease Control"; and Bayer and Dupuis, "Tuberculosis, Public Health, and Civil Liberties."

68. Ronald Bayer and David Wilkinson, "Directly Observed Therapy: History of an Idea," *The Lancet* 345, no. 8694 (June 17, 1995): 1545–8.

69. Bayer, "Ethics and Infectious Disease Control"; Bayer and Dupuis, "Tuberculosis, Public Health, and Civil Liberties."

70. Bayer, "Ethics and Infectious Disease Control"; Bayer and Dupuis, "Tuberculosis, Public Health, and Civil Liberties"; and M. Rose Gasner, Khin Lay Maw, Gabriel E. Feldman, Paula Fujiwara, and Thomas R. Frieden, "Use of Legal Action in New York City to Ensure Treatment of Tuberculosis," *New England Journal of Medicine* 340 (February 4, 1999): 359–66, http://www.nejm.org/doi/full/10.1056/NEJM199902043400506#t=article.

71. See Gostin, Burris, and Lazzarini, "Law and the Public's Health."

72. Gasner et al., "Use of Legal Action," 359.

73. Ibid.

74. Centers for Disease Control and Prevention, "Pneumocystis Pneumonia—Los Angeles," *MMWR* 30 (1981).

75. See Clarence Page, "The Rise and Fall of Jerry Falwell," *Chicago Tribune*, May 20, 2007, http://articles.chicagotribune.com/2007-05-20/news/0705190543_1_thomas-road-baptist-church-lynchburg-baptist-nation-of-islam-minister.

76. Kaiser Family Foundation, *HIV/AIDS at 30: A Public Opinion Perspective* (Washington, DC: Kaiser Family Foundation, 2011).

77. Mike Thomas, "Arson Cause of Fire at Rays—Boys Start School Today," *Orlando Sentinel*, September 23, 1987, http://articles.orlandosentinel.com/1987-09-23/news/0150050182_1_andy-ray-ray-family-varnadore.

78. Lawrence O. Gostin, "The Isolation of HIV—Positive Patients Reply," *JAMA* 262 (1989): 208–9; John Waller, "Sex, Sin, and Science: The HIV/AIDS Crisis," 2014, accessed May 1, 2015, http://history.msu.edu/hst425/resources/online-essays/sin-sex-and-science-the-hivaids-crisis/.

79. Eleanor Singer, Theresa F. Rogers, and Mary Corcoran, "The Polls—A Report: AIDS," *Public Opinion Quarterly* 51, no. 4 (Winter 1987): 580.

80. Philip J. Tiemeyer, *Plane Queer: Labor, Sexuality, and AIDS in the History of Male Flight Attendants* (Berkeley: University of California Press, 2013), 170.

81. Gostin, "Isolation of HIV."

82. J. Stan Lehman, Meredith H. Carr, Allison J. Nichol, Alberto Ruisanchez, David W. Knight, Anne E. Langford, Simone C. Gray, and Jonathan H. Mermin, "Prevalence and Public Health Implications of State Laws That Criminalize Potential HIV Exposure in the United States," *AIDS and Behavior* 18 (2014): 997–1006.

83. Ibid.

84. Lawrence O. Gostin, *The AIDS Pandemic: Complacency, Injustice, and Unfulfilled Expectations* (Chapel Hill: University of North Carolina Press, 2004).

85. Office of the President of the United States of America, "National HIV/AIDS Strategy," July 2010, accessed January 9, 2017, 37, https://www.whitehouse.gov/sites/default/files/uploads/NHAS.pdf.

86. "Prevalence and Public Health Implications of State Laws That Criminalize Potential HIV Exposure in the United States," Center for HIV Law and Policy, March 2014, accessed January 9, 2017, http://hivlawandpolicy.org/resources/prevalence-and-public-health-implications-state-laws-criminalize-potential-hiv-exposure.

87. Katherine Beckett and Bruce Western, "Governing Social Marginality: Welfare, Incarceration, and the Transformation of State Policy," *Punishment and Society* 3, no. 1 (2001): 43–59.

88. Erica Meiners and Maisha T. Winn, "Resisting the School to Prison Pipeline: The Practice to Build Abolition Democracies," *Race Ethnicity and Education* 13, no. 3 (2010): 271–76.

89. Becky Pettit and Bruce Western, "Mass Imprisonment and the Life Course: Race and Class Inequality in U.S. Incarceration," *American Sociological Review* 69, no. 2 (2004): 151–69.

90. Allan Brandt, "Behavior, Disease, and Health in the Twentieth-Century United States: The Moral Valence of Individual Risk," in *Morality and Health*, ed. Allan M. Brandt and Paul Rozin (New York: Routledge, 1997), 69.

CHAPTER 2. "HIV STOPS WITH ME"

1. Walt Odets, "Prevention for Positives," *POZ Magazine,* January 1, 2004, https://www.poz.com/article/Prevention-for-Positives-179-7702.

2. Centers for Disease Control and Prevention, "Advancing HIV Prevention: New Strategies for a Changing Epidemic—United States, 2003," *Morbidity and Mortality Weekly Report* 52, no. 15 (April 18, 2003): 329–32.

3. Notably, I am not the first scholar to take notice of this transition. In 2001, for example, Kane Race argued that new treatment protocols had the potential to responsibilize HIV-positive people in unexpected and potentially problematic ways. Kane Race, "The Undetectable Crisis: Changing Technologies of Risk," *Sexualities* 4, no. 2 (May 2001): 167–89. Also see Barry Adam and colleagues' concern that the "onus of responsibility may be shifting back toward HIV-positive people" in Canadian HIV legal discourse. Barry Adam, Richard Elliot, Winston Husbands, James Murray, and John Maxwell, "Effects of the Criminalization of HIV Transmission in *Cuerrier* on Men Reporting Unprotected Sex with Men," *Canadian Journal of Law and Society* 23, no. 1–2 (2008): 144.

4. It is not difficult to find comparisons between AIDS and the Holocaust. For just one example, see Larry Kramer, *Reports from the Holocaust: The Story of an AIDS Activist* (New York: St. Martin's, 1989).

5. Advisory Committee of the People with AIDS, "Denver Principles (1983)," http://www.actupny.org/documents/Denver.html.

6. For a useful brief review of this history, see Sean Strub, "Denver Principles Empowerment Index and a Brief History of the Empowerment Movement," *POZ Blogs,* July 7, 2011, https://blogs.poz.com/sean/archives/2011/07/denver_principles_em.html.

7. Steven Epstein has written the most comprehensive analysis of ACT UP and its impact on science. Steven Epstein, *Impure Science: AIDS, Activism, and the Politics of Knowledge* (Berkeley: University of California Press, 1993).

8. Centers for Disease Control and Prevention, *HIV/AIDS Surveillance Report* 11, no. 2 (1999), https://www.cdc.gov/hiv/pdf/library/reports/surveillance/cdc-hiv-surveillance-report-1999-vol-11-2.pdf.

9. Chris Collins, Stephen F. Morrin, Michael D. Shriver, and Thomas J. Coates, *Designing Primary Prevention for People Living with HIV* (San Francisco: AIDS Policy Research Center and Center for AIDS Prevention Studies, 2000), 2.

10. Ibid., 5.

11. For a thorough analysis of the Williams case and its media portrayal, see Thomas Shevory, *Notorious HIV: The Media Spectacle of Nushawn Williams* (Minneapolis: University of Minnesota Press, 2004).

12. Although Williams was due to be released upon completion of his twelve-year prison sentence in 2010, authorities invoked a then-new "civil commitment" procedure against him; it allowed the state to keep sex offenders deemed a threat behind bars forever. "HIV-Positive Convict Nushawn Williams to Remain in Civil Confinement," *POZ Magazine*, May 12, 2016, https://www.poz.com/article /hivpositive-convict-nushawn-williams-remain-civil-confinement.

13. Gary Marks, Scott Burris, and Thomas A. Peterman, "Reducing Sexual Transmission of HIV from Those Who Know They Are Infected: The Need for Personal and Collective Responsibility," *AIDS* 13, no. 3 (March 3, 1999): 301.

14. Judith D. Auerbach, "Principles of Positive Prevention," suppl., *Journal of Acquired Immune Deficiency Syndromes* 37, no. S2 (October 2004): S123.

15. Robert S. Janssen, David R. Holtgrave, Ronald O. Valdiserri, Melissa Shepherd, Helene D. Gayle, and Kevin M. De Cock, "The Serostatus Approach to Fighting the HIV Epidemic: Prevention Strategies for Infected Individuals," *American Journal of Public Health* 91, no. 7 (July 2001): 1019–24.

16. Ibid., 1019–20.

17. These figures come from searches for these phrases between 1992 and 2013 on Google Scholar. While roughly 25 publications cite these phrases in 2003, that number increases to over 150 in 2008 and over 250 in 2013. Google Scholar, http://www.google.com/scholar.

18. Sue Rochman, "You Are Your Brother's Keeper," *HIV Plus*, March 1, 2003, http://www.hivplusmag.com/issue-features/2003/03/01/you-are-your-brother8217s-keeper.

19. According to Les Pappas, president of Better World Advertising (the social marketing firm behind HIV Stops with Me), iterations of the campaign have made their way into thirteen markets—six in California (Los Angeles, West Hollywood, San Diego, Orange County, San Francisco, and Oakland) and seven outside California (Oregon, Seattle, New York, Virginia, Maryland, Alaska, and Boston). Les Pappas, e-mail message to the author, December 21, 2016.

20. It was not possible to independently verify whether HIV Stops with Me is definitely the most widely disseminated positive prevention campaign. According to the advertising agency's president, Les Pappas, "We would not have any way of verifying this either. However, we have not heard of any other positive prevention campaigns implemented in so many jurisdictions." Les Pappas, e-mail message to the author, December 21, 2016.

21. Better World Advertising, "Bold HIV Prevention Campaign Claims 'Cure' in Three Cities," PR Newswire, November 10, 2006, http://www .thefreelibrary.com/Bold+HIV+Prevention+Campaign+Claims+%27Cure%27 +in+Three+Cities.-a0154242388.

22. For just a few examples, see Jonathan Elford, Graham Bolding, Mark Maguire, and Lorraine Sherr, "Combination Therapies for HIV and Sexual Risk Behavior among Gay Men," *Journal of Acquired Immune Deficiency Syndrome* 23, no. 3 (April 2000): 266–71; Perry Halkitis, "Barebacking among

Gay and Bisexual Men in New York City: Explanations for the Emergence of Intentional Unsafe Behavior," *Archives of Sexual Behavior* 32, no. 4 (August 2003): 351–57; Linda A. Valleroy, Duncan A. MacKellar, John M. Karon, Daniel H. Rosen, William McFarland, Douglas A. Shehan, and the Young Men's Survey Study Group, "HIV Prevalence and Associated Risks in Young Men Who Have Sex with Men," *JAMA* 284, no. 2 (July 12, 2000): 198–204; Paul Van de Ven, Danielle Campbell, Susan Kippax, Stephanie Knox, Garrett Prestage, June Crawford, Paul Kinder, and David Cooper, "Gay Men who Engage Repeatedly in Unprotected Anal Intercourse with Casual Partners: The Sydney Men and Sexual Health Study," *International Journal of STD and AIDS* 9, no. 6 (June 1998): 336–40; and Jacob C. Warren, M. Isabel Fernandez, Gary W. Harper, Marco A. Hidalgo, Omar B. Jamil, and Rodrigo S. Torres, "Predictors of Unprotected Sex among Young Sexually Active African American, Hispanic, and White MSM: The Importance of Ethnicity and Culture," *AIDS and Behavior* 12, no. 3 (May 2008): 459–68.

23. See, for example, Linda A. Valleroy, Duncan A. MacKellar, John M. Karon, Daniel H. Rosen, William McFarland, Douglas A. Shehan, Susan R. Stoyanoff, et al., "HIV Prevalence and Associated Risks in Young Men Who Have Sex with Men," *JAMA* 284, no. 2 (July 12, 2000): 198–204; Warren et al., "Predictors of Unprotected Sex."

24. Michael Gross, "The Second Wave Will Drown Us," *American Journal of Public Health* 93, no. 6 (June 2003): 874.

25. Supachai Rerks-Ngarm, Punnee Pitisuttithum, Sorachai Nitayaphan, Jaranit Kaewkungwal, Joseph Chiu, Robert Paris, Nakorn Premsri, et al., "Vaccination with ALVAC and AIDSVAX to Prevent HIV-1 Infection in Thailand," *New England Journal of Medicine* 361, no. 23 (December 3, 2009): 2209–20.

26. See, for example, Ronald H. Gray, Godfrey Kigozi, David Serwadda, Frederick Makumbi, Stephen Watya, Fred Nalugoda, Noah Kiwanuka, et al., "Male Circumcision for HIV Prevention in Men in Rakai, Uganda: A Randomised Trial," *Lancet* 369, no. 9562 (February 24, 2007): 657–66.

27. Paul J. Feldblum, Adesina Adeiga, Rashidi Bakare, Silver Wevill, Anja Lendvay, Fatimah Obadaki, M. Onikepe Olayemi, Lily Wang, Kavita Nanda, and Wes Rountree, "SAVVY Vaginal Gel ($C_{31}G$) for Prevention of HIV Infection: A Randomized Controlled Trial in Nigeria," *PLoS ONE* 3, no. 1 (January 23, 2008): e1474.

28. Quarraisha Abdool Karim, Salim S. Abdool Karim, Janet A. Frohlich, Anneke C. Grobler, Cheryl Baxter, Leila E. Mansoor, Ayesha B. M. Kharsany, et al., "Effectiveness and Safety of Tenofovir Gel, an Antiretroviral Microbicide, for the Prevention of HIV Infection in Women," *Science* 329, no. 5996 (September 3, 2010): 1168–74.

29. Salim S. Abdool Karim, Barbra Richardson, Gita Ramjee, Irving Hoffman, Zvavahera M. Chirenje, Taha, Muzala Kapina, et al., "Safety and Effectiveness of BufferGel and 0.5% PRO2000 Gel for the Prevention of HIV Infection in Women," *AIDS* 25, no. 7 (April 24, 2011): 957–66.

30. National Institutes of Health, "NIH Discontinues Tenofovir Vaginal Gel in 'VOICE' HIV Prevention Study," news release, November 25, 2011, https://www.nih.gov/news/health/nov2011/niaid-25.htm.

31. Ann Swidler, "AIDS and the Moral Imagination" (paper presented at Second International HIV Social Science and Humanities Conference, Paris, France, July 7–10, 2013).

32. Gary Smith and Paul Van de Ven, *Reflecting on Practice: Current Challenges in Gay and Other Homosexually Active Men's HIV Education* (Sydney: National Centre in HIV Social Research, September 2001), 18.

33. Pietro Vernazza, Bernard Hirschel, Enos Bernasconi, and Markus Flepp, "Les personnes séropositives ne souffrant d'aucune autre MST et suivant un traitement antirétroviral efficace ne transmettent pas le VIH par voie sexuelle," *Bulletin des médecins suisses* 89, no. 5 (2008): 165–69.

34. Quoted in Alice Park, "Are Some HIV Patients Non-Infectious?" *Time,* February 4, 2008, http://www.time.com/time/health/article/0,8599,1709841,00 .html.

35. Myron S. Cohen, "HIV Treatment as Prevention and 'The Swiss Statement': In for a Dime, in for a Dollar?," *Clinical Infectious Diseases* 51, no. 11 (December 1, 2010): 1323.

36. Richard Berkowitz, *Stayin' Alive: The Invention of Safer Sex* (New York: Basic Books, 2003).

37. L. V. Anderson, "We Should Have a Better Condom by Now. Here's Why We Don't," *Slate,* April 2, 2015, http://www.slate.com/articles/health_and_ science/science/2015/04/latex_condoms_are_the_worst_why_after_all_these_ years_don_t_we_have_a_better.html.

38. Susan C. Weller, "A Meta-analysis of Condom Effectiveness in Reducing Sexually Transmitted HIV," *Social Science and Medicine* 36, no. 12 (June 1993): 1642.

39. Thomas C. Quinn, Maria J. Wawer, Nelson Sewankambo, David Serwadda, Chuanjun Li, Fred Wabwire-Mangen, Mary O. Meehan, Thomas Lutalo, and Ronald H. Gray, "Viral Load and Heterosexual Transmission of HIV Type 1," *New England Journal of Medicine* 342, no. 13 (March 30, 2000): 921–29; and Deborah Donnell, Jared M. Baeten, James Kiarie, Katherine K. Thomas, Wendy Stevens, Craig R. Cohen, James McIntyre, Jairam R. Lingappa, and Connie Celum, "Heterosexual HIV-1 Transmission after Initiation of Antiretroviral Therapy: A Prospective Cohort Study," *Lancet* 375, no. 9731 (June 2010): 2092–98.

40. Myron S. Cohen, Ying Q. Chen, Marybeth McCauley, Theresa Gamble, Mina C. Hosseinipour, Nagalingeswaran Kumarasamy, James G. Hakim, et al., "Prevention of HIV-1 Infection with Early Antiretroviral Treatment," *New England Journal of Medicine* 365, no. 6 (August 11, 2011): 493–505.

41. Jon Cohen, "Breakthrough of the Year: HIV Treatment as Prevention," *Science* 334, no. 6063 (December 2011): 1628.

42. Alison Rodger, Tina Bruun, Valentina Cambiano, Pietro Vernazza, Vicente Estrada, Jan Van Lunzen, Simon Collins, Anna Maria Geretti, Andrew Phillips, and Jens Lundgren, "HIV Transmission Risk through Condomless Sex if HIV+ Partner on Suppressive ART: PARTNER Study" (paper presented at the Twenty-First Conference on Retroviruses and Opportunistic Infections, Boston, MA, March 3–6, 2014).

43. Gus Cairns, "No-One with an Undetectable Viral Load, Gay or Heterosexual, Transmits HIV in First Two Years of PARTNER Study," *NAM Aidsmap,*

March 4, 2014, http://www.aidsmap.com/No-one-with-an-undetectable-viral-load-gay-or-heterosexual-transmits-HIV-in-first-two-years-of-PARTNER-study/page/2832748/.

44. Alison J. Rodger, Valentina Cambiano, Tina Bruun, Pietro Vernazza, Simon Collins, Jan van Lunzen, Giulio Maria Corbelli, et al., "Sexual Activity without Condoms and Risk of HIV Transmission in Serodifferent Couples When the HIV-Positive Partner Is Using Suppressive Antiretroviral Therapy," *JAMA* 316, no. 2 (2016): 171–81.

45. See, for example, "Risk of Sexual Transmission of HIV from a Person Living with HIV Who Has an Undetectable Viral Load: Messaging Primer and Consensus Statement," Prevention Access Campaign, November 16, 2016, http://www.preventionaccess.org/consensus.

46. These figures come from searches run on Google Scholar for "treatment as prevention" between 2004 and 2014. While almost no publications cited this phrase before the Swiss Statement in 2008, the number rapidly escalated to over two hundred in 2011, when the Centers for Disease Control announced HIP. See http://www.google.com/scholar.

47. Jonathan Mermin, "The Science and Practice of HIV Prevention in the United States" (paper presented at the Eighteenth Conference on Retroviruses and Opportunistic Infections, Boston, MA, February 27–March 2, 2011).

48. Centers for Disease Control and Prevention, *High-Impact HIV Prevention: CDC's Approach to Reducing HIV Infections in the United States,* August 2011, https://www.cdc.gov/hiv/pdf/policies_NHPC_Booklet.pdf.

49. Stephen J. Fallon, "Who Moved my DEBI? Preparing Your Agency to Fit the New High Impact HIV Prevention Priorities," October 2012, http://www.skills4.org/wp-content/uploads/2012/10/AdaptingAgencyHIP.pdf.

50. *The U.S. President's Emergency Plan for AIDS Relief: Fiscal Year 2007: Operational Plan June 2007 Update* (Washington, DC: United States State Department, 2007), https://2009-2017.pepfar.gov/about/82477.htm.

51. Many thanks to Judith Auerbach for pointing this out to me in discussions.

52. Although the Centers for Disease Control launched the HIV Treatment Works campaign in 2016, the campaign focuses on the idea that HIV-positive people can lead happy, health lives—not on the notion that HIV treatment can prevent transmission. CDC, "Act against AIDS: HIV Treatment Works," last modified May 1, 2017, www.cdc.gov/actagainstaids/campaigns/hivtreatmentworks/index.html.

53. See, for example, Keith Boykin, *Beyond the Down Low: Sex, Lies, and Denial in Black America* (New York: Carroll & Graf, 2004).

54. For example, in a recent study involving focus groups of women across the United States discussing pre-exposure prophylaxis (PrEP), one participant noted that PrEP would let her "know for sure, no matter what he's doing, I know what I'm doing. And I know I'm protecting myself from the virus." Judith Auerbach, Suzanne Kinsky, Gina Brown, and Vignetta Charles, "Knowledge, Attitudes, and Likelihood of Pre-Exposure Prophylaxis (PrEP) Use Among U.S. Women at Risk of Acquiring HIV," *AIDS Patient Care and STDs,* 29, no. 2 (2015): 108.

55. Many thanks to Judith Auerbach for highlighting this reality.

56. CDC, "Act against AIDS: HIV Treatment Works."

57. One medical expert asked, "Does one really need to put couples through this expensive and time-consuming process when the risk of transmission is unmeasurably tiny, if not zero, if the man is on suppressive ART and the woman is taking PrEP? Can you imagine the number needed to treat to prevent one additional case of HIV transmission with sperm washing in addition to ART and PrEP?" Paul E. Sax, "Can't HIV Serodiscordant Couples Now Just Have Children the Regular Way?," *Body PRO*, June 4, 2017, http://www.thebodypro.com/content/79996/cant-hiv-serodiscordant-couples-now-just-have-chil.html?ap=1100. For the original CDC report, see Jennifer F. Kawwass, Dawn K. Smith, Dmitry M. Kissin, Lisa B. Haddad, Sheree L. Boulet, Saswati Sunderam, and Denise J. Jamieson, "Strategies for Preventing HIV Infection Among HIV-Uninfected Women Attempting Conception with HIV-Infected Men—United States," *Mortality and Morbidity Weekly Report* 66, no. 21 (June 2, 2017): 554–57.

58. Centers for Disease Control and Prevention, *There Are Lots of Things You Want to Share ... And Some You Don't*, 2011, 3, https://www.cdc.gov/actagainstaids/pdf/campaigns/pic/cdc-pic-serodiscordant-couples.pdf.

59. Ibid.

60. Ibid.

61. See, for example, Robert H. Remien, Michael J. Stirratt, Curtis Dolezal, Joanna S. Dognin, Glenn J. Wagner, Alex Carballo-Dieguez, Nabila El-Bassel, and Tiffany M. Jung, "Couple-Focused Support to Improve HIV Medication Adherence: A Randomized Controlled Trial," *AIDS* 19, no. 8 (May 20, 2005): 807–14.

62. Such practices could include HIV-positive men engaging only in receptive anal intercourse with HIV-negative partners, as it carries a greatly reduced risk of transmission. For a more thorough set of examples, see Willi McFarland, Yea-Hung Chen, H. Fisher Raymond, Binh Nyugen, Grant Colfax, Jason Mehrtens, Tyler Robertson, Ron Stall, Deb Levine, and Hong-Ha M. Truong, "HIV Seroadaptation among Individuals, within Sexual Dyads, and by Sexual Episodes, Men Who Have Sex with Men, San Francisco, 2008," *AIDS Care* 23, no. 3 (March 2011): 261–68. For an empirical study documenting these practices among HIV-positive men who have sex with men, see J. Jeff McConnell, Larry Bragg, Stephen Shiboski, and Robert M. Grant, "Sexual Seroadaptation: Lessons for Prevention and Sex Research from a Cohort of HIV-Positive Men Who Have Sex with Men," *PLOS ONE* 5, no. 1 (January 21, 2010): e8831.

63. For the most well-known example of this line of critique, see Alan Petersen and Deborah Lupton, *The New Public Health: Health and Self in the Age of Risk* (Newbury Park, CA: Sage, 1997). For a recent example, see Paul Crawshaw, "Governing at a Distance: Social Marketing and the (Bio)Politics of Responsibility," *Social Science and Medicine* 75, no. 1 (July 2012): 200 7.

64. Tyler Curry, "How PrEP Empowers Bottoms," *Advocate*, September 25, 2015, http://www.advocate.com/hiv-aids/2015/9/25/how-prep-empowers-bottoms.

65. Robert M. Grant, Javier R. Lama, Peter L. Anderson, Vanessa McMahan, Albert Y. Liu, Lorena Vargas, Pedro Goicochea, et al., "Preexposure Chemoprophylaxis for HIV Prevention in Men Who Have Sex with Men,"

New England Journal of Medicine 363, no. 27 (December 30, 2010): 2587–99.

66. Sheena McCormack, David T. Dunn, Monica Desai, David I. Dolling, Mitzy Gafos, Richard Gilson, Ann K. Sullivan, et al. "Pre-exposure Prophylaxis to Prevent the Acquisition of HIV-1 Infection (PROUD): Effectiveness Results from the Pilot Phase of a Pragmatic Open-Label Randomised Trial," *Lancet* 387 (September 10, 2015): 53–60.

67. Staci Bush, David Magnuson, M. Keith Rawlings, Trevor Hawkins, Scott McCallister, and Robertino M. Giler, "Racial Characteristics of FTC/TDF for Pre-Exposure Prophylaxis (PrEP) Users in the U.S." (presentation at American Society for Microbiology 2016, Boston, MA, June 16–20, 2016).

68. Centers for Disease Control and Prevention, *HIV Surveillance Report: Diagnoses of HIV Infection in the United States and Dependent Areas, 2015,* November 2016, https://www.cdc.gov/hiv/pdf/library/reports/surveillance/cdc-hiv-surveillance-report-2015-vol-27.pdf.

69. Ibid.

70. For a discussion of these debates, see Judith Auerbach and Trevor Hoppe, "Beyond 'Getting Drugs into Bodies': Social Science Perspectives on Pre-Exposure Prophylaxis for HIV," *Journal of the International AIDS Society* 18, suppl. 3 (July 20, 2015): 19983.

71. David Duran, "Truvada Whores?," *Huffington Post,* November 12, 2012, accessed February 10, 2015, www.huffingtonpost.com/david-duran/truvada-whores_b_2113588.html.

72. David Tuller, "A Resisted Pill to Prevent H.I.V.," *New York Times,* December 30, 2013, D1.

73. Hasina Samji, Angela Cescon, Robert S. Hogg, Sharada P. Modur, Keri N. Althoff, Kate Buchacz, Ann N. Burchell, et al., "Closing the Gap: Increases in Life Expectancy among Treated HIV-Positive Individuals in the United States and Canada," *PLoS ONE* 8, no. 12 (December 18, 2013): e81355.

74. J. Stan Lehman, Meredith H. Carr, Allison J. Nichol, Alberto Ruisanchez, David W. Knight, Anne E. Langford, Simone C. Gray, and Jonathan H. Mermin, "Prevalence and Public Health Implications of State Laws That Criminalize Potential HIV Exposure in the United States," *AIDS and Behavior* 18, no. 6 (June 2014): 996–1006.

CHAPTER 3. THE PUBLIC HEALTH POLICE

1. Bruce Evatt, "The Tragic History of AIDS in the Hemophilia Population, 1982–1984," *Journal of Thrombosis and Haemostasis* 4, no. 11 (2006): 2295–301.

2. Mary Lou Lindegren, Robert H. Byers Jr., Pauline Thomas, Susan F. Davis, Blake Caldwell, Martha Rogers, Marta Gwinn, John W. Ward, and Patricia L. Fleming, "Trends in Perinatal Transmission of HIV/AIDS in the United States," *JAMA* 282, no. 6 (August 11, 1999): 531–38.

3. Thomas R. Freiden, Moupali Das-Douglas, Scott E. Kellerman, and Kelly J. Henning, "Applying Public Health Principles to the HIV Epidemic," *New England Journal of Medicine* 353, no. 22 (December 1, 2005): 2397–402.

4. Lawrence O. Gostin, John W. Ward, and A. Cornelius Baker, "National HIV Case Reporting for the United States: A Defining Moment in the History of the Epidemic," *New England Journal of Medicine* 337, no. 16 (October 16, 1997): 1162–67.

5. This incident in Pinellas County was widely reported in media outlets across the country. See, for example, "Official Is Dismissed in AIDS List Scandal," *Los Angeles Times,* October 10, 1996, http://articles.latimes.com/1996-10-10/news/mn-52512_1_list-scandal

6. Dudley C. Smith and William A. Brumfield, "Tracing the Transmission of Syphilis," *JAMA* 101, no. 25 (1933): 1955–57; Thomas B. Turner, Abraham Gelperin, and James R. Enright, "Results of Contact Investigation in Syphilis in an Urban Community," *American Journal of Public Health* 29, no. 7 (1939): 768–76.

7. To this day, contact tracing remains somewhat contested though it is nearly universally implemented. Modeling studies comparing random screening and contact tracing suggest that deciding whether contact tracing was more effective hinged on assumptions about how the disease is spread and who is spreading it. In other words, in some scenarios, randomly screening people for HIV may be better suited to controlling HIV. The researchers, however, were not able to determine conclusively which method was better suited for HIV because of the large number of variables that shape the epidemic. James M. Hyman, Jia Li, and E. Ann Stanley, "Modeling the Impact of Random Screening and Contact Tracing in Reducing the Spread of HIV," *Mathematical Biosciences* 181, no. 1 (January 2003): 17–54.

8. Julie Gerberding, CDC Director, "Recommendation That All States and Territories Adopt Confidential Name-Based Surveillance Systems to Report HIV Infections" (dear colleague letter), Centers for Disease Control and Prevention, July 5, 2005, https://npin.cdc.gov/publication/recommendation-all-states-and-territories-adopt-confidential-name-based-surveillance.

9. Centers for Disease Control and Prevention, *HIV/AIDS Surveillance Report,* 2005 17 (rev. June 2007), https://www.cdc.gov/hiv/pdf/library/reports/surveillance/cdc-hiv-surveillance-report-2005-vol-17.pdf; and Allyn K. Nakashima, Rosemarie Horsley, Robert L. Frey, Patricia A. Sweeney, J. Todd Weber, and Patricia L. Fleming, "Effect of HIV Reporting by Name on Use of HIV Testing in Publicly Funded Counseling and Testing Programs," *JAMA* 280, no. 16 (October 28, 1998): 1421–26.

10. Tracy Peterson-Jones, "Partner Services Guidelines," (presentation to the Michigan Department of Community Health Strategic Planning Committee for HIV/AIDS, Detroit, MI, November 13, 2009).

11. Cicely Bolden was murdered in September 2012 by her boyfriend, Larry Dunn Jr. Anthony Bartkewicz, "Man Stabbed Girlfriend Who Told Him She Had HIV, Left Her Body for Kids to Find: Cops," *New York Daily* News, September 9, 2012, http://www.nydailynews.com/news/national/man-stabbed-girlfriend-told-hiv-left-body-kids-find-cops-article-1.1155389. Elisha Henson was strangled to death in June 2014 by Justin Welch when he learned of her status after they engaged in oral sex. Alia Malik, "Man Arrested in San Antonio Suspected of Killing Woman Because She Had HIV," *San Antonio News-*

Express, June 17, 2014, http://www.mysanantonio.com/news/local/article
/Deputies-Man-caught-in-San-Antonio-killed-woman-5558852.php.

12. "Man Sentenced in AIDS Case," *Grand Rapids Press,* April 27, 2000, B2.

13. Centers for Disease Control and Prevention, "HIV Prevention: Questions and Answers," 2017, accessed June 6, 2017, https://www.cdc.gov/hiv/basics/prevention.html.

14. Denise Chrysler, "Re: Legal Counsel / Macomb CHD," e-mail message obtained by Freedom of Information Act request from Todd Heywood, 2008. Quoted in Todd Heywood, "State HIV Disclosure Forms Legally Inaccurate," *Michigan Messenger,* February 7, 2011, accessed April 4, 2011, http://michiganmessenger.com/46295/state-hiv-disclosure-forms-legally-inaccurate.

15. Michigan Department of Community Health, e-mail message to author, October 11, 2011.

16. Health officials either directly described using such a form ($n = 2$) or they provided me with policy documents that included one ($n = 5$).

17. This is a public document, and its inclusion should not be read as an indication that Macomb County did or did not participate in this study.

18. "Deadly Secret Gets Man 5–15 Years," *WWMT News* (West Michigan), March 8, 2007, accessed January 20, 2012, http://www.wwmt.com/news/willis-34782-russell-convictions.html.

19. Heywood, "State HIV Disclosure Forms Legally Inaccurate."

20. A string of articles from journalist Todd Heywood reported these developments. Todd Heywood, "State HIV Disclosure Forms"; Todd Heywood, "Equality Michigan Calls For Investigation of HIV Documents," *Michigan Messenger,* February 9, 2011, accessed April 4, 2011, http://michiganmessenger.com/46408/equality-michigan-calls-for-investigation-of-hiv-documents; Todd Heywood, "State Civil Rights Officials Want Investigation of HIV Documents," *Michigan Messenger,* February 10, 2011, accessed April 4, 2011, http://michiganmessenger.com/46433/state-civil-rights-officials-confirm-interest-in-hiv-documents-controversy; and Todd Heywood, "MDCH Reverses Position on HIV Documents," *Michigan Messenger,* February 11, 2011, accessed April 4, 2011, http://michiganmessenger.com/46475/mdch-reverses-position-on-hiv-documents.

21. Quoted in Heywood, "State HIV Disclosure Forms."

22. Heywood, "State Civil Rights Officials."

23. Heywood, "MDCH Reverses Position."

24. Michigan Department of Community Health, *Recalcitrant Behaviors among HIV/AIDS Diagnosed Populations: Guidance for Local Public Health Department Response to Health Threat to Other Situations* (Lansing, MI: Michigan Department of Community Health, 2006), 3–4.

25. Anxieties about Black male sexuality have fueled considerable HIV panic in the United States. See, for example, Cathy Cohen, *Boundaries of Blackness: AIDS and the Breakdown of Black Politics* (Chicago: University of Chicago Press, 1999); and Keith Boykin, *Beyond the Down Low: Sex, Lies, and Denial in Black America* (New York: Carroll & Graf, 2004). Studies also suggest Black communities are invested in policing Black women's sexuality. For example,

Bronwen Lichtenstein found that Black health workers in the Deep South expected their Black female clients to be "ladylike" and held stigmatizing views of "bad girls" whose sexualities did not conform to those expectations. Bronwen Lichtenstein, "Stigma as a Barrier to Treatment of Sexually Transmitted Infection in the American Deep South: Issues of Race, Gender and Poverty," *Social Science and Medicine* 57, no. 12 (December 2003): 2435–45. While the findings reported in this chapter are not conclusive in demonstrating a gender bias in Black communities' informal social control of sexuality, they do suggest there may be a trend worth exploring in future research.

26. Michael G. Walsh, "HIV Virus Victim: Isolation 'Unfair,'" *Muskegon Chronicle,* June 12, 1992, 1–2A.

27. "Court Upholds Validity of Michigan's HIV Exposure Law," *AIDS Policy and Law* 13, no. 18 (October 22, 1998): 3.

28. Lisa Medendorp, "Woman Charged for Not Disclosing HIV-Positive Status with Sex Partner," *Muskegon Chronicle,* May 22, 2003, A1.

29. Ibid.

30. Todd Heywood, "Mich. Health Dept. Puts HIV Criminal Law Review 'On Hold,'" *Between the Lines News,* August 23, 2013, http://www .pridesource.com/article.html?article=61814.

31. Matt Comer, "House Arrest for Gay DJ's Second HIV Violation," *Q-Notes,* no. 2134, November 1, 2008, http://goqnotes.com/994/house-arrest-for-gay-dj%E2%80%99s-second-hiv-violation/.

32. In addition to the informational form, prior health-department-initiated HTTO proceedings against the defendant directly informed the later criminal sentencing of the defendant. At the sentencing, the judge justified the application of a sentence enhancement factor by citing these health-department-related documents and proceedings: "Factor #10, 'That the defendant had no hesitation about committing a crime when the risk to human life was high.' The Court does find that as an appropriate enhancing factor. Specifically, The Court finds that he was warned over and over and over again by the Health Department that he could not have unprotected sex with anyone. . . . More so than being warned by the Health Department, he was ordered by the General Sessions Court Judge . . . at that time, not to have unprotected sex with anyone and that if he did have any sex—sexual encounters he had to tell that person about his HIV condition. So, you know, he was warned by The Court. He was warned by the Health Department more than once. And so, The Court does find that that is an appropriate factor to consider and will give it some weight because it does appear that [the defendant] just went out and had sex, knowing that he shouldn't be having sex because of his HIV condition." Transcript of Sentencing Hearing at 64–65, People v. Michael H., No. 00-544 (Madison County, Tenn., Cir. Ct., March 9, 2001).

33. "HIV Interview Form No. 917, Mississippi State Department of Health," Center for HIV Law and Policy, August 2009, http://www.hivlawandpolicy .org/resources/hiv-interview-form-no-917-mississippi-state-department-health; and Sean Strub, "Did You Sign a Form When You Tested Positive for HIV?" *POZ Blogs,* September 23, 2010, http://blogs.poz.com/sean/archives/2010/09 /did_you_sign_a_form.html.

34. According to the prosecutor, "The victim stated that she went to the Health Department on November the 27th of 2001, tested positive for STD and at that time she gave the suspect's name to the Health Department and told that he was HIV positive." Transcript of Plea Hearing at 5–6, People v. Claude A., No. 02–03915 (Shelby County, Tenn., Cir. Ct., December 6, 2002).

35. Examples of this research include studies on battered women; see Michael A. Rodriguez, Seline Szkupinkski-Quiroga, and Heidi Bauer, "Breaking the Silence: Battered Women's Perspectives on Medical Care," *Archives of Family Medicine* 5, no. 3 (March 1996): 153–58. For research on men who have sex with men, see Matthew J. Miamaga, Hilary Goldhammer, Candice Belanoff, Ashley Tetu, and Kenneth Mayer, "Men Who Have Sex with Men: Perceptions about Sexual Risk, HIV and Sexually Transmitted Disease Testing, and Provider Communication," *Sexually Transmitted Diseases* 34, no. 2 (February 2007):113–19. For research on sex workers, see Deborah L. Cohan, Alexander Lutnick, Peter Davidson, Charles Cloniger, Antje Herlyn, Johanna Breyer, Cynthia Cobaugh, Daniel Wilson, and Jeffrey Klausner, "Sex Worker Health: San Francisco Style," *Sexually Transmitted Infections* 82, no. 5 (October 2006): 418–22.

36. Lawrence O. Gostin, Scott Burris, and Zita Lazzarini, "The Law and the Public's Health: A Study of Infectious Disease Law in the United States," *Columbia Law Review* 99 (1999): 59–128.

CHAPTER 4. MAKING HIV A CRIME

1. "Overreacting to AIDS," *Oklahoman*, August 4, 1983.

2. "House Backs Bill to Shut Bathhouses Used by Gays," *Akron Beacon Journal*, October 3, 1985, A10.

3. "Despite a contemporary federal presence," said public health law expert Lawrence Gostin, "the states and localities have had the predominant public responsibility for population-based health services since the founding of the republic." Lawrence O. Gostin, *Public Health Law: Power, Duty, Restraint* (Berkeley: University of California Press, 2000), 46.

4. For a discussion of state versus federal public health powers, see Lawrence O. Gostin, "Public Health in the Constitutional Design," in *Public Health Law*, chap. 2; Institute of Medicine, *The Future of Public Health* (Washington, DC: National Academy Press, 1988), appendix A, https://www.nap.edu/read/1091/chapter/10; and Frank P. Grad, *The Public Health Law Manual*, 3rd ed. (Washington, DC: American Public Health Association, 2005). There are exceptions to this, of course. In North Carolina, the legislature only maintains a skeleton system of codes that simply refer out to rules that are enacted and maintained by the State Department of Public Health. Thus, changing public health policy in North Carolina does not depend on the actions of the state legislature to the extent that it does in other states.

5. Lawrence O. Gostin, Scott Burris, and Zita Lazzarini, "The Law and the Public's Health: A Study of Infectious Disease Law in the United States," *Columbia Law Review* 99 (1999): 102–3.

6. Lawrence Gostin wrote in 1989 that "isolation is a particularly antiquated public health notion. It was designed in a very different era and intended for

diseases of a character wholly different from that of AIDS." Lawrence O. Gostin, "The Politics of AIDS: Compulsory State Powers, Public Health, and Civil Liberties," *Ohio State Law Review* 49 (1989): 1027.

7. There were many instances of children being removed from classes for being HIV-positive. For example, see "No Reason to Bar Girl, Officials Say," *Richmond Times-Dispatch,* December 31, 1987, B-4.

8. For example, Republican presidential candidate Pat Robertson claimed that the government was being dishonest with Americans in saying the disease was difficult to transmit. He claimed, "If say, we're in a room with 25 people with AIDS and they're breathing various things into the atmosphere, the chance of somebody catching it has become quite strong." Maralee Schwartz, "Robertson Disputes Doctors on AIDS," *Washington Post,* December 20, 1987, A12.

9. See, for example, Jane Gross, "Funerals for AIDS Victims: Searching for Sensitivity," *New York Times,* February 13, 1987, http://www.nytimes.com/1987/02/13/nyregion/funerals-for-aids-victims-searching-for-sensitivity.html?pagewanted=all

10. For example, in a floor debate in the Michigan House of Representatives over whether to codify strict privacy safeguards for HIV testing, the chairman of the House Public Health Committee, Representative Michael Bennane, argued, "If we don't have such standards of confidentiality for AIDS, we're very afraid that there may be special groups of people—especially those who are most likely to contract the disease—to be afraid to become tested without special confidentiality standards." Michigan House of Representatives, floor session, December 1, 1988, audio recording. For a broader news analysis, see Lawrence K. Altman, "Privacy Called Vital to AIDS Screening," *New York Times,* March 1, 1987, E26.

11. "The Times Poll: 42% Would Limit Civil Rights in AIDS Battle," *Los Angeles Times,* July 31, 1987, 1.

12. Many public health experts at the time noticed as much. For example, Dr. Ronald Bayer told New Jersey media that "both the fear of the illness and the hatred of homosexuals and drug users create a broad social context where gestures ostensibly designed to control the spread of the illness become gestures of repression, particularly against gays. . . . All those measures draw their energy from a history of antihomosexual posturing. I don't think they have any public health justification." Quoted in Elliot Pinsely, "Will the Remedy Feed the Phobia?" (Hackensack) *Record,* December 29, 1985, A1.

13. Ryan White CARE Act, Pub.L. 101-381, 104 Stat. 576 (1990).

14. "Officials Defend AIDS Letters," *Dallas Morning News,* October 19, 1985, 32A.

15. Ibid.

16. Ibid.

17. "Letters to AIDS Victims Called 'Hysterical,'" *Dallas Morning News,* October 22, 1985, 13A.

18. S.B. 1064—Enrolled Version, 1983 Leg., 68th Sess. (Tex. 1983).

19. A contemporary news report suggests that the health department did not defend or elaborate on the rationale behind how they selected who received a letter: "Seventeen people are known to have AIDS in the San Antonio area, but

letters were sent to only 14, Rothe said. There is no concern about the three others spreading the disease, he said, but declined to elaborate." "AIDS Sex Becomes a Felony—San Antonio Warns 14 Victims to Abstain," *Orlando Sentinel,* October 18, 1985, A1.

20. This was perhaps not the intent of legislators who enacted the 1983 provision. During the legislative session immediately following the San Antonio controversy, Texas lawmakers amended the 1983 law by reclassifying failing to comply with a health department directive as a misdemeanor rather than a felony. See H.B. 1829—Enrolled Version, 1987 Leg., 70th Sess. (Tex. 1987).

21. Pat Flynn, "Man Accused of Biting Officer, Claiming AIDS, Pleads Not Guilty," *San Diego Union-Tribune,* December 6, 1985, B4.

22. Jackie Fitzpatrick, "No Bail Cut for Avowed AIDS Victim Charged in Biting," *San Diego Union-Tribune,* November 14, 1985, B3.

23. Quoted in ibid.

24. Pat Flynn, "Sentencing of Biter Is Delayed for AIDS Tests," *San Diego Union-Tribune,* February 25, 1985, B3.

25. "San Diego: Policeman Bitten at Rally Sues Gay; Countersuit Filed," *Los Angeles Times,* June 10, 1987.

26. Barlow v. Ground Id., 943 F. 2d 1132 (9th Cir. 1991).

27. Ibid.

28. Russell Minick, "No Felony Charges in AIDS Case: Infected Woman and Alleged Pimp Will Face Lesser Counts," *Fresno Bee,* June 19, 1987, A1.

29. Linda Deutsch, "AIDS Case Murder Charges Dismissed," *Daily Breeze,* December 2, 1987, A3.

30. "Possible AIDs Carrier Acquitted in Bite Case," *Milwaukee Journal,* July 29, 1986, A11. John Curtis Richards was originally charged with assault with intent to murder in Flint, Michigan. He later pled guilty to resisting and obstructing a police officer after the judge dismissed the felony assault charge. See "AIDS Victim Charged in Assault against Policemen," *Houston Chronicle,* December 7, 1985, 12; "Fight after Wedding Lands Groom in Jail," *Miami Herald,* August 5, 1986, A13.

31. "AIDS: Educate, Motivate," *Orlando Sentinel,* January 6, 1988, A10.

32. Fran Smith, "Mood Shifts to the Right on AIDS Legislation," *San Jose Mercury News,* August 16, 1987, 1A.

33. "There Ought to Be a Law," *Daily News of Los Angeles,* December 4, 1987, N24.

34. Lawrence Gostin, "Applying Tough Penalties Will Not Curtail AIDS," *Providence Journal,* July 7, 1987, A15.

35. Quoted in Marc Lifsher, "Quarantine: 2 Lawmakers Call for Stricter Measures against Contagion," *Orange County Register,* March 22, 1987, M8.

36. "Surgeon General Koop: The Right, the Left and the Center of the AIDS Storm," *Washington Post Health Magazine,* March 24, 1987, 6–8.

37. Under Dr. Archer's "HIV parole system," the ability of people living with HIV to move freely would "be permitted only under a parole system—just as is done with criminals." Victor E. Archer, "Psychological Defenses and Control of AIDS," *American Journal of Public Health* 79, no. 7 (1989): 876.

38. Leonard Robbins and Charles Backstrom, "The Role of State Health Departments in Formulating Policy: A Survey on the Case of AIDS," *American Journal of Public Health* 84 (1994): 905–9.

39. *Report of the Presidential Commission on the Human Immunodeficiency Virus Epidemic* (Washington, DC, 1988), https://archive.org/details /reportofpresidenoopres, 130.

40. Ibid.

41. Some scholars argue that the presidential commission's report was a key impetus in driving states to start drafting HIV-specific criminal laws. However, as this chapter shows, by the time the commission issued its report in the spring of 1988, lawmakers in sixteen states had already (during the 1985, 1986, and 1987 legislative sessions) introduced two dozen bills that would impose some form of criminal sanction against HIV-positive people.

42. For example, a 1985 study of Rwanda sex workers found that twenty-nine of thirty-three (87.9 percent) sex workers screened had antibodies for the disease. Philippe van de Perre, Michel Carael, Marjorie Robert-Guroff, Nathan Clumeck, Elie Nzabihimana, Patrick De Mol, Pierre Freyens, Robert C. Gallo, Jean-Paul Butzler, and Jean-Baptiste Kanyamupira, "Female Prostitutes: A Risk Group for Infection with Human T-Cell Lymphotropic Virus Type III," *Lancet* 2 (1985): 524–27. A study published the next year found that 66 percent of low-income sex workers screened in Nairobi, Kenya were HIV-positive. Joan K. Kreiss, Davy Koech, Francis A. Plummer, King K. Holmes, Marilyn Lightfoote, Peter Piot, Allan R. Ronald, et al., "AIDS Virus Infection in Nairobi Prostitutes: Spread of the Epidemic to East Africa," *New England Journal of Medicine* 314, no. 7 (1986): 414–18.

43. Robert R. Redfield, Phillip D. Markham, Syed Zaki Salahuddin, D. Craig Wright, M.G. Sarngadharan, and Robert C. Gallo, "Heterosexually Acquired HTLV-III/LAV Disease (AIDS-Related Complex and AIDS): Epidemiological Evidence for Female-to-Male Transmission," *JAMA* 254, no. 15 (1985): 2094–96.

44. Randy Shilts, "Laws on Prostitution Don't Help," *San Francisco Chronicle*, August 28, 1989, A4.

45. Ibid.

46. Beth Bergman, "AIDS, Prostitution, and the Use of Historical Stereotypes to Legislate Sexuality," *John Marshall Law Review* 21 (1988–1989): 783.

47. Gail Epstein, "Fulton to Go after Repeat Prostitutes Who Fail AIDS Tests," *Atlanta Journal-Constitution*, July 11, 1987, A1.

48. Mark Mayfield, "Atlanta—A Prostitute Group Sued the State Thursday over a New Health Regulation Requiring Anyone Convicted of Prostitution to Be Tested for AIDS," *USA Today*, August 6, 1987.

49. Paul Edward Parker, "Judge Wants Prostitutes to Be Tested for AIDS," *Providence Journal*, August 7, 1987, A1.

50. "Minneapolis—Judge to Hear Prostitution Case of Prostitution Who May Carry AIDS Virus," *Star Tribune*, September 25, 1987, 3B.

51. Valerie Jenness, "Explaining Criminalization: From Demography and Status Politics to Globalization and Modernization," *Annual Review of Sociology* 30 (2004): 141–71.

52. A.B. 3577, 1986 Leg., 202nd Sess. (N.J. 1986).

53. Bruce Rosen, "Penalties Proposed for Transmitting AIDS," (Hackensack) *Record,* December 5, 1985, A1.

54. Susan Taylor-Martin, "Nevada Brothels Battle for Business amid AIDS Scare," *Tampa Bay Times,* November 1, 1987, 1A.

55. Jim Boren, "Haaland Blasts Bronzan for AIDS Votes—Republican's Attack of Democratic Opponent Ranges from Health Care to Office Rent," *Fresno Bee,* March 19, 1988, B1.

56. Amy Pyle, "Bill on AIDS Testing Past Initial Hearing," *Fresno Bee,* March 9, 1988, B1.

57. Daniel C. Carson, "Governor Decides Fate of 166 Bills—Urges Legislators to Scale Back on Number of New Laws," *San Diego-Tribune,* October 2, 1988, A3.

58. Jenness, "Explaining Criminalization."

59. Kristen Gallagher, "Prosecution Becomes AIDS Fight Weapon Orlando Prostitute Who Has Virus Faces 2 Charges of Attempted Manslaughter," *Orlando Sentinel,* January 3, 1988, A7.

60. Michelle Ruess, "Prostitute with AIDS Sentenced," *Fort Lauderdale Sun Sentinel,* January 21, 1988, 3B.

61. "Society Should Try to Help Hooker, but If That Fails, Then Protect Others," *Fort Lauderdale Sun Sentinel,* January 23, 1988, 14A.

62. Ibid.

63. "Elections Chief Gets Job Back—Child Support Rules Passed—AIDS Bill Turned Back—The Day in Tallahassee," *Fort Lauderdale Sun Sentinel,* May 29, 1987, p. 12A.

64. Kirsten Gallagher, "Legislators: Jail Prostitutes with AIDS for 5 Years," *Orlando Sentinel,* February 3, 1988, D1.

65. Quoted in ibid.

66. Committee Substitute for H.B. 1519, 1988 Leg. (Fla. 1988).

67. Kris Newcomer, "Prostitute Frustrates Denver Cops," *Rocky Mountain News,* January 6, 1990, 12.

68. Ibid.

69. John C. Ensslin, "Prostitutes Spreading AIDS—Streetwalkers Aware of Fatal Infection, Still Ply Their Trade," *Rocky Mountain News,* January 31, 1990, 7.

70. Steve Garnaas, "Courts Do Little to Stop Prostitutes with AIDS," *Denver Post,* February 5, 1990.

71. For example, a national study published in JAMA the same month as Avis's arrest found that 6.7 percent of female sex workers nationwide and 2.2 percent of sex workers in Colorado Springs were HIV-positive. Rima F. Khabbaz, William W. Darrow, Trudie M. Hartley, John Witte, Judith B. Cohen, John French, Parkash S. Gill, et al., "Seroprevalence and Risk Factors for HTLV-I/II Infection among Female Prostitutes in the United States," *JAMA* 263 (1990): 60–64. Moreover, the preliminary findings from this study were readily accessible as early as 1987. See Judith Cohen, Constance Wofsy, Parkash Gill, S. Aguilar, John Witte, William Bigler, Robert K. Sikes et al., "Antibody to Human

Immunodeficiency Virus in Female Prostitutes," *Morbidity and Mortality Weekly Reports* 36, no. 11 (1987):157–61.

72. Khabbaz et al., "Seroprevalence and Risk Factors."

73. Garnaas, "Courts Do Little to Stop Prostitutes with AIDS."

74. "Hookers with AIDS," *Rocky Mountain News*, February 9, 1987, 84.

75. Ibid.

76. Ensslin, "Prostitutes Spreading AIDS."

77. Hardwick v. Bowers, 760 F. 2d 1202 (11th Cir. 1985).

78. Frederick Allen, "AIDS Threat New Factor in Sodomy Fight," *Atlanta Journal and Constitution*, September 3, 1985, A2.

79. Ibid.

80. Oral Argument, Bowers v. Hardwick, 478 U.S. 186 (1986) (No. 85-140), March 31, 1986, https://apps.oyez.org/player/#/burger8/oral_argument_audio /18346.

81. At least one other amicus brief filed made the argument that sodomy laws helped to combat AIDS. Law professor David Robinson reportedly filed a brief making this case. See Tracy Thompson, "Sodomy Law Challenge Goes to U.S. Supreme Court," *Atlanta Journal and Constitution*, March 16, 1986, B1.

82. Ibid.

83. "State Sodomy Laws in the United States," *Wikipedia*, accessed July 10, 2016, https://en.wikipedia.org/wiki/Sodomy_laws_in_the_United_States.

84. S.B. 466 [Senate Committee Substitute], 1993 Leg., 67th Sess. (Nev. 1993).

85. According to the minutes of the May 24, 1993, Senate Committee hearing at which the bill was debated, lawyer Myra Sheehan argued that the law and its amendments "accomplish the goal of making it unlawful to commit certain acts against minors, protects prisoners from those who engage in acts which could spread the Acquired Immunodeficiency Syndrome (AIDS) virus." Nevada Senate Judiciary Committee, Minutes, May 24, 1993, 6.

86. Paul Cameron was a notoriously antigay activist at the time who worked under the banner of the Family Research Institute. His pamphlets were distributed to Nevada lawmakers, according to committee hearing minutes. Nevada Senate Judiciary Committee hearing, Minutes, June 10, 1993. See also Family Research Institute, *Medical Consequences of What Homosexuals Do* (Washington, DC: Family Research Institute, 1993).

87. Nevada Senate Judiciary Committee, May 24, 1993, 39.

88. In legislative procedure, a bill is read three times before being voted on for passage. Once it is passed, it is then sent to the other legislative body—generally the House of Representatives or the Senate—for consideration.

89. Nevada State Legislature, *Senate Daily Journal*, May 28, 1993, 17.

90. Senator Matt Callister remarked, "On the amendment, I share the concern which is raised by the maker of the amendment in regards to the HIV issue. . . . However, I am not supportive of addressing it in this measure. . . . We don't need to further muddy the water on this bill." Ibid., 19.

91. Ibid.

92. These figures were distributed to lawmakers by the Family Research Institute in *Medical Consequences of What Homosexuals Do*. Senate Judiciary

Committee minutes reported: "to determine the longevity of individuals involved in the homosexual lifestyle, Dr. Cameron pronounced researchers from the Family Research Institute had gathered information from obituaries published in homosexual publications over the previous twelve years, Exhibit H. The research data disclosed homosexual males who died of AIDS had a median age at death of 39 years and 1 percent attained old age." Nevada Senate Committee on the Judiciary, Minutes, June 10, 1993, 15.

93. Nevada State Legislature, *Senate Daily Journal*, 24.

94. "Repealing Anti-homosexual Law Overdue," *Reno Gazette-Journal*, June 3, 1993, 7A.

95. Nevada Senate Committee on Judiciary, Minutes, June 7, 1993.

96. House of Delegates, February 1, 2000, Library of the State of Virginia, video.

97. Ibid.

98. Barry Malone, "Uganda's 'Kill the Gays' Bill Shelved Again," Reuters, May 13, 2011, http://af.reuters.com/article/topNews/idAFJOE74C0HP20110513.

99. Uganda Parliament, The Anti-Homosexuality Bill, 2009, http://www.publiceye.org/publications/globalizing-the-culture-wars/uganda-antigay-bill.php#april.

100. "Uganda Court Annuls Anti-homosexuality Law," *BBC News*, August 1, 2014, http://www.bbc.com/news/world-africa-28605400.

101. For a history of the eugenics movement, see Diane Paul, *Controlling Human Heredity: 1865 to the Present* (Atlantic Highlands, NJ: Humanity Books, 1995).

102. *Report of the Presidential Commission on the HIV Epidemic*, 130.

103. Robert Manor and Kathleen Best, "Missouri Legislature Follows Illinois Lead, Considers AIDS Bills," *St. Louis-Dispatch*, January 17, 1988, 1C.

104. Michael Tanner and the ALEC National Working Group on State AIDS Policy, *The Politics of Health: A State Response to the AIDS Crisis* (Washington, DC: American Legislative Exchange Council, 1989).

105. Todd Heywood, "The Crime of Being HIV-Positive," *Advocate*, April 1, 2013.

106. Amendment 1 to S.B. 1180, 1989 Leg., 86th Gen. Assembly (Ill. 1989).

107. Although the ALEC report does not have a specific date, the report is known to post-date the Illinois legislation as it cites Illinois' criminal law in its description of Illinois state policies. "It is a criminal act for an infected individual to put another person at risk of infection without alerting the endangered party." Tanner and ALEC National Working Group, *Politics of Health*, 151.

108. Legislation considered in the following states reference the phrase "intimate contact" and use a similar structure: Alaska (S.B.91 of 1995, S.B. 14 of 1997); Connecticut (H.B. 5434 of 1999); Hawai'i (S.B. 2602 of 2000); North Carolina (H.B.973 of 1993, H.B. 801 of 1995); Mississippi (S.B. 2124 and 2542 of 1997, S.B. 2545 and 2657 of 1998, S.B. 2450 and 2006 of 1999, S.B. 2249 and 2044 of 2000, S.B. 2065 and 2080 of 2001, S.B. 2010 of 2002, S.B. 2082 of 2003, S.B. 2810 of 2004); Tennessee (H.B. 1673 and S.B. 1676 of 1992, H.B. 585 and S.B. 398 of 1993, H.B. 1686 of 1994); and Utah (H.B. 331 of 1995).

109. Manor and Best, "Missouri Legislature Follows Illinois."

110. Nevada Senate Committee on Judiciary meeting, Minutes, June 11, 1993, 2.

111. Ibid.

112. For example, lawmakers reference the fact that Illinois's statute does not require proof of intent: "Senator James stated the Illinois statute states, 'engages in intimate contact.' In that statute, there is no secondary intent." They also note that the Illinois language of "exposure in a manner that could result" is "comparable to the term 'likely'" in the Nevada bill. Ibid., 4.

113. Alaska Senate Health Education and Social Services Committee, Minutes, April 11, 1997.

114. S.B. 17 [as introduced], 1997 Leg., 20th Sess. (Alas. 1997).

115. Alaska Senate Health Education and Social Services Committee, Minutes, April 14, 1997.

CHAPTER 5. HIV ON TRIAL

1. Throughout this chapter, I identify the defendants by first name and last initial. Although criminal records are public record, I do not use the defendants' full name because of concerns that doing so implicitly reveals the HIV status of defendants. In an era in which the contents of books are searchable online via Google, it seemed to me important to do what I can to protect the confidentiality of the men and women whose cases I review in this chapter. For more on the methods used in this chapter, see appendix 1.

2. "Michigan," *USA Today*, June 24, 1991, 10A.

3. Fred Bruning, "Prosecution in the Age of AIDS," *Newsday*, September 23, 1991, 2C.

4. Sarah Kellogg, "Engler Blasted for His Actions in AIDS Case," *Grand Rapids Press*, June 22, 1999, A4.

5. Transcript of Preliminary Examination Hearing at 81, People v. Jeffrey H., No. 91-301-FH (Lake Cty. Dist. Ct., Oct. 22, 1991).

6. Louis Weisberg, "Jeffrey [H.] Free on Bail," *Windy City Times*, January 23, 1992, 4.

7. Transcript of Preliminary Examination Hearing at 47, *People v. Jeffrey H.*

8. Phil Donahue, "People Who Intentionally Spread the AIDS Virus," *Donahue*, show 1227-91, transcript 3368 (New York: Multimedia Entertainment, 1991). As cited in Stephanie Kane, *AIDS Alibis: Sex, Drugs, and Crime in the Americas* (Philadelphia: Temple University Press, 2010).

9. Transcript of Preliminary Examination Hearing at 37, *People v. Jeffrey H.*

10. Alan R. Lifson, Paul M. O'Malley, Nancy A. Hessol, Susan P. Buchbinder, Lyn Cannon, and George W. Rutherford, "HIV Seroconversion in Two Homosexual Men after Receptive Oral Intercourse with Ejaculation: Implications for Counseling Concerning Safe Sexual Practices," *American Journal of Public Health* 80, no. 12 (December 1990): 1509-11.

11. Ibid., 1509: "Studies of homosexual and bisexual men have shown that anal intercourse, especially receptive anal intercourse with ejaculation, is the sexual practice associated with the greatest risk of human immunodeficiency virus (HIV) infection. Although orogenital contact has not been statistically associated

in these studies with HIV infection, many subjects engaged in multiple sexual practices, making a relatively lower risk more difficult to detect statistically."

12. Transcript of Motion Hearing at 103, People v. Jeffrey H., No. 91-2793-FH (Lake Cty. Cir. Ct., Feb. 27, 1992).

13. Ibid., 21.

14. Court Opinion on Briefs at 20, People vs Jeffrey H., No. 91-2793-FH (Lake Cty. Cir. Ct., Apr. 30, 1992.

15. News reports reveal a scattered number of cases in the years leading up to Jeffrey's conviction. None were covered by the media extensively. See, for example, news coverage of cases in South Carolina in September 1988; an Idaho case in October 1989; and a Missouri case in May 1991. Karen Garloch, "AIDS Activists Fear Signal in S.C. Charges," *Charlotte Observer,* September 1, 1988, 1A; Bill Miller, "AIDS Exposure Trial Begins," *USA Today,* October 29, 1989, accessed February 5, 2016, via Access World News; Alan Bavley and Diane Carroll, "Prison Term Possible in AIDS Cases," *Kansas City Star,* May 1, 1991, C1.

16. John Hogan and Chris Murphy, "Ice Broken with AIDS Disclosure Case," *Grand Rapids Press,* May 31, 1992, A1.

17. Ibid.

18. Charis E. Kubrin and Erik Neilson, "Rap on Trial," *Race and Justice* 4, no. 3 (2014): 185–211.

19. Erik Neilson and Charis E. Kubrin, "Rap Lyrics on Trial," *New York Times,* January 13, 2014, A27.

20. John M. Conley and William O'Barr, *Just Words: Law, Language, and Power,* rev. 2nd ed. (Chicago: University of Chicago Press, 2005).

21. Because Michigan authorities reported the precise number of cases to the author, it was possible to calculate the exact number of cases represented by these records. In Tennessee, however, the precise number of cases is not reported by the state; only the number of counts is reported. Since Tennessee cases frequently involve numerous counts (one defendant was charged in a single case with twenty-six counts, for example), it is impossible to deduce the number of unique cases from the number of counts reported by Tennessee authorities. For more on this, see appendix 1.

22. Court transcripts were available from 78 of the 103 criminal cases analyzed. As four defendants in Michigan and three defendants in Tennessee were charged twice in separate years, these 78 cases represent 71 defendants.

23. Michael G. Walsh, "AIDS Virus Prompts 'Quarantine,'" *Muskegon Chronicle,* June 11, 1992, 2A.

24. Michael B. First, Allen Frances, and Harold A. Pincus, *DSM-IV-TR Guidebook: The Essential Companion to the Diagnostic and Statistical Manual of Mental Disorders,* rev. 3rd ed. (Arlington, VA: American Psychiatric Association, 2004), 373.

25. Mich. Public Health Code MCL § 333.5207.

26. Walsh, "AIDS Virus Prompts 'Quarantine.'"

27. Transcript of the Jury Trial, vol. II., at 203, People v. Brenda J., No. 94-37564-FH (Muskegon Cty. Cir. Ct., Mar. 29, 2005).

28. For a discussion of the inability of the prosecution to locate the witness, see Transcript of the Preliminary Examination, vol. I., at 4–5, *People v. Brenda J.* (Aug. 5, 1994).

29. In the jury trial, for example, the prosecutor included the following in his opening statement: "But you'll also learn in order to allay those fears, the Prosecutor's Office told him: We're not planning to charge you, but to make sure that you're not concerned about that, and in fact we will give you what is called immunity so you don't have to worry about that as far as your testimony is concerned. Testimony will also indicate in this case that—that [he] had a number of traffic tickets that he hadn't paid. The Prosecutor's Office didn't do anything as far as a sentence is concerned. But they did tell him: We will get all those cases and we'll get you in court on those cases so they can be taken care of concurrently at the same time." Transcript of the Jury Trial, vol. I, at 84–85, *People v. Brenda J.* (March 28, 1995).

30. Transcript of the Jury Trial, vol. I., at 74, *People v. Brenda J.*

31. Transcript of the Jury Trial, vol. III, at 392, *People v. Brenda J.* (Mar. 30, 1995).

32. Ibid.

33. Pamela Block, "Sexuality, Fertility, and Danger: Twentieth-Century Images of Women with Cognitive Disabilities," *Sexuality and Disability* 18, no. 4 (2000): 239–54.

34. Given the inconsistency with which this information was available, it is likely these figures are underreported. It is difficult to say how this maps to the general population. The CDC reports that 10.6 percent of Americans in 2013 had a cognitive disability. Centers for Disease Control and Prevention, "Key Findings: Prevalence of Disability and Disability Type among Adults, United States— 2013," August 20, 2015, http://www.cdc.gov/ncbddd/disabilityandhealth/features /key-findings-community-prevalence.html.

35. Transcript of the Sentencing Hearing at 6–9, *People v. Brenda J.* (Apr. 25, 1992).

36. Tenn. Code Ann. § 39-13-109.

37. Transcript of Plea and Sentence Hearing, People v. Ronald T., No. 8873 (Sumner Cty., Tenn., Cir. Ct., Nov. 9, 1995).

38. "Gallatin: HIV-Positive Man Pleads in Spitting Case," *Nashville Banner,* November 14, 1995, B2.

39. Erik Eckholm, "Poll Finds Many AIDS Fears That the Experts Say Are Groundless," *New York Times,* September 12, 1985, http://www.nytimes .com/1985/09/12/us/poll-finds-many-aids-fears-that-the-experts-say-are-groundless.html.

40. Kaiser Family Foundation, *The AIDS Epidemic at 20 Years: The View from America* (Kaiser Family Foundation: Washington, DC, 2001).

41. Kaiser Family Foundation, "Public Attitudes and Knowledge about HIV/ AIDS in Georgia," November 19, 2015, http://kff.org/hivaids/poll-finding /public-attitudes-and-knowledge-about-hivaids-in-georgia/.

42. This distinction is commonly used by researchers evaluating attitudes toward individuals living with mental illness. They define *explicit stigma* as

outwardly expressed negative attitudes toward people living with mental illness. *Implicit stigma* is defined as unconscious or unspoken negative attitudes that the individual may not even be aware of holding. See, for example, Claire O'Driscoll, Caroline Heary, Eilis Hennessy, and Lynn McKeague, "Explicit and Implicit Stigma towards Peers with Mental Health Problems in Childhood and Adolescence," *Journal of Child Psychology and Psychiatry* 53, no. 10 (2012): 1054–62.

43. Transcript of the Jury Trial, vol. I, at 143, People v. Franklin C., No. 2000-172553-FH (Oakland Cty. Cir. Ct., Aug. 8, 2000).

44. Transcript of the Jury Trial, vol. II, at 132, *People v. Franklin C.* (Aug. 21, 2000).

45. Ibid., at 141.

46. Alison J. Rodger, Valentina Cambiano, Tina Bruun, Pietro Vernazza, Simon Collins, Jan van Lunzen, Giulio Maria Corbelli, et al., "Sexual Activity without Condoms and Risk of HIV Transmission in Serodifferent Couples When the HIV-Positive Partner Is Using Suppressive Antiretroviral Therapy," *JAMA* 316, no. 2 (2016): 171–81.

47. For an early reference to the suspicion that undetectable viral loads mitigated HIV transmission, see, for example, Gary Smith and Paul Van de Ven, *Reflecting on Practice: Current Challenges in Gay and Other Homosexually Active Men's HIV Education* (Sydney, Australia: National Centre in HIV Social Research, 2001), 18. The first scientific statement to that effect came out of Switzerland in 2008 with the "Swiss Statement." See Pietro Vernazza, Bernard Hirschel, Enos Bernasconi, and Markus Flepp, "Les personnes séropositives ne souffrant d'aucune autre MST et suivant un traitement antirétroviral efficace ne transmettent pas le VIH par voie sexuelle," *Bulletin des médecins suisses* 89, no. 5 (2008): 165–69.

48. People v. Jensen (On Remand), 231 Mich. App. 439 (1998).

49. Transcript of the Jury Trial, vol. II, at 138, *People v. Franklin C.*

50. Ibid., at 139–40.

51. Mich. Code of Criminal Procedure, MCL § 777.33.

52. Transcript of the Sentencing Hearing at 6, *People v. Franklin C.* (Oct.3, 2000).

53. Ibid., at 10.

54. Centers for Disease Control and Prevention, "HIV Basics: Testing," last modified December 6, 2016, accessed January 13, 2017, https://www.cdc.gov /hiv/basics/testing.html.

55. Transcript of the Sentencing Hearing at 22, People v. Gerald C., No. 08-M-10957-FH (Montcalm Cty. Cir. Ct., Jan. 29, 2008).

56. Ibid., at 24.

57. Under Tenn. Code Ann. § 40–38–103, a crime victim has the right to "(2) Whenever possible, be advised and informed of plea bargaining discussions and agreements prior to the entry of any plea agreement, where such victim is a victim of violent crime, involving death of a family member or serious bodily injury, speak at parole hearings, submit a victim impact statement to the courts and the board of probation and parole and give impact testimony at court sentencing hearings."

58. Transcript of the Sentencing Hearing at 15, People v. Antonio F., No. 2003-D-2897 (Davidson Cty., Tenn., Cir. Ct., Apr. 16, 2004).

59. Ibid., at 49.

60. Ibid., at 53.

61. Transcript of the Sentencing Hearing at 11–12, People v. Scott B., No. 2007-I-1516 (Davidson Cty., Tenn., Cir. Ct., Feb. 1, 2008).

62. Ibid., at 14.

63. Tenn. Code Ann. § 40–35–313.

64. Transcript of the Sentencing Hearing at 43, *People v. Scott B.*

65. Ibid., at 43–44.

66. Ibid., at 50.

67. Transcript of the Sentencing Hearing at 48, People v. Chester B., No. 216721-216725 (Hamilton Cty. Cir. Ct., Apr. 27, 1998).

68. Ibid., at 96.

69. Ibid.

70. In criminal courts, applying a sentencing factor that is necessarily tied to the offense in question would effectively punish the defendant twice for the same offense. Specifically, the judge ruled: "Regarding the aggravation factor, the defendant had no hesitation committing a crime when the risk to human life was high; I think there have been plenty of unreported cases, as well as a few reported cases, where the courts have determined and there have been many cases where the court says you cannot use something as an aggravator that is part of the underlying offense. My argument would be that this factor of committing a crime when the risk to human life was high is, in fact, part of the nature and element of the offense. The fact that the legislature created this statute was in response to the fact that knowing exposure of another to HIV is an inherently dangerous act and there is a risk to human life. So to enhance with this factor in my estimation would be double-dipping I guess is the best thing to call it. So I do not feel that that enhancement factor is appropriate in this case." Ibid., at 79.

71. Specifically, the judge ruled that "I think if this law is going to have any effect there has to be some teeth in it; I think that's why the legislature created it because they could see this type of thing happening and being a prevalent thing and one of the reasons for incarceration is to avoid depreciating the seriousness of this offense; I think to do anything other than to require [Chester] to be incarcerated would be saying to the public out there, 'If you've got HIV and you're infected, it's okay to have sex with someone else and not tell them because if you are caught when you do it, then what's going to happen to you is if you're taking care of yourself and you're participating in the programs then you'll probably get placed on probation,' and I think it's not going to mean anything." Ibid., at 97.

72. Mich. Code of Criminal Procedure, MCL § 777.31.

73. Transcript of the Sentencing Hearing at 13, People v. Valerie J., No. 10-003899-FH (Clare Cty. Cir. Ct., Aug. 27, 2010).

74. Douglas Stanglin, "Judge to Rule If Bite from HIV-Positive Man Counts as Bioterrorism," *USA Today,* May 11, 2010, http://content.usatoday.com /communities/ondeadline/post/2010/05/judge-to-rule-if-bite-from-hiv-positive-man-counts-as-bioterrorism/1#.UgEy6JLh2So.

75. The defense attorney specifically notes, "There has been a decision by a circuit court judge—Honorable . . . Peter J. Maceroni . . . ruled that saliva of an HIV positive man is not a harmful biological substance, and dismissed one count of a three-count Complaint, and so, our argument on OV 1 and 2 is a combination argument, that I believe that they should be both scored at zero." Ibid., at 6. For more on the Macomb County ruling, see Jameson Cook, "Bio-Terrorism Charged against HIV-Positive Man Tossed in Biting Case," *Macomb Daily,* June 3, 2010, http://www.macombdaily.com/article/MD/20100603/FINANCE01/306039984.

76. Transcript of the Sentencing Hearing at 7–8, *People v. Valerie J.*

77. Transcript of the Sentencing Hearing, People v. Billy T., No. 00-1617-FC (Washtenaw Cty. Cir. Ct., Jan.25, 2001).

78. Ibid., at 21.

79. Ibid., at 16.

80. Ibid., at 25.

81. Ibid., at 26.

82. Karen R. Davis and Susan C. Weller, "The Effectiveness of Condoms in Reducing Heterosexual Transmission of HIV," *Family Planning Perspectives* 31 (1999): 272–79.

83. Benedicte Leynaert, Angela M. Downs, and Isabelle de Vincenzi, "Heterosexual Transmission of Human Immunodeficiency Virus: Variability of Infectivity throughout the Course of Infection," *American Journal of Epidemiology* 148 (1998): 88–96.

84. Lou Mumford, "Strip Club Padlocked in Raid Aftermath," *South Bend Tribune,* April 28, 2009, http://articles.southbendtribune.com/2009-04-28/news/26761240_1_strip-club-hiv-raid-aftermath.

85. Transcript of the Plea Hearing at 12–13, People v. Melissa G., No. 09-10107 (Cass Cty. Cir. Ct., Jul. 10, 2009).

86. Transcript of the Sentencing Hearing at 3, *People v. Melissa G.* (Sept. 18, 2009).

87. Transcript of the Sentencing Hearing at 38, People v. David S., No. 17264 (Rhea Cty. Cir. Ct., May 7, 2010).

88. See, for example, Tara Parker-Pope, "Kept From a Dying Partner's Bedside," *New York Times,* May 18, 2009, http://www.nytimes.com/2009/05/19/health/19well.html.

89. The prosecutor noted at sentencing that "Your Honor . . . in the presentence report it says, you know, I think they took this from the warrant, on Friday July 17, 2009, at 12:31 a.m., I was dispatched to the emergency room." Transcript of the Sentencing Hearing at 51 *People v. David S.* (May 7, 2010).

90. Ibid., at 52.

91. Prison Policy Initiative, *Detaining the Poor: How Money Bail Perpetuates an Endless Cycle of Poverty and Jail Time* (Northhampton, MA: Prison Policy Initiative, 2016); and John H. Blume and Rebecca K. Helm, "The Unexonerated: Factually Innocent Defendants Who Plead Guilty," *Cornell Law Review* 100 (2015): 157–92.

92. Transcript of the Sentencing Hearing at 54, *People vs. David S.*

93. Binh An Diep, Henry F. Chambers, Christopher J. Graber, John D. Szumowski, Loren G. Miller, Linda L. Han, Jason H. Chen, et al., "Emergence of

Multidrug-Resistant, Community-Associated, Methicillin-Resistant *Staphylococcus aureus* Clone USA300 in Men Who Have Sex with Men," *Annals of Internal Medicine* 148, no. 4 (2008): 249–57.

94. Michael Petrelis, "Newsweek Questions Panicky Staph Coverage," *Petrelis Files* (blog), January 19, 2008, https://mpetrelis.blogspot.com/2008/01/newsweek-questions-panicky-gay-staph.html.

95. Transcript of the Sentencing Hearing at 55, *People v. David S.*

96. Ibid.

97. Transcript of the Sentencing Hearing at 4–5, People v. William K., No. 04-13718-FH (Allegan Cty. Cir. Ct., Aug. 20, 2004).

98. Calculated by multiplying the risk reduction estimated for condoms (87 percent) in Davis and Weller's 1999 paper by the odds estimated of insertive anal intercourse without condoms (0.06 percent), in the paper also published in 1999 by Vittinghoff and colleagues. Davis and Weller, "Effectiveness of Condoms"; Eric Vittinghoff, John Douglas, Frank Judson, Kate MacQueen, and Susan Buchbinder, "Per-Contact Risk of Human Immunodeficiency Virus Transmission between Male Sexual Partners," *American Journal of Epidemiology* 150, no. 3 (1999): 306–11.

99. Transcript of the Probation Violation Arraignment at 2, *People v. William K.* (Aug. 5, 2005).

100. Michelle Phelps, "The Paradox of Probation: Community Supervision in the Age of Mass Incarceration," *Law and Policy* 35, no. 1–2 (2013): 51–80.

101. Transcript of the Probation Violation Arraignment at 3, *People v. William K.*

102. Ibid., at 5.

103. Transcript of the Probation Violation Hearing at 5–6, *People v. William K.* (Aug. 18, 2005).

104. Ibid., at 12.

105. "Obituary," (Cedar Rapids) *Gazette,* September 4, 2005, retrieved from Newsbank.

106. Kent County Death Certificate, William K., Michigan State File No. 2673413.

107. See, for example, Rebecca Tiger, *Judging Addicts* (New York: New York University Press, 2013).

108. See, for example, Sabrina Brugel, Marie Postma-Nilsenova, and Kiek Tates, "The Link between Perception of Clinical Empathy and Nonverbal Behavior: The Effect of a Doctor's Gaze and Body Orientation," *Patient Education and Counseling* 89, no. 10 (2015): 1260–66.

109. Joseph R. Gusfield, "Moral Passage: The Symbolic Process in Public Designations of Deviance," *Social Problems* 15 (1967): 175–88.

110. For a discussion of the thin line between medicalization and criminalization for pregnant women, see Elizabeth Armstrong, *Conceiving Risk, Bearing Responsibility: Fetal Alcohol Syndrome and the Diagnosis of Moral Disorder* (Princeton, NJ: Princeton University Press, 2008).

111. In the case against Ronald D. in 2002, the judge told the defendant, "I want you to take the kind of medication that they are developing now that will take care of AIDS. They have new medications coming out that apparently are

having a positive effect. And I hope that helps you." Transcript of the Sentencing Hearing at 9, People v. Ronald D., No. 02-9827-FH (Lenawee Cty. Cir. Ct., June 13, 2002).

CHAPTER 6. VICTIM IMPACT

1. "Down Low AIDS Wrestler Sharing the Love," Chimpmania (online discussion forum), 2013, accessed August 25, 2016, http://chimpmania.com /forum/showthread.php?39410-Down-low-AIDS-wrestler-sharing-the-love/.

2. Steven Thrasher, "A Black Body on Trial: The Conviction of HIV-Positive 'Tiger Mandingo,'" *Buzzfeed News,* November 30, 2015, https://www .buzzfeed.com/steventhrasher/a-black-body-on-trial-the-conviction-of-hiv-positive-tiger-m.

3. Kenneth Pass, Charles Stephens, Martez Smith, Darnell L. Moore, Craig Washington, Damian J. Denson, David Roscoe Moore, et al., "Open Letter to Michael [J.]," *POZ Magazine,* June 6, 2017, https://www.poz.com/article /michael-johnson-27220-2596.

4. Rod McCullom, "The Reckless Prosecution of 'Tiger Mandingo,'" *Nation,* May 29, 2015, https://www.thenation.com/article/reckless-prosecution-tiger-mandingo/.

5. Thrasher, "Black Body on Trial."

6. Jurors 6, 8, 9, 16, 19, 23, 44, 69, 76, 85, 89, 99, 101, 115, 127, 128, and 130. Of those, only juror 44 was selected to serve. It is worth noting that five jurors who said explicitly that they did *not* view homosexuality as a sin were seated (jurors 25, 35, 38, 52, and 64). Transcript of the Jury Trial, vol. I., at 68–82, People v. Michael J., no. 1311-CR0591-01 (St. Charles Cty. Cir. Ct. Case, May 11, 2015).

7. Thrasher, "Black Body on Trial."

8. Transcript of the Jury Trial, vol. II, at 201, *People v. Michael J.* (May 12, 2015).

9. Ibid., at 211.

10. Ibid., at 212.

11. Thomas Shevory, *Notorious HIV: The Media Spectacle of Nushawn Williams* (Minneapolis, MN: University of Minnesota Press, 2004).

12. Kansas v. Hendricks, 521 U.S. 346 (1997).

13. Matter of State of New York v. Nushawn W., 2016 N.Y. Slip Op 03625.

14. In this chapter, I speak in stark terms of *gay* and *straight* for ease of reading and understanding. However, the sexual identities of many of these men are often unknown; I am inferring sexual identity based on the gender of their partners. Men accused by other men of not disclosing their status are referred to as "gay," while men accused by women of not disclosing their status are "straight." An earlier version of this manuscript attempted to use the more accurate terms of *MSM* (men who have sex with men) and *MSW* (men who have sex with women). This approach, while more accurate, proved to be extremely cumbersome and confusing to readers; after a while, the constant references to Black MSM, Black MSW, White MSM, and White MSW become difficult to differentiate. Thus, this footnote serves as a warning to close readers that the discussion

of the data is simplified in admittedly problematic ways.

15. Becky Pettit and Bruce Western, "Mass Imprisonment and the Life Course: Race and Class Inequality in U.S. Incarceration," *American Sociological Review* 69, no. 2 (2004): 151–69.

16. Michelle Alexander, *The New Jim Crow: Mass Incarceration in the Age of Colorblindness* (New York: New Press, 2010).

17. For a useful overview of the conceptual debates, see Samuel R. Lucas, *Theorizing Discrimination in an Era of Contested Prejudice* (Philadelphia: Temple University Press, 2008).

18. Andrew Gellman, Jeffrey Fagan, and Alex Kiss, "An Analysis of New York City Police Department's 'Stop-and-Frisk' Policy in the Context of Claims of Racial Bias," *Journal of the American Statistical Association* 102, no. 479 (2007): 813–23.

19. For a review, see Doris Marie Provine, "Race and Inequality in the War on Drugs," *Annual Review of Law and Social Science* 7 (2011): 41–60.

20. Jawjeong Wu and Cassia Spohn, "Does an Offender's Age Have an Effect on Sentence Length? A Meta-analytic Review," *Criminal Justice Policy Review* 20, no. 4 (2009): 379–413; and S. Fernando Rodriguez, Theodore R. Curry, and Gang Lee, "Gender Differences in Criminal Sentencing: Do Effects Vary Across Violent, Property, and Drug Offenses?," *Social Science Quarterly* 87, no. 2 (2006): 318–39.

21. Jill. K. Doerner, and Stephen Demuth, "The Independent and Joint Effects of Race/Ethnicity, Gender, and Age on Sentencing Outcomes in U.S. Federal Courts," *Justice Quarterly* 27, no. 1 (2010): 1–27; and Darrell Steffensmeier, Jeffery Ulmer, and John Kramer, "The Interaction of Race, Gender, and Age in Criminal Sentencing: The Punishment Cost of Being Young, Black, and Male," *Criminology* 36, no. 4 (1998): 763–98.

22. David C. Baldus, Charles Pulaski, and George Woodworth, "Comparative Review of Death Sentences: An Empirical Study of the Georgia Experience," *Journal of Criminal Law and Criminology* 74, no. 3 (1983): 661–753; and Jefferson E. Holcomb, Marian R. Williams, and Stephen Demuth, "White Female Victims and Death Penalty Disparity Research," *Justice Quarterly* 21, no. 4 (2004): 877–902.

23. Katherine Beckett, Kris Nyop, and Lori Pfingst, "Race, Drugs, and Policing: Understanding Disparities in Drug Delivery Arrests," *Criminology* 44, no. 1 (2006): 105–37.

24. Michael L. Radelet and Glenn L. Pierce, "Race and Prosecutorial Discretion in Homicide Cases," *Law and Society Review* 19, no. 4 (1985): 587–622.

25. Robert W. Hymes, Mary Leinart, Sandra Rowe, and William Rogers, "Acquaintance Rape: The Effect of Race of Defendant and Race of Victim on White Juror Decisions," *Journal of Social Psychology* 133, no. 5 (1993): 626–34.

26. David B. Mustard, "Racial, Ethnic, and Gender Disparities in Sentencing: Evidence from the U.S. Federal Courts," *Journal of Law and Economics* 44, no. 1 (2001): 285–314.

27. Transcript of the Jury Trial, vol. 1, at 174, People v. Franklin C., No. 2000-172553-FH (Oakland Cty. Cir. Ct., Aug. 8, 2000).

28. Ibid., at 173.

29. Ibid., at 176.

30. Ibid., at 177.

31. William L. F. Felstiner, Richard L. Abel, and Austin Sarat, "The Emergence and Transformation of Disputes: Naming, Blaming, Claiming . . . ," *Law and Society Review* 15, no. 3–4 (1980–81): 631–54.

32. Notably, eight of the thirteen cases involving additional sexual-assault-related charges were in Tennessee. This may bear some relationship to the wording of Tennessee and Michigan statutes. In Michigan, the crime of nondisclosure would appear a nonsensible charge in a rape case: Would it actually matter if defendants disclosed being HIV-positive before raping their victim? In other words, the Michigan statute is written in such a way that implies consent—perhaps making it a less obvious choice for prosecutors seeking to punish defendants accused of rape. Tennessee law, on the other hand, criminalizes "HIV exposure."

33. Mich. Public Health Code, MCL Annotated § 333.5131.

34. For a description of how these data were collected, see the appendix 1. For a thorough description of some of the analytic methods used in this chapter, see Trevor Hoppe, "Disparate Risks of Conviction under Michigan's Felony HIV Disclosure Law: An Observational Analysis of Convictions and HIV Diagnoses, 1992–2010," *Punishment and Society* 17, no. 1 (2015): 73–93.

35. Centers for Disease Control and Prevention, "1996 HIV/AIDS Trends Provide Evidence of Success in HIV Prevention and Treatment" (press release), February 1, 1996, https://www.cdc.gov/media/pressrel/aids-d1.htm.

36. Centers for Disease Control and Prevention, "HIV in the United States: At a Glance," December 2, 2016, https://www.cdc.gov/hiv/statistics/overview/ataglance.html.

37. Sentencing Project, *Women in the Criminal Justice System: Briefing Sheets* (Washington, DC: Sentencing Project, 2007).

38. Ibid.

39. Toby Miles-Johnson, "LGBTI Variations in Crime Reporting," *SAGE Open* 3 (April–June 2013): 1–15; Timothy C. Hart and Callie M. Rennison, *Reporting Crime to the Police, 1992–2000* (Washington, DC: Bureau of Justice Statistics, 2003), http://www.bjs.gov/index.cfm?ty=pbdetail&iid=1142.

40. Wendy Wang, "The Rise of Intermarriage," Pew Research Center, February 16, 2012, http://www.pewsocialtrends.org/2012/02/16/the-rise-of-intermarriage/.

41. David W. Purcell, Christopher H. Johnson, Amy Lansky, Joseph Prejean, Renee Stein, Paul Denning, Zaneta Gaul, Hillard Weinstock, John Su, and Nicole Crepaz, "Estimating the Population Size of Men Who Have Sex with Men in the United States to Obtain HIV and Syphilis Rates," *Open AIDS Journal* 6 (2012): 98–107.

42. Cindy Brooks Dollar, "Racial Threat Theory: Assessing the Evidence, Requesting Redesign," *Journal of Criminology* 2014 (2014): 1–7.

43. In 2013, the CDC estimated that of the 933,941 Americans living with a diagnosed HIV infection, 9,382 were White men infected through heterosexual contact; 25,595 were White women infected through heterosexual contact; and

544,392 were men classified whose risk was classified as either "male-to-male sexual contact" or "male-to-male sexual contact and injection drug use." Centers for Disease Control and Prevention, *Diagnoses of HIV Infection in the United States and Dependent Areas, 2014* (Washington, DC: CDC, 2014), http://www.cdc.gov/hiv/pdf/library/reports/surveillance/cdc-hiv-surveillance-report-us.pdf.

44. Lesbians are not considered to be at risk of contracting HIV. The CDC does not tabulate data on new HIV infections among women who have sex with women. No convictions were identified in which a female complainant was accused of not disclosing her HIV-status before having sex with a female complainant. There have been a small number of cases in which a female defendant was accused of having sex with a male and female complainant without disclosing her status. These cases are excluded from analysis.

45. Peter Glick and Susan T. Fiske, "The Ambivalent Sexism Inventory: Differentiating Hostile and Benevolent Sexism," *Journal of Personality and Social Psychology* 70, no. 3 (1996): 491–512.

46. Anthony Walsh, "Homosexual and Heterosexual Child Molestation: Case Characteristics and Sentencing Differentials," *International Journal of Offender Therapy and Comparative Criminology* 38, no. 4 (1994): 339–53.

47. For a brief discussion of victim-impact statements and their role in courtrooms, see legal scholar Susan Bandes's 2016 essay. Susan Bandes, "What Are Victim-Impact Statements For?" *Atlantic*, July 23, 2016, http://www.theatlantic.com/politics/archive/2016/07/what-are-victim-impact-statements-for/492443/.

48. Amnesty International, *Stonewalled: Police Abuse and Misconduct against Lesbian, Gay, Bisexual and Transgender People in the U.S.* (New York: Amnesty International, 2005), 3.

49. Mary Bernstein and Constance Kostelac, "Lavender and Blue: Attitudes about Homosexuality and Behavior toward Lesbians and Gay Men among Police Officers," *Journal of Contemporary Criminal Justice* 18, no. 3 (2002): 302–28.

50. Gregory M. Herek, Jeanine C. Cogan, and J. Roy Gillis, "Victim Experiences in Hate Crimes Based on Sexual Orientation," *Journal of Social Issues* 58, no. 2 (2002): 319–39.

51. Kristina B. Wolff and Carrie L. Cokely, "'To Protect and to Serve?': An Exploration of Police Conduct in Relation to the Gay, Lesbian, Bisexual, and Transgender Community," *Sexuality and Culture* 11, no. 2 (2007): 1–23.

52. Victor Rios, *Punished: Policing the Lives of Young Black and Latino Men* (New York: New York University Press, 2011); Alexander, *New Jim Crow*; and Loic Wacquant, "Class, Race and Hyperincarceration in Revanchist America," *Daedalus* 193, no. 3 (2010): 74–90.

53. For a review, see Angela J. Davis, "Prosecution and Race: The Power Privilege of Discretion," *Fordham Law Review* 67, no. 1 (1998): 13–68.

54. Amira Hasenbush, Ayako Miyashita, and Bianca D.M. Wilson, *HIV Criminalization in California: Penal Implications for People Living with HIV/AIDS* (Los Angeles: Williams Institute, 2015).

CONCLUSION

1. I have permission to use Corey Rangel's full name in discussing this case, which I have written about in popular media elsewhere. Trevor Hoppe, "The County in Michigan Where HIV is a Crime," *Huffington Post,* April 4, 2016, http://www.huffingtonpost.com/trevor-hoppe/the-county-in-michigan-wh_b_9602758.html.

2. Todd Heywood, "HIV Bias, Discrimination Alleged in Cass County," *Pridesource,* April 5, 2016, http://pridesource.com/article.html?article=75945.

3. Molly Jirasek, "Public Outcry over Police Allegedly Disclosing a Man's HIV Status with Contacts in His Cell Phone," *FOX 28,* April 4, 2016, accessed June 1, 2016, http://www.fox28.com/story/31641203/2016/04/Monday/public-outcry-over-police-allegedly-disclosing-a-mans-hiv-status-with-contacts-in-his-cell-phone.

4. Audio recording of Amended Show Cause Hearing, People v. Corey Rangel, No. 15–010061-FH (Cass Cty. Cir. Ct., May 2, 2016).

5. Louise Wrege, "HIV-Positive Dowagiac Man Sentenced to Prison," *Herald Palladium,* June 18, 2016, http://www.heraldpalladium.com/news/local/hiv-positive-dowagiac-man-sentenced-to-prison/article_a1c84854–7eac-5ca7-a761-fbc6c0fb79ba.html.

6. Centers for Disease Control and Prevention, "Transmission of HIV Possibly Associated with Exposure of Mucous Membrane to Contaminated Blood," *MMWR* 46, no. 27 (July 11, 1997): 620–23.

7. Lawrence K. Altman, "Case of H.I.V. Transmission Is First to Be Linked to Kiss," *New York Times,* July 11, 1997, http://www.nytimes.com/1997/07/11/us/case-of-hiv-transmission-is-first-to-be-linked-to-kiss.html.

8. Donald J. Trump, "Protecting the Nation from Foreign Terrorist Entry into the United States," January 27, 2017, White House Office of the Press Secretary, https://www.whitehouse.gov/the-press-office/2017/01/27/executive-order-protecting-nation-foreign-terrorist-entry-united-states.

9. "6 Dead, 8 Wounded in Mosque Shooting; Trump's Travel Ban Triggers Global Condemnation; Democrats Fight Against Travel Ban" (transcript), January 30, 2017, *New Day,* CNN, http://www.cnn.com/TRANSCRIPTS/1701/30/nday.01.html.

10. See Maurice Possley, "Nick Rhoades," National Registry of Exonerations, October 9, 2014, last modified July 11, 2016, https://www.law.umich.edu/special/exoneration/Pages/casedetail.aspx?caseid=4514.

11. See the press release issued by One Iowa, the state's leading LGBT rights group. "Iowa Revamps Harsh HIV Criminalization Law" press release, One Iowa (blog), June 4, 2014, http://oneiowa.org/2014/06/iowa-revamps-harsh-hiv-criminalization-law/.

12. Carol L. Galletly and Zita Lazzarini, "Charges for Criminal Exposure to HIV and Aggravated Prostitution Filed in Nashville, Tennessee Prosecutorial Region 2000–2010," *AIDS and Behavior* 17, no. 8 (October 2013): 2624–36.

13. This framework draws on Edmund McGarrell and Thomas C. Castellano's integrative conflict model of criminal law formation. I am adapting it here to describe not just how criminal laws are enacted but also how they are enforced. Edmund McGarrell and Thomas Castellano, "An Integrative Conflict

Model of the Criminal Law Formation Process," *Journal of Research on Crime and Delinquency* 28, no. 2 (1991): 174–96.

14. Obviously, any conceptual map is artificial in the sense that all of these levels do not really exist in a separate time or space; they are necessarily interwoven and overlapping. Despite its artificiality, however, it is useful for collectively communicating the key drivers of criminalization identified in the book, which do involve different kinds of social phenomena.

15. Roman Jimenez, "SDGLN Exclusive: Accuser in HIV-Infection Case Speaks Out for the First Time," *San Diego Gay and Lesbian News*, September 9, 2014, http://sdgln.com/news/2014/09/09/sdgln-exclusive-accuser-hiv-infection-case-speaks-out-first-time-sandiego.

16. Staci Bush, David Magnuson, M. Keith Rawlings, Trevor Hawkins, Scott McCallister, and Robertino Mera Glier, "Racial Characteristics of FTC/TDF for Pre-Exposure Prophylaxis (PrEP) Users in the US" (abstract #2651, American Society for Microbiology Annual Meeting, Boston, MA, June 16–20, 2016); and Centers for Disease Control and Prevention, *HIV Surveillance Report: Diagnoses of HIV Infection in the United States and Dependent Areas, 2015*, November 2016, https://www.cdc.gov/hiv/pdf/library/reports/surveillance/cdc-hiv-surveillance-report-2015-vol-27.pdf.

17. For a more robust description of some of the issues facing PrEP's rollout from a social science perspective, see Judith Auerbach and Trevor Hoppe, "Beyond 'Getting Drugs into Bodies': Social Science Perspectives on Pre-Exposure Prophylaxis for HIV," suppl., *Journal of the International AIDS Society* 18, no. Suppl-3 (2015): 19983.

18. For a description of Canadian law, see Canadian HIV/AIDS Legal Network, "The Obligation to Disclose HIV-Positive Status under Canadian Criminal Law," 2014, accessed January 10, 2017, http://www.aidslaw.ca/site/wp-content/uploads/2014/09/CriminalInfo2014_ENG.pdf.

19. H. Irene Hall, Qian An, Tian Tang, Ruiguang Song, Mi Chen, Timothy Green, and Jian Kang, "Prevalence of Diagnosed and Undiagnosed HIV Infection—United States, 2008–2012," *Morbidity and Mortality Weekly Report* 64, no. 24 (2015): 657–62.

20. Gary Marks, Nicole Crepaz, and Robert S. Janssen, "Estimating Sexual Transmission of HIV from Persons Aware and Unaware That They Are Infected with the Virus in the USA," *AIDS* 20 (2006): 1447–50.

21. Devah Pager, "The Mark of a Criminal Record," *American Journal of Sociology* 108, no. 5 (2003): 937–75.

22. Jonathan Simon, "Project Exile: Race, the War on Crime, and Mass Imprisonment," in *Governing through Crime: How the War on Crime Transformed American Democracy and Created a Culture of Fear* (New York: Oxford University Press, 2007).

23. Douglas Husak, "The Criminal Law as Last Resort," *Oxford Journal of Legal Studies* 24, no. 2 (2004): 207–35.

24. Hasina Samji, Angela Cescon, Robert S. Hogg, Sharada P. Modur, Keri N. Althoff, Kate Buchacz, Ann N. Burchell, et al., "Closing the Gap: Increases in Life Expectancy among Treated HIV-Positive Individuals in the United States and Canada," *PLoS ONE* 8, no. 12 (December 18, 2013): e81355. For a

discussion on why men die younger than women on average, see Robert H. Schmerling, "Why Men Often Die Earlier Than Women," *Harvard Health Blog*, February 19, 2016, http://www.health.harvard.edu/blog/why-men-often-die-earlier-than-women-201602199137.

25. Harinder S. Chahal, Elliot A. Marseille, Jeffrey A. Tice, Steve D. Pearson, Daniel A. Ollendorf, Rena K. Fox, and James G. Kahn, "Cost-Effectiveness of Early Treatment of Hepatitis C Virus Genotype 1 by Stage of Liver Fibrosis in a US Treatment-Naïve Population," *JAMA Internal Medicine* 176, no. 1 (2016): 65–73.

26. Scott Burris, Leo Beletsky, Joseph Burleson, Patricia Case, and Zita Lazzarini, "Do Criminal Laws Influence HIV Risk Behavior? An Empirical Trial," *Arizona State Law Journal* 39 (2007): 467–519.

27. Keith J. Horvath, Richard Weinmeyer, and Simon Rosser, "Should It Be Illegal for HIV-Positive Persons to Have Unprotected Sex without Disclosure? An Examination of Attitudes among US Men Who Have Sex with Men and the Impact of State Law," *AIDS Care* 22, no. 10 (2010): 1221–28.

28. Carol Galletly, Steven D. Pinkerton, and Wayne DiFrancesico, "A Quantitative Study of Michigan's Criminal HIV Exposure Law," *AIDS Care* 24, no. 2 (2012): 174–79.

29. Patricia Sweeney, Simone C. Gray, David W. Purcell, Jennya Sewell, Aruna Surenderab Babu, Brett A. Tarver, Joseph Prejean, and Jonathan Mermin, "Association of HIV Diagnosis Rates and Laws Criminalizing HIV Exposure in the United States," *AIDS* 31, no. 10 (June 19, 2017): 1483–88.

30. UNAIDS, *Ending Overly Broad Criminalization of HIV Non-Disclosure, Exposure, and Transmission: Critical Scientific, Medical, and Legal Considerations,* May 2013, http://www.unaids.org/sites/default/files/media_asset/20130530_Guidance_Ending_Criminalisation_0.pdf.

31. Ramon Gardenhire, "How Illinois's HIV Criminalization Law Has Changed," *AIDS Foundation of Chicago,* July 27, 2012, http://www.aidschicago.org/page/news/all-news/how-illinois-hiv-criminalization-law-has-changed.

32. State of Tennessee v. Ronnie Ingram, No. W2011–02595-CCA-R3-CD (Tenn. Ct. App. October 31, 2012); Stephanie Norton, "Woman Charged with Criminal Exposure to HIV after Allegedly Biting Memphis Police," (Memphis) *Commercial Appeal,* August 4, 2016, http://archive.commercialappeal.com/news/crime/woman-charged-with-criminal-exposure-to-hiv-after-allegedly-biting--memphis-police-officer-3942cf01--389200481.html.

33. The title of this final section borrows from a preconference to the 2016 International AIDS Conference in Durban, South Africa, where activists and experts from around the world gathered under the banner of Beyond Blame. For a video review of the meeting, see HIV Justice Network, *Beyond Blame: Challenging HIV Criminalization,* YouTube video, 28:59, September 7, 2016, https://youtu.be/YKdkkbAoyHg.

34. Los Angeles LGBT Center, "F Without Fear is Message of New Los Angeles LGBT Center Campaign to Reduce HIV Infection Rate by Promoting PrEP," January 6, 2017, PR Newswire, http://www.prnewswire.com/news-releases/f-without-fear-is-message-of-new-los-angeles-lgbt-center-campaign-to-reduce-hiv-infection-rate-by-promoting-prep-300386908.html.

35. Associated Press, "Divide over HIV Prevention Drug Truvada Persists," *USA Today*, April 6, 2014, http://www.usatoday.com/story/news/nation/2014/04/06/gay-men-divided-over-use-of-hiv-prevention-drug/7390879/; and AIDS Healthcare Foundation, "'PrEP: The Revolution That Didn't Happen' Declares New AHF Ad," December 17, 2015, https://www.aidshealth.org/#/archives/24286.

36. AIDS Healthcare Foundation, "AHF's 'Condom Nation' Big Rig Hits The Road," February 13, 2012, https://www.aidshealth.org/#/archives/7558; and Ballotpedia, "California Proposition 60, Condoms in Pornographic Films (2016)," 2016, https://ballotpedia.org/California_Proposition_60,_Condoms_in_Pornographic_Films_(2016).

37. For a discussion, see Tyler Curry, "PrEP Goes Primetime," *Out*, September 25, 2015, http://www.out.com/popnography/2015/9/25/prep-goes-primetime-abc-hit-how-get-away-murder.

38. Kate Langrall Folb, "When It Comes to HIV, TV Can Be Good for Your Health," *The Body*, December 1, 2015, http://www.thebody.com/content/76794/when-it-comes-to-hiv-tv-can-be-good-for-your-healt.html.

39. Ibid.

40. For an overview of restorative justice, see Centre for Justice and Reconciliation, "Tutorial: Introduction to Restorative Justice," Prison Fellowship International, n.d., http://restorativejustice.org/restorative-justice/about-restorative-justice/tutorial-intro-to-restorative-justice/. For a survey of such programs, see American Bar Association, *Mediation in Criminal Matters: Survey of ADR and Restorative Justice Programs*, March 11, 2016, http://www.americanbar.org/content/dam/aba/publications/criminaljustice/mediationsurvey.authcheckdam.pdf.

APPENDIX I

1. For useful review, see Celeste Watkins-Hayes, "Intersectionality and the Sociology of HIV/AIDS: Past, Present, and Future Research Directions," *Annual Review of Sociology* 40 (2014): 431–57.

2. Claire Decoteau, *Ancestors and Antiretrovirals: The Biopolitics of HIV/AIDS in Post-Apartheid South Africa* (Chicago: University of Chicago Press, 2013); Sanyu Mojola, *Love, Money and HIV: Becoming a Modern African Woman in the Age of AIDS* (Berkeley: University of California Press, 2014); and Robert Wyrod, *AIDS and Masculinity in the African City: Privilege, Inequality, and Modern Manhood* (Oakland: University of California Press, 2016).

3. Marian Burchardt, *Faith in the Time of AIDS: Religion, Biopolitics, and Modernity in South Africa* (New York: Palgrave-Macmillan, 2015); and Iddo Tavory and Ann Swidler, "Condom Semiotics: Meaning and Condom Use in Rural Malawi," *American Sociological Review* 74, no. 2 (2009): 171–89.

4. Steven Epstein, *Impure Science: AIDS, Activism, and the Politics of Knowledge* (Berkeley: University of California Press, 1998).

5. See, for example, Bruce Western, *Punishment and Inequality in America* (Thousand Oaks, CA: Sage, 2006).

6. For example, see David C. Baldus, Charles Pulaski, and George Woodworth, "Comparative Review of Death Sentences: An Empirical Study of the Georgia Experience," *Journal of Criminal Law and Criminology*, 74, no. 3 (1983): 661–753.

7. For a recent example, see Jamie Small, "Trying Male Rape: Legal Renderings of Masculinity, Vulnerability, and Sexual Violence" (PhD diss., University of Michigan, 2015), https://deepblue.lib.umich.edu/handle/2027.42/113289.

8. Stefan Timmermans and Jonathan Gabe, "Introduction: Connecting Criminology and Sociology of Health and Illness," *Sociology of Health and Illness* 24, no. 5 (2002): 501–16.

9. For a description of the methods behind such tools, see Jean-Baptiste Michel, Yuan Kui Shen, Aviva Presser Aiden, Adrian Veres, Matthew K. Gray, Google Books Team, Joseph P. Pickett, et al., "Quantitative Analysis of Culture Using Millions of Digitized Books," *Science* 331, no. 6014 (January 14, 2011): 176–82.

10. Tenn. Code Ann. § 40-39-207.

11. Louisiana State Police, "Sex Offender Registry: Offenses," n.d. http://www.lsp.org/socpr/offenses.html.

12. Trevor Hoppe, "Disparate Risks of Conviction under Michigan's Felony HIV Disclosure Law: An Observational Analysis of Convictions and HIV Diagnoses, 1992–2010," *Punishment and Society* 17, no. 1 (2015): 73–93.

Index

abstinence, 61
acquired immune deficiency syndrome, naming, 101
Adler, Ernest, 120
advertising. *See* marketing campaigns
Advocate (gay and lesbian publication), 132
Africa, 18, 29, 122; circumcision initiatives, 52–53; sex workers in, 110, 243n42
African Americans. *See* Black people
age, 162
aggravated prostitution, 112. *See also* sex workers
aggravation, defined, 111
AIDS. *See* HIV/AIDS
AIDS Coalition to Unleash Power (ACT UP), 45–47, 230n7
AIDS exceptionalism, 68–73, 103
AIDS Healthcare Foundation (AHF), 205–206
AIDS-victim narrative, 45–47
Alaska, 127–129
alcoholics, 24, 29
Alexander, Michelle, 4
Allen, Frederick, 116–117
American Civil Liberties Union (ACLU), 18, 114
American Journal of Public Health, 49, 52, 109
American Legislative Exchange Council (ALEC), 11, 123, 124, 125–127, 246n107

American Public Health Association, 117
Amnesty International, 183
anal sex, 52, 54, 62, 153, 247n11, 253n98
Anderson, Andy, 118
And the Band Played On (Shilts), 29, 38, 41, 123
Annals of Internal Medicine, 152
antibiotics: infectious disease eradication through, 5, 10, 19, 30, 223n29, 227n45; resistance to, 34, 35, 151–152; TB treatment, 23–24, 35–37. *See also* vaccines
Anti-Drug Abuse Act (1986), 3
antiretroviral drugs and treatment, 40, 47, 53–58, 68; PrEP, 63–66, 195, 202, 205–206, 234n54, 235n57. *See also* treatment as prevention (TasP)
anti-sodomy laws, 105, 117–121, 131, 245n81
Archer, Victor E., 109
Arkansas, 167–170, 177–179, 213–214
Army, U.S., 25–26, 29
arrest patterns, 4, 162, 163, 165. *See also* conviction data
Atlanta Journal and Constitution, 116
attention deficit hyperactivity disorder (ADHD), 6, 223n30
Auerbach, Judith, 48–49
Avis, 114
azidothymidine (AZT), 70